The Patient Particulars

The Patient Particulars

American Modernism
and the Technique of Originality

Christopher J. Knight

Lewisburg
Bucknell University Press
London: Associated University Presses

Associated University Presses
440 Forsgate Drive
Cranbury, NJ 08512

Associated University Presses
25 Sicilian Avenue
London WC1A 2QH, England

Associated University Presses
P.O. Box 338, Port Credit
Mississauga, Ontario
Canada L5G 4L8

The paper used in this publication meets the requirements
of the American National Standard for Permanence of Paper
for Printed Library Materials Z39.48-1984.

Library of Congress Cataloging-in-Publication Data

Knight, Christopher J., 1952–
    The patient particulars : American modernism and the technique of
originality / Christopher J. Knight.
        p.   cm.
    Includes bibliographical references and index.
    ISBN 0-8387-5296-9 (alk. paper)
    1. American literature—20th century—History and criticism.
2. Modernism (Literature)—United States.   3. Creation (Literary,
artistic, etc.)   4. Originality (Aesthetics)   I. Title.
PS228.M63K57   1995
810.9'1—dc20   94-23967
                                                                          CIP

PRINTED IN THE UNITED STATES OF AMERICA

For my parents

Blessed are the patient particulars.

—Gertrude Stein

Contents

List of Abbreviations   9
Preface   11
Acknowledgments   15

1. The Problems of Representing an American Literary
   Modernism   19
   Thesis   19
   Authorial Intention   27
   Foucault/Words and Things   30
   How Do We Periodize?   37
   Periodizing (American) Literary Modernism   '43
2. Shifting Paradigms: Emerson, James and Hulme   50
   Emerson's "Nature"   50
   Shifting Paradigms   55
   James and Pragmatism   63
   The Modernist Imagination   69
   Stein, Hemingway, Williams, Moore, and the Technique of
      Originality   74
3. Gertrude Stein and *Tender Buttons*   80
   Monet, Stein, and The Innocent Eye   80
   Stein's Early Typologies   83
   Three Lives, The Making of Americans, and the Present
      Moment   87
   Tender Buttons   97
   Picasso   108
   Celebrating the Patient Particulars   110
   Stein and the Postmodern   113
4. Ernest Hemingway and *In Our Time*   117
   The Influence of Stein   117
   Omission as a Form of Apophasis   124
   Adjudicating Aesthetic Value   133
   Thinking about the Self   139
   The Technique of Originality   146
5. William Carlos Williams and *Spring and All*   152
   Tradition, Modernism, and the Innocent Eye   152
   The Poet and His World   159
   Polemicizing the Imagination   166

The Technique of Originality   173
6. Marianne Moore and *Observations*   182
    Epistemological Assumptions   182
    The Value of Observation   186
    The Value of Naturalness   191
    The Value of Imagination   194
    The Technique of Originality   198
    Curiosity and a Sacred World   203
Conclusion   206

Notes   215
Bibliography   238
Index   247

List of Abbreviations

ABT   Gertrude Stein, *The Autobiography of Alice B. Toklas*
CP   Marianne Moore, *The Complete Prose*
DIA   Ernest Hemingway, *Death in the Afternoon*
GHA   Gertrude Stein, *Geographical History of America*
HWW   Gertrude Stein, *How Writing is Written*
LIA   Gertrude Stein, *Lectures in America*
MF   Ernest Hemingway, *A Moveable Feast*
N   Ralph Waldo Emerson, *Nature*
NA   Wallace Stevens, *The Necessary Angel*
P   William James, *Pragmatism*
PI   Ludwig Wittgenstein, *Philosophical Investigations*
Pic   Gertrude Stein, *Picasso*
Psych   William James, *The Principles of Psychology*
RE   William James, *Essays in Radical Empiricism*
RT   Paul de Man, *Resistance to Theory*
SL   Ernest Hemingway, *Selected Letters*
Spec   T. E. Hulme, *Speculations*
T   Ludwig Wittgenstein, *Tractatus Logico-Philosophicus*

Preface

While chapter 1 functions, in many respects, as an introduction, I am conscious of the ways in which it veers from this purpose; accordingly, I would like to supply the reader with a précis of what follows.

In addition to serving as an introduction to the book's topic—i.e., the technique of originality as illustrated by Gertrude Stein's *Tender Buttons,* Ernest Hemingway's *In Our Time,* William Carlos Williams's *Spring and All,* and Marianne Moore's *Observations*—the first chapter also offers a necessary statement with regard to my own methodology. The need follows from the type of project undertaken: a literary history, of sorts. That is, as my design here is to investigate the technical affinities which link four prominent American modernist texts, it is incumbent upon me to address the theoretical difficulties inherent in the project, particularly as these difficulties, or issues—e.g., history, periodization, modernism, intention, etc.—are very much at the fore of current debates. I, for one, am deterred by the objections raised against the writing of literary histories by a theorist such as Paul de Man, who basically distrusts such projects for the reason that they seem too anxious to reify literature. I, too, share this distrust, yet at the same time believe that categorization—of which history is one segment—is an inescapable human endeavor and that even when we profess no interest, we do not necessarily avoid the case. Chapter 1, then, works as an introduction as well as an attempt to foreground philosophical issues which bear upon the project as a whole.

Chapter 2, meanwhile, is offered as something of a fore-history, vis-à-vis which the texts *Tender Buttons, In Our Time, Spring and All,* and *Observations* stand in a relation of culmination. Of course, this is a retrospective observation, and whatever necessitous relations these texts might appear to have vis-à-vis one another are understood to be at least nine-tenths metaphoric. Necessity hardly exists except as it finds itself ensconced in some trope. In any event, the history of which I speak here begins with a discussion of Emerson's "Nature," particularly as that essay addresses the question of how "the world" is to be cognized, and then, keeping to the same question, follows

11

with a discussion of William James's *Pragmatism* and T. E. Hulme's *Speculations*. It concludes with a discussion of how the question finds itself manifested in the work of the American modernists.

In brief, my overall thesis is that while the Stein, Hemingway, Williams, and Moore texts are conventionally identified as representative examples of American literary modernism—a judgment with which I can, more or less, concur—one does not want to conceive of modernism too monolithically. Therefore, it is imperative that we specify the problems which attract our attention and acknowledge that when the problem is, say, one of gender relations or of literary technique, a given work may, or may not, be said to be modern. That is, in the same instance one text may be both modern and not modern, depending on which questions are being asked of it. We should then more correctly speak of *modernisms* than modernism, even when the discussion attends to the seemingly self-enclosed field of American literary modernism.

In the present instance, as I have said, I am particularly interested in the problem of epistemology, the problem of subjects attempting to cognize their world. I think (as I hope I make clear in the first chapter) there are ways—and perhaps these are the most important—in which this problem is, *more or less,* ahistorical. Still, there will always be ways in which a problem is historicized, and it is these which I most wish to attend to with respect to the epistemological problem. Meanwhile, of the four texts to which I attend to here, three of them—*In Our Time* (1925), *Spring and All* (1923) and *Observations* (1924)—were published within three years of one another, and when *Tender Buttons* (1914) is included, within but eleven years. They are, as such, conjoined by their identification with a single historical moment as they are also conjoined by their similarity in technique. In the following chapters I speak of the latter as a technique of originality, a technique which promotes the suggestion that the world's objects are being presented as objects qua objects, rather than as their representations. In a sense, then, we find a technique which its authors should like to imagine as no technique at all, for if these texts reflect the authorial intention to see whether representation might be pressed to the point of presentation, as I argue they do, anything which should remind one of the artifice of the undertaking must be, more or less, downplayed.

Thus if we might understand these four texts as examples of extraordinarily focused attentions, attentions which, while undoubtedly quixotic, nevertheless have formal consequences, including the assumption of a literary still life character, we might also, I think, infer from their intentional and technical likenesses some consequences with respect to American literary modernism itself. That is, if these writers and these texts are conventionally represented as being in the vanguard of modernism, or as being brand new and irruptive of all that previously stood in their place, I should like to argue that there is also a way in which they represent less the beginning of something new than the conclusion of something—i.e., an episteme—old. Hence in many ways I find these texts representative of the end of a way of seeing, of thinking about the world as something out there, waiting to be discovered and redeemed, just as the interpretative frustrations in these same texts signal the beginning of a way of being in the world in which the relation between mind and object is construed as less oppositional than as interlaced.

Chapters 3 through 6 focus, respectively, upon the said texts: Stein's *Tender Buttons,* Hemingway's *In Our Time,* Williams's *Spring and All,* and Moore's *Observations.* I discuss them separately not only for the reason that they are each full-scale literary works and thus require individual attention, but also for the reason that, despite their resemblances to one another, they remain different texts. However much I understand these texts as determined, I do not wish to stop here. They are as disruptive of one another's aesthetic claims as they are of the history in which I place them, and I do not wish to deny this any more than my own separate purposes require. In short, I would like to imagine my efforts in the subsequent pages as constituting a negotiation among these texts—one which respects the separate virtues of each text even as it makes the point that separateness does not preclude commonality.

Acknowledgments

I am grateful to the following for the permission to quote and use the said materials in *The Patient Particulars:*

To Random House, Inc., for the right to quote from Gertrude Stein, The Autobiography of Alice B. Toklas (1933, reprint. New York: Random House—Vintage, 1961); *Lectures in America* (1935, reprint. New York: Random House—Vintage, 1975); and *The Geographical History of America* (New York: Random House, 1936).

To Liveright and to David Higham Associates, for permission to quote from Gertrude Stein, *Picasso* (Boston: Beacon Press, 1959).

To Sun & Moon Press, for permission to quote from Gertrude Stein, *Tender Buttons* (1914, reprinted. Los Angeles, Sun & Moon Press, 1991).

To Macmillan Publishing and the Hemingway Estate, for the right to quote from Ernest Hemingway, *In Our Time* (1925, reprint. Scribner, 1970); *Selected Letters, 1917–1961,* ed. Carlos Baker (New York: Scribner, 1981); and a letter to Robert Morgan Brown (14 July 1954) housed in the Humanities Research Center, Austin, Texas.

To New Directions Publishing Corporation, for the right to quote from William Carlos Williams, *Spring and All, in The Collected Poems of William Carlos Wlliams, vol. I, 1909–1939* (New York: New Directions, 1986).

To Viking Penguin, a division of Penguin Books USA Inc., and Clive E. Driver, Literary Executor of the Estate of Marianne C. Moore, for permission to quote from Marianne Moore, *The Complete Prose of Marianne Moore,* ed. Patricia C. Willis (New York: Viking, 1986); *The Complete Poems of Marianne Moore* (New York: The Macmillan Company/The Viking Press, 1981); and from her essays "Precision," "Monsieur Testes," "Review of My Trip Abroad," and a letter to William Carlos Williams (12 May 1934), housed in The Rosenbach Museum & Library, Philadelphia.

To the Charles Cowles Gallery (New York) and the Curt Marcus Gallery (New York) for permission to reproduce Mark Tansey's "The Innocent Eye Test."

★ ★ ★

For their valued comments in response to *The Patient Particulars* and more general support, I would especially like to thank Dale Bauer, John Cassidy, Barry Chabot, Mary Jean Corbett, Jim Sosnoski, and Keith Tuma.

The Patient Particulars

1

The Problems of Representing an American Literary Modernism

THESIS

THESIS

In what follows, I will study four well-known examples of American literary modernism—Gertrude Stein's *Tender Buttons,* Ernest Hemingway's *In Our Time,* William Carlos Williams's *Spring and All,* and Marianne Moore's *Observations*—within an Occidental history of literary representation, and at the same time argue that the rules of this representation are, more or less, ahistorical. That is, led by the example of Paul de Man's resurrection of the classical *trivium* "which considers the sciences of language as consisting of grammar, rhetoric, and logic (or dialectics),"[1] I shall accentuate the interdependence of these matters, and likewise view them as a "set of unresolved tensions powerful enough to have generated an infinitely prolonged discourse of endless frustration" (RT, 13). I shall also take note of the isomorphic relationship between logic and grammar, wherein logic ("the rational 'grammar' of thought") and grammar ("the 'logic' of linguistic structures")[2] seem to work in tandem so as to bridge the space separating language from its ground, "reality," only to have their work undermined by rhetoric.[3]

Yet to say that "[g]rammar stands in the service of logic which, in turn, allows for the passage to the knowledge of the world" (RT, 14), or to say (de Man's real point) that they "seem" to do so, *is itself an historically contingent observation.* For, in truth, logic and grammar do not do this, or if they in any way either effect or adumbrate an affinity between language and the world, they do so in a manner that, again, is not free from the play of rhetoric. Logic, grammar, and rhetoric are inseparable—at least in linguistic representation. But this does not mean that we cannot imagine historical moments wherein a significant number of practitioners did not think they could do away with one or another part of the equation. That de Man himself thinks it necessary to resurrect the equation—

forceably to remind us that rhetoric is also integrative—is a statement with historical import. It bespeaks a concern that many of his contemporaries, in fact, do not acknowledge the interdependence of logic, grammar and rhetoric, that in an age dominated by scientific discourse many are quite ready to repress rhetoric's part in the equation.

In the seventeenth century, John Locke wrote that "if we would speak of things as they are, we must allow that all the art of rhetoric, besides order and clearness, all the artificial and figurative application of words eloquence hath invented, are for nothing else but to insinuate wrong ideas, move the passions, and thereby mislead the judgment, and so indeed are perfect cheat!"[4] The seventeenth century is not the twentieth, yet one acknowledges the link, by which I mean that Locke's distrust of rhetoric goes hand in hand with his epoch's celebration of reason, with the project of the Enlightenment. We still live, or think of ourselves as living, in this discourse, even as we should discount Locke's antipathy for rhetoric as wrongheaded and intellectually naive. We should prefer to complicate the question of reason further, to see it (and its practical offshoot, science) not as something that might ever discretely separate itself from rhetoric but as something which is inescapably intertwined with it.

Of course, the bringing in of rhetoric is a mixed blessing. Rhetoric, or language, is, in Wittgenstein's words, "a labyrinth of paths. You approach from one side and know your way about; you approach the same place from another side and no longer know your way about."[5] And if we conceive of rhetoric as part of the Enlightenment project, it also seems to threaten it, to raise, once again, the specter of scholasticism. Yet if scholasticism still has the power to frighten us, we must nevertheless acknowledge that the choice of whether to bring in rhetoric or not is, in fact, no choice at all. Or it is not our choice to make. We live surrounded by, even in, language, and if we find ourselves, in Wittgenstein's words, doing "battle against the bewitchment of our intelligence by means of language" (PI, 47), we also know that there is no escaping this battle.

Still, as I have noted, the Enlightenment project has often been about the repression of rhetoric. The project has a history. And if we, living at the end of the twentieth century, think it imperative that we rejoin rhetoric to logic and grammar, we also wish to make it clear that until recently the tide mostly went the other way— toward rhetoric's repression. The reason had something to do with what Wallace Stevens, in *The Necessary Angel,* called "the pressure of reality,"[6] with the sense (particularly reinforced by modern science) that a deference, perhaps even an obsequiousness, toward "nature's facts" was the best path to truth. Truth lay outside ourselves, and while language might serve as a bridge here, it should find itself undermined were we to accent its rhetoric over its grammar. Grammar, not rhetoric, was the path to the outside world, and grammar not so much by itself but as it was allied with logic. Such was the essence of Wittgenstein's argument in the *Tractatus Logico-Philosophicus* (1921),[7] a beautiful articulation of this aspect of Enlightenment thinking even as the author (as we have already seen) later repudiated the book's anti-rhetorical thrust. (In the preface to *Philosophical Investigations* [1945], Wittgenstein wrote, "I have been forced to recognize grave mistakes in what I wrote in that first book" [PI, vi].)

For the Wittgenstein of the *Tractatus,* rhetoric was an unwelcome obstacle to truth, which like colloquial "[l]anguage disguises the thought; so that from the external form of the clothes one cannot infer the form of the thought they clothe, because the external form of the clothes is constructed with quite another object than to let the form of the body be recognized" (T, 63). Wittgenstein wanted, as Lady Ottoline Morrell said of him, "to find out how things really are,"[8] and one way to do this, he theorized, was to distinguish that which could be said clearly from all other more spurious statements: "What can be said at all can be said clearly; and whereof one cannot speak thereof one must be silent" (T, 27).[9] In this vein, Wittgenstein sought to constrict the connotative range of signs. He granted that it was often the case "that the same word signifies in two different ways," the way, for instance, in the statement "Green is green . . . the first word is a proper name and the last an adjective" (T, 55). Nevertheless, the situation troubled him ("Thus there easily arise the most fundamental confusions" [T, 55]), and he thought there should be a way to escape, or to avoid, such "errors":

> In order to avoid these errors, we must employ a symbolism which excludes them, by not applying the same sign in different symbols and by not applying signs in the same way which signify in different ways. A symbolism, that is to say, which obeys the rules of logical grammar—of logical syntax. (T, 55)

The way was, of course, to wed grammar to logic. "It is clear," said Wittgenstein, "that however different from the real one an imagined world may be, it must have something—a form—in common with the real world" (T, 35). That is, the grammar of the picture or representation (i.e., language) should be likened to the grammar of reality. What ties them together is their mutual form or logic. Thus while one granted that there was something quite arbitrary about signs, nevertheless there remained something quite necessary about the way in which signs symbolized the world:

> A particular method of symbolizing may be unimportant, but it is always important that this is a possible method of symbolizing. And this happens as a rule in philosophy: The single thing proves over and over again to be unimportant, but the possibility of every single thing reveals something about the nature of the world. (T, 59)

Yet if Wittgenstein sought to foreground grammar and logic at the expense of rhetoric, so as to circumscribe any particular sign's valency, he appears to have underestimated the disruptive force of rhetoric. One need go no further than the *Tractatus's* first series of propositions to see how troubling rhetoric may be. For instance, if we take the statement "The world is the totality of facts, not of things" ("*Die Welt ist die Gesamtheit der Tatsachen, nicht der Dinge*") (T, 31, 30), we find ourselves recalling Wittgenstein's prefactory remark that "[t]his book will perhaps only be understood by those who have themselves already thought the thoughts which are expressed in it" (T, 27). The reason is that while Wittgenstein aims to "make clear and delimit sharply the thoughts which otherwise are, as it were, opaque and blurred" (T, 77), the statement immediately raises a question of interpretation, immediately sets up a situation wherein rather than "[t]he name mean[ing] its object" (T, 47), it ends up meaning not one thing but many. So whereas "[n]ames [might] resemble points; [and] propositions arrows, [for] they have sense" (T, 47), there is also the sense that both names and propositions, while indexical, also refuse such usage. The sign, simultaneously, both speaks of a path between the "I" and the "that" and blurs that path. For example, the first discrimination we find here is between "facts" and "things." Yet this proves confusing not only for the reason that our dictionary defines a "fact" as "something that actually exists" but also because Wittgenstein himself (in proposition 2.01) defines a fact in terms of things: "An atomic fact is a combination of objects (entities, things)" ("*Der Sachverhalt ist eine Verbindung von Gegenstanden. [Sachen, Dingen]*") (T, 31, 30). The discrete proves readily assimilable. It always does. And the sign which we purport to use in order to discriminate one fact or thing from another— e.g., the Macintosh computer as opposed to the apple or the coat— inevitably ends up blurring the distinction, so that we find ourselves using the very same sign to refer to the distinct entities which are your computer and mine, or your coat and mine. Thus, Witt-

genstein's remark to a friend that the *Tractatus* "is strictly philosophical and at the same time literary" proves more true than even he
himself knew.[10] Yet this said, we must again remind ourselves that
as much as Wittgenstein wishes to avoid the "error" which is rhetoric, he does not insist that every sign corresponds to some fact or
thing. What he does insist upon is that every sign has, aside from
its conventional or arbitrary aspect, a necessary logical relation to
that which it refers:

> Herein lies the decisive point. We said that in the symbols which we use
> something is arbitrary, something not. In logic only this expresses: but
> this means that in logic it is not we who express, by means of signs,
> what we want, but in logic the nature of the essentially necessary signs
> itself asserts. That is to say, if we know the logical syntax of any sign
> language, then all the propositions of logic are already given. (T, 165)

For Wittgenstein, logic grounds language in reality; it makes their
relation necessary, even as it "shows" itself without being in any
way representable:

> That [logical form] which mirrors itself in language, language cannot
> represent. That which expresses itself in language, we cannot express by
> language. The propositions show the logical form of reality. They ex-
> hibit it. (T, 79)

Perhaps they do, and perhaps the grammar of language—or languages (of English, Russian, Chinese, etc.)—is, or are, identical to
the grammar of reality; but if so, is this not something that needs
to be proven—or, if one thinks it true yet unprovable, fideistically
assented to—rather than asserted ("It is clear . . ." [T, 35]). The
Wittgenstein of *Philosophical Investigations* thought so, stressing their
relatedness rather than their identicalness: "The concept of a representation of what is seen, like that of the copy, is very elastic, and
so together with it is the concept of what is seen. The two are
intimately connected. (Which is not to say that they are alike)" (PI,
198). And more recently, de Man has restated the objection: "Literature is fiction not because it somehow refuses to acknowledge 'reality,' but because it is not a priori certain that language functions
according to principles which are those, or which are like those, of
the phenomenal world" (RT, 11).

One assumes the existence of a transcendental reality—of a universe—yet as both Wittgenstein and de Man here suggest, one does
not want, therefore, to reduce everything to likeness, to equate the
ordering principle of one language—e.g., English—with that of an-

other—e.g., "reality," or more concretely, the Australian emu. It is easy enough to do, however; witness not only Wittgenstein in the *Tractatus* but also Stevens in *The Necessary Angel*. There, Stevens argues that "[t]he accuracy of accurate letters is an accuracy with respect to the structure of reality," and that should "we desire to formulate an accurate theory of poetry, we [will] find it necessary to examine the structure of reality, because reality is the central reference for poetry" (NA, 71). Like Wittgenstein, Stevens does not say that poetry is identical with reality: the poem is not the thing, but a metamorphosis of the thing, "a satisfying of the desire for resemblance" (NA, 77). Yet if something (e.g., metaphor, rhetoric) prevents poetry from being the thing, from being other than an "intensification" of reality, poetry and reality nevertheless do share a common grammar or essence:

> We have been trying to get at the truth about poetry, to get at one of the principles that compose the theory of poetry. It comes to this, that poetry is a part of the structure of reality. If this has been demonstrated, it pretty much amounts to saying that the structure of poetry and the structure of reality are one, or should be. (NA, 81)

For Stevens, "the structure[s]" of poetry and reality may be one, yet poetry and reality themselves are not one, for the already stated reason that resemblances intercede. A difficulty perhaps, though Stevens himself treats it as an opportunity. He relishes resemblances: "If resemblance is described as a partial similarity between two dissimilar things, it complements and reinforces that which the two dissimilar things have in common. It makes it brilliant. When the similarity is between things of adequate dignity, the resemblance may be said to transfigure or to sublimate them" (NA, 77). Resemblance, here a synonym for the poetic imagination, creates reality anew—it enhances it, "heightens it, intensifies it" (NA, 77)—and leaves Stevens feeling thoroughly satisfied. And yet resemblance remains not reality but reality transformed.

Today, we should conflate reality and its transformation, and not grant the distinction. But Stevens did not imagine things this way. Rather, he acknowledged two different ways of beholding the world: with the eye and the mind. The first offers one thing: "What the eye beholds may be the text of life. It is, nevertheless, a text that we do not write. The eye does not beget in resemblance. It sees" (NA, 76). The second another: "[T]he mind begets in resemblance as the painter begets in representation; that is to say, as the painter makes his world within a world; or as the musician begets in music,

in the obvious small pieces having to do with gardens in the rain or
the fountains of Rome and in the obvious larger pieces having to do
with the sea, Brazilian night or those woods in the neighborhood
of Vienna in which the hunter was accustomed to blow his horn"
(NA, 76). Of the two ways, Stevens clearly prefers the latter. He
values the mind's genius too much to wish for the "I" to become
merely an "eye."

With Wittgenstein, things are somewhat different however, at
least in the era of the *Tractatus*. In a notebook entry from 1916,
he writes,

> I know that this world exists. That I have a place in it like that of my
> eye in its visible field.[11]

The suggestion here, and later in the second half of the *Tractatus,* is
that the subject does not exist accept as it becomes synonymous with
its world:

> The world and life are one.
>   I am my world. (The microcosm.)
>   The thinking, presenting subject; there is no such thing.
> (T, 151)

What one notes here—or what one thinks one notes, for this part
of the *Tractatus* is famously difficult, its rhetoric admitting to the
most contradictory readings—is a desire to merge the self with the
world, to transmute the "I" into an "eye," or into a transparent
eyeball. The thrust is no longer logical, as it is in the first half of the
Tractatus, but mystical. Language no longer acts as an intermediary
between the "I" and the "that" but is superceded by a relation of
immediacy, wherein subject and predicate change places, or, better
yet, cease to exist, their prior bifurcation constituting a statement of
essential disunion. Or as de Man, in another context ("Hegel on the
Sublime"), writes, "The only thing the misleading metaphor of a
two-sided world accomplishes is to radicalize the separation between
sacred and human in a manner that no dialectic can surmount."[12]

And yet the metaphor of a two-sided world (e.g., language and
world, or consciousness and nature) fails only if one thinks this the
end of the story, only if one does not see the necessity of positing
this experienced binary as co-extensive with a more extensive transcendental. Wittgenstein himself does not make this mistake; his
error, as I have already said, is rather that of confusing the grammar
of one material order (e.g., the German or English language) with

another, and then shunting rhetoric to the side as he attempts to reconcile the two orders through the means of a logic allied with a grammar. For while the spoken of transcendental undoubtedly includes these said orders, it is, at the same time, not to be reduced to them. Meanwhile, if Wittgenstein, in the *Tractatus,* seems to err by privileging two sides (logic and grammar) of the classical *trivium* at the expense of the third (rhetoric), it is an error with a history. By this I mean, as I suggested earlier, that while the *trivium* functions, more or less, as an ahistorical equation in literary representation, the tendency to accent one aspect of the equation against another often has historical significance. For instance, I do not think we can dissociate Wittgenstein's attempt to circumscribe the field of what we can sensibly talk about from the scientific thought of his day. This is not because he says as much when he calls attention to his engineering studies, but because certain intellectual problems crossed over disciplines. Similarly, if we find a concerted attempt in the disciplines of science and philosophy to promote one kind of knowledge (e.g., "objective") over others, we should do well to anticipate its spread to other disciplines, literature included. Again, this is not because all intellectual grammars, or paradigms, transcend their disciplines; they do not, but the more powerful ones do.

In the present instance, as I first noted, I am especially interested in the way that representation is enacted in four prominent literary texts: Stein's *Tender Buttons* (1914), Hemingway's *In Our Time* (1925), Williams's *Spring and All* (1923) and Moore's *Observations* (1924).[13] This means attending to the way in which the authors bend the *trivium* to their own purposes, and it also means attending to what the said authors share—or do not share—in common. Here the attention is to a set of texts mostly written within a few years—and at most within eleven years—of one another. Accordingly, I am also interested in the significance, within the history of literary representation, of their strategies. The reader should thus be forewarned that I do not intend to foreground the four texts as individual masterworks (though they are) and from there offer a close reading of their excellences. I do not discount such an approach, yet I would like to go in another direction—toward the examination of a prevalent desire among American literary modernists to understand their art as a vertical, veridical act of discovery. Particularly, I wish to focus upon the manner in which Stein, Hemingway, Williams, and Moore almost seem to conceive of representation as something that might be pressed forward as presentation, even revelation. Of course, the ambition is quixotic, and fails to deliver these authors to the point intended. Yet the ambition, as we have already seen with

Wittgenstein, if not quite with Stevens, was very much a part of the historical moment, and if it was carried out within the parameters of what George Steiner refers to as the classical "covenant between word and world,"[14] it also set the stage for a more radical questioning of that covenant, a project vigorously pursued by a subsequent generation of authors, often under the banner of postmodernism.

AUTHORIAL INTENTION

As stated, I plan to study the Stein, Hemingway, Williams, and Moore texts as examples of a kind of modernist literary still life, wherein the authors, much like Wittgenstein in the *Tractatus,* aspire to bridge the space between word and world by means which promote logic and grammar over rhetoric. Such a study, however, cannot be undertaken without reference to authorial intention. Without this reference, we should tend to read their texts otherwise, in the light of not only their logic and grammar but also of their rhetoric. In fact, this is the way we wish to read these texts; yet we cannot go very far toward understanding their distinctiveness if we do not investigate the contexts in which they have meaning, including those of their creation. Part of our task, then, entails reading the said texts against the grain of the authors' expressed representational ambitions—of measuring mimetic ambitions which are often quite radical against boundaries which yield but do not break. Perhaps the story of the artist attempting to know his or her world—the story of subjects and objects; of minds and things—may not be what these texts are exclusively about. Texts are, in fact, never exclusively about any one thing. Still, the story does shed light on the form these texts take, and helps to explain their structural affinity.

Meanwhile, to speak of intention is not to suppress the problem of the author itself, to naively posit an author who is completely responsible for the work, and to whose authority, in Romantic fashion, appeal may be made. As Roland Barthes writes, "To give a text an Author is to impose a limit on that text, to furnish it with a final signified, to close the writing."[15] But if it is misleading to think of the author as the final arbiter of meaning, it is perhaps just as misleading to elide the question of the author altogether. Certainly, it makes a difference to our reading of *The Autobiography of Alice B. Toklas* to know that Stein, not Toklas, is the author, in the same way that Borges's protagonist in "Pierre Menard, Author of the Quixote" reads *Don Quixote* one way when its author is Cervantes and another way when it is Menard. So, if we do not wish to say that authors exclusively determine meaning, we also do not wish—after the poem, the essay, the novel, etc. is a "fact"—summarily to exclude the author (i.e., his or her intentions) from the determinations which we ourselves make. As Donald Davidson reminds us, interpreting any speech act requires us to be familiar with a whole grammar or pattern of linguistic behavior, of which the text before us is but a part: "We have a full grasp of what a man said when he uttered certain sounds only if we know his language, that is, are prepared to interpret a large number of things he might say."[16]

Perhaps it was a familiarity of this sort which led the New Critics to forget that literary texts are also authored texts. In their well known essay "The Intentional Fallacy," W. K. Wimsatt and Monroe C. Beardsley write, "The poem is not the critic's own and not the author's (it is detached from the author at birth and goes about the world beyond his power to intend about it or control it)."[17] More recently, post-structuralist critics have also demonstrated a propensity for discounting the author, and while such critics (among others) would be unhappy with Wimsatt and Beardsley's birthing metaphor, many would readily extend the reach of their statement by foregrounding the matter of the linguistic grammar at the expense of both author and critic. Michel Foucault, for instance, in an equally famous essay, "What Is an Author?," writes: "Using all the contrivances that he sets up between himself and what he writes, the writing subject cancels out the signs of his particular individuality. As a result, the mark of the writer is reduced to nothing more than the singularity of his absence; he must assume the role of the dead man in the game of writing."[18]

Yet if we accept that the author/self is inextricably inscribed in discourse, this does not necessarily entail an acceptance of the author/self's insignificance or, worse, "death." For one, the denial of the author/self can be as much a matter of fiat as its celebration. And given the importance of the discussion, we should do well to speak with a degree of caution. (Here, there seems to be an inescapable irony in Foucault's positioning himself at the point of authority in order to deny it.) Maybe the best response should be to acknowledge the difficulty without giving way to it, much in the manner of Milan Kundera's pronouncement: "The quest for the self has always ended, and always will end, in a paradoxical dissatisfaction. I don't say defeat."[19]

Meanwhile, if we should wish to reimagine rather than to banish the idea of the author/self, there are no guarantees that intentions shall be readily discerned. "[I]ntentions are just as hard to interpret as utterances," says Davidson. "It makes no sense to suppose we can first intuit all of a person's intentions and beliefs and then get at what he means by what he says. Rather we refine our theory of each in the light of the other."[20] Thus, we need to situate utterances, to estimate intention in the light of a grammar of meaning. And to be prepared to answer when Foucault mischievously asks, "What difference does it make who is speaking?," that it makes a very real difference. Or as Cheryl Walker responds: "It can never be shown that the treatment of the author as speaking makes *no* difference, since every way of constructing the text makes *some* difference. The point is to consider what difference such a difference makes."[21] In sum, then, our knowledge of an author's intention *always* has a consequence in terms of the way we read the text. If we are given to understand that an author meant to say one thing rather than another, then we are perforce either going, one, to accept this additional information and read the text in accordance with this light; two, reject it, and argue for another reading; three, ignore it; or, four, move among the various alternatives, here accepting what we know of the authorial intention as an interpretative guide and there rejecting it. But whatever the case, once we make some judgment respecting an author's intention, it becomes a determinant to our understanding. And while we would not wish to posit an author who is completely self-present, standing less inside discourse than outside it, we would not, at the same time, wish to reduce authorial intention, after de Man, to the "intentionality of the structure":

> the concept of intentionality is neither physical nor psychological in its nature, but structural, involving the activity of a subject regardless of its empirical concerns, except as far as they relate to the intentionality of the structure. . . . The structure of the chair is determined in all its components by the fact that it is destined to be sat on, but this structure in no way depends on the state of mind of the carpenter who is in the process of assembling its parts.[22]

Here the problem is that de Man's formulation appears to beg the question. For instance, the concept of "structure" appears both too abstract and too mysterious. Too abstract, in the sense that all the detailed gestures on the part of the carpenter which would make one chair different from another, and which might even mean that the intended object (i.e., a chair) is transformed into something else (e.g., a table), are suppressed. Too mysterious, in the sense that "structure" appears to be given anthropomorphic status ("the intentionality of the structure") only so that it may be denied the carpenter, or human being. Nor is our disagreement likely to be resolved by drawing a distinction between "self" and "subject," even as we might suggest that the self speaks of something which stands both inside and outside language; and the subject speaks of something that comes into being through language, through its grammatical—or structural—relation to an object. Somewhat in this vein, Emile Benveniste writes:

> Language is possible only because each speaker sets himself up as *subject* by referring to himself as an *I* in his discourse. Because of this, *I* posits another person, the one who, being, as he is, completely exterior to 'me,' becomes my echo to whom I say *you,* and who says *you* to me. This polarity of persons is the fundamental condition in language.[23]

I do not deny that both self and the subject are alike in that they require not only an other by which they might set themselves apart, but also an order by which they might find themselves determined. The difference is that whereas I am willing to grant the view which sees language as determining the subject, I am not willing to do this for the self. Neither language nor structure (as used by de Man) appear sufficiently large enough to encompass the self, and like Derrida who (in answer to Jean-Luc Nancy's question "Who comes after the subject?") aptly responded, "I would not want to see the 'who' restricted to the grammar of what we call Western language, nor even limited by what we believe to be the very humanity of language,"[24] I, too, would hold out for a determining order—a transcendental—which resisted a too familiar formalization. Also, I would like to think that this transcendental resists being completely known by us, even, as in Wittgenstein's *Tractatus,* one feels it there all the time, that it "shows" itself without being representable. Like de Man's "structure," this formulation also begs the question. Begging the question itself, however, is not the problem, for begging the question is something that we each do; there is no avoiding it, unless one should find a way altogether to avoid belief, both large and small. Meanwhile, with the young Wittgenstein, I would prefer to beg the question in the direction of what escapes our understanding, of the sublime, rather than in the direction of things as comparatively commonplace as structure, language, law, logic, nature, poetry, and discourse. Finally, what matters is not whether one begs the question, but where one begs it, and the consequent advantages or disadvantages of this choice.

FOUCAULT/WORDS AND THINGS

As I said at first, I wish to study *Tender Buttons, In Our Time, Spring and All,* and *Observations* within the history of Occidental representation. There are aspects about representation which remain, more or less, the same, yet any narrative also constitutes itself as a history, wherein differences ensue. In fact, a history would be the charting of those differences, be they differences of large scale events, philosophical accents, or whatever. This much is obvious. Yet I would also like to argue here that the four texts bear an extraordinary similarity (i.e., intentional and structural) to one another, and that this follows from a cause which stands outside the invention of the individual authors themselves. What this cause is, I hesitate to say, for I do not wish to make it appear absolute, or to reduce it to a law. It is not as determining as a Foucauldian episteme, yet not inconsequential either.

This said, I would still like to pause and pay heed to Foucault's discussion, in *The Order of Things*,[25] of epistemes; for if Foucault's work does not determine my own, it nevertheless holds a sway over it and the way that I conceive the Stein, Hemingway, Williams, and Moore texts. Thus I would like to remind the reader of the way in which Foucault divides the last five hundred years of Western history into three ages: the Renaissance, the Classical, and the Modern. The Renaissance, says Foucault, ended sometime in the seventeenth century and was characterized, in its way of seeing, by the four similitudes—*convenienta, aemulatio, analogy,* and *sympathy*—all held together by a system of signatures. Here, *convenienta* "is a resemblance connected with space in the form of a graduated scale of proximity" (O, 18); *aemulatio* is a resemblance that operates from a distance, mirrorlike; *analogy* is the superimposition of *convenienta* and *aemulatio,* speaking not only of the "confrontation of resemblances across space" but also of adjacencies, bonds, and joints; and *sympathy* is a force of attraction, "so strong and so insistent that it will not rest content to be merely one of the forms of likeness" (O, 23). Each of these resemblances functions separately, in its own space. As resemblances, they remain invisible; yet if they only remain invisible, they will go unrecognized. Thus the system of signatures, the glue that brings all together into a hylomorphic unity:

The system of signatures reverses the relation of the invisible form of that which, from the depths of the world, made things visible; but in order that this form may be brought out into the light in its turn there must be a visible figure that will draw it out from its profound invisibility. That is why the face of the world is covered with blazons, with characters, with ciphers and obscure words—with "hieroglyphics," as Turner calls them. (O, 26–27)

In short, argues Foucault, the Renaissance required that the realm of the visible (the microcosm) be understood as a sign of a larger, more encompassing invisible reality, the macrocosm. Strung together by the system of signatures, the latter world folds over the former, giving it both number and justification. The visible world may appear to be a plethora of forms, yet the truth is that in the Renaissance view these forms are both limited and unchanging. It is all one big Platonic world, with real mirroring ideal, and Creation forever complete. However, in the Classical age, this neoplatonism, this correspondence of real to ideal, gives way to identity and difference. With Bacon and Descartes leading the way, a growing scientific temper begins to set aside the magical beliefs of the recent past. This new age substitutes analysis for the hierarchy of analogies, and it makes comparison, linked with a new *mathesis,* not an order in itself but a function of order, designed to facilitate the most comprehensive enumeration and classification of the visible world. Lastly, it fosters a state of mind more busily engaged in discrimination, in establishing identities, than in *"drawing things together"* (O, 55). Intuition—that is, distinct perception—replaces language as a way to the truth of things. Language itself is now conceived as neutral and transparent, capable perhaps of translating the intuition's truth, but "no longer hav[ing] the right to be considered a mark of it" (O, 56).

Neither is it any longer possible to understand the sign as the form of the world, something existing anterior to its discovery. For if the Renaissance individual thought it imperative "to uncover a language which God had previously distributed across the face of the earth" (O, 59), the descendant does not. Not seeing the world analogically, this person is less likely to see it as being replete with symbols. Things are what they are and language, as such, does not seem to be "bound to what it marks by the solid and secret bonds of resemblance or affinity" (O, 58). Instead, from the seventeenth century onward, the sign, in respect to its accuracy of representation, is understood to work somewhere in the territory between the probable and the certain. Here the sign is not something absolute, but something "built up step by step in accordance with a knowledge of what is probable" (O, 60). Signs still remain divided between the natural (found) and the conventional (invented), yet now it is the conventional sign which offers the benefits of convenience and elasticity, "that draws the dividing-line between man and animal[,] . . . transform[ing] imagination into voluntary memory, spontaneous attention into reflection, and instinct into rational knowledge" (O, 62). What has most significantly changed is that the sign is now considered a demonstration of the "act of knowing." Man, not God, names the world's objects. ("Man" represents humankind in this episteme.)

Knowing itself is a most important aspect of the Classical. Man here stands not inside his world but outside it, outside, so to speak, the picture frame. He is man thinking and everything that is not thought—his body, world, etc.—comes under the heading "external world," the grist for the mind's mill. Yet the Classical is not the Modern, and if the Classical saw man as apart from the world, the Modern sees the human as very much in the middle of his or her world, one relation among many. When this occurs, language is one of the first things to experience transformation. By this, one means that Classical thought depends on sight, on the enumeration, demarcation, and classification of the visible world. From this viewpoint, the world is less inclusive than selective. In fact, argues Foucault, it might be said "that the Classical age used its ingenuity, if not to see as little as possible, at least to restrict deliberately the area of experience" (O, 132). Tastes and smells are dismissed as vehicles of knowledge for reason of their uncertainty, and touch is "narrowly limited to the designation of a few fairly evident distinctions (such as that between smooth and rough)" (O, 132–33). And even sight is not completely utilizable; colors, for instance, are not fitful foundations for knowledge. Still, sight is the privileged faculty. And because it is, language finds itself construed as representation. That is, language acts as a grid of organization, setting up a one to one correspondence between signs and the things of the visible world. So that if in the Renaissance the theory of the sign entailed three distinct elements— the signified, the sign, and resemblance, or "that which made it possible to see in the first the mark of the second" (O, 64)—then in the Classical age the number of elements appears reduced to two: the signified and the sign. As Foucault writes, "The relation of the sign to the signified now resides in a space in which there is no longer any intermediary figure to connect them: what connects them is a bond established, inside knowledge, between the *idea of one thing* and the *idea of another*" (O, 63). This bond, in short, is "psycholinguistic."

The conception of language as a plane situated parallel to the world depended in large part on the assumption that reality was to be easily demarcated, that it was atomistic, continuous and solid. Yet, says Foucault, what started to become evident with Georges Cuvier's investigation into sub-kingdoms in the nineteenth century was that space was really "without essential continuity." It was, in fact, a "space that is posited from the very outset in the form of fragmentation. A space crossed by lines which sometimes diverge and sometimes intersect" (O, 272). Thus if the Classical age celebrated both man and language as the former made use of the latter in pursuit of epistemological ends, of knowing the *external world,* the Modern age celebrates no such thing. It acknowledges no such privileged position vis-à-vis the world for either humans or language. Instead, both are construed as already integrated integers in that world, of which there is no other. Here, men and women are unable to step back from what they survey because they are always intertwined with that world. Epistemology gives way to conversation, to a mode of questioning which predicates no "finished signified."[26] No longer does the object present itself as something veiled, awaiting discovery. Instead, in David Couzens Hoy's words, "objects are themselves functions of the conceptions of what sorts of things we could desire to know about."[27] Meanwhile, mind and language, their mirroring function seeming less certain, withdraw, says Foucault, "into their own essence, taking up their place at last within the force that animates them, within the organic structure that maintains them" (O, 239).

In the Modern scheme of things, then, the event is the ultimate paradigm. By "event" is meant a nexus of relations, those between humans included. In *The Order of Things,* for instance, Foucault argues that human knowledge has historical, social, and economic (among other) conditions, that it is formed within the relations that are woven among people, and that it is not independent of the particular form they take here or there; in short, there is a *history* of human knowledge which could both be given to empirical knowledge and prescribe its forms. What people know and what they have hopes of knowing are constricted by finite, particular relations. They can never step outside the conditions in which they find themselves or realize an objective, god-like knowledge of the world. They are as much the "difficult object" of knowledge as they are its "sovereign subject." As part of the world, they are subject to its laws, yet as thinking subjects, they are able to turn about upon themselves and contemplate those same laws which govern them.

Giving inspection to those laws, however, humans note something their ancestors did not: each and every law, be it that of biology, economics, grammar, history, etc., is to be known only as it is spatialized, only as it works its way in a given context. Of universal laws and logics, they not only, like their ancestors, know nothing but they also, unlike their ancestors, care not to know anything, believing that such purported essences are merely examples of unenlightened misconstructions. So, if in modernity epistemology gives way to conversation, representation (as classically constructed) also gives way to something else. That is, classical representation is based upon a belief in a universal logic. One did not pretend that one could single out this logic and point to it; still, one did assume that it existed, standing mid-way between the planes of reality and language and guaranteeing their connection. To return to Wittgenstein's *Tractatus:*

> Propositions can represent the whole of reality, but they cannot represent what they must have in common with reality in order to represent it—logical form.
>
> In order to be able to represent logical form, we should have to be able to station ourselves with propositions somewhere outside logic, that is to say outside the world. (26)

Wittgenstein here displays an unusual confidence that the logic of language and the logic of reality are one and the same. As I have already indicated, to posit a transcendental, I think, is necessary, though one wants also to distinguish the ways in which the logic of language (or "propositions") and "reality" can be different. Meanwhile, Foucauldian modernists, as well as the later Wittgenstein, have distanced themselves from this same Tractarian confidence. They tend to pass the whole matter off as an elaborate superstition. If, without stationing ourselves outside logic, we can neither represent nor point to this logical form, then how can we be so presumptuous as to assume its existence? Positing this logic, this transcendental, may allow us to maintain the superstructure of classical representation, yet many a modernist has questioned the need to do so. In *The Philosophical Investigations,* Wittgenstein himself dropped the search for an ideal structure within language and began to play with the analogy of language as a game. Might we not, he argued, see the rules of language as originating and acquiring form much as in the way that when children start to toss a ball about, they soon set themselves to playing a game, creating and evolving rules as they go along? "Doesn't the analogy between language and games throw light here?" (PI, 39).

The analogy certainly did throw light of a sort upon the philosopher's understanding of language, even as it umbriferously sets aside Wittgenstein's prior contention respecting language's ideality. At once, the analogy's effect was to shift attention to language as something eccentric and evolving, something that was never so profound a thing as when it presented itself without pretension:

> We are under the illusion that what is peculiar, profound, essential, in our investigation, resides in its trying to grasp the incomparable essence

of language. That is, the order existing between the concepts of proposition, word, proof, truth, experience, and so on. This order is a *superorder* between—so to speak—*super*-concepts. Whereas, of course, if the words "language," "experience," "world," have a use, it must be as humble a one as that of the words "table," "lamp," "door." (PI, 44)

What did this mean for representation? Well, if language was no longer to be thought of as a grid that stands parallel to reality and, at the same time, finds itself affixed to it by the glue of logical form, then it followed that language's meaning was going to be understood less and less as a matter of cross reference and more and more as something self-referential. A word's first meaning was not going to be found in its indexical function, but rather in its contextual significance, what it meant in the frame of the language in which it resided. Said Wittgenstein, "For a *large* class of cases—though not for all—in which we employ the word 'meaning' it can be defined thus: the meaning of a word is its use in the language" (PI, 20–21). The planes of language and "reality" were two different things, and the result, argued Foucault, was that language was less a matter of what one saw than of what one did:

> It [language] is no longer a system of representations which has the power to pattern and recompose other representations; it designates in its roots the most constant of actions, states, and wishes; what it is trying to say, originally, is not so much what one sees as what one does or what one undergoes; and though it does eventually indicate things as though by pointing at them, it does so only in so far as they are the result, or the object, or the instrument of that action. (O, 289–90)

Foucault would argue that, in the movement from the Classical to the Modern, we experience a shifting of attention away from the external object and toward the "active subject." Or, toward the notion that these terms—subject and object—are inextricably intertwined. One cannot speak of a subject without constituting it in terms of its objects; nor can one speak of objects without reference, implicit or explicit, to a subject. And so, the traditional conception of language and its referents as distinct entities gives way to another understanding, that of "discourse." Discourse implies the inseparability of the signifier and the signified. At the same time, it inverts the classical subordination of language to things, and suggests that things themselves come into being through language, or discourse. So that if the Modernist has set an agenda, it is "[t]o substitute for the enigmatic treasure of 'things' anterior to discourse, the regular formation of objects that emerge only in discourse. To define these *objects* without reference to the *ground,* the *foundation of things,* but by relating them to the body of rules that enable them to form as objects of a discourse and thus constitute the conditions of their . . . appearance."[28] Finally, says Foucault, it is to move away from a conception of language as "a spontaneous grid for the knowledge of things" (O, 304) to a conception that envisions discourse as the supreme arbiter of reality.

How Do We Periodize?

I hope I have not dwelled too long upon Foucault's epistemic descriptions, yet as I said from the onset, the descriptions have influenced me, even though I would like to distance myself from the suggestion that epistemes are discontinuous. If they were truly this, Foucault would not be able so brilliantly to map the discourse of, say, the Renaissance, using the idiom of the Modern. There must be something the two discourses share in common—again, something almost ahistorical—to allow the translation. Otherwise, there would be nothing to say. So if Foucault seems to situate himself in an episteme (the Modern) wherein epistemology is construed as a way of doing philosophy that begins with Descartes's search for clear and distinct ideas and ends with the post-structuralists' theory of signs, then his own epistemic representations would appear to involve an inherent contradiction. As Richard Rorty notes, in *The Order of Things* Foucault "is not content simply to give a genealogy of epistemology, to show how this genre came into being (something he does very well). Rather, he wants to *do* something like epistemology."[29] And I, refusing the implication of Rorty's statement, would argue that literary representation always entails an epistemological dimension, whatever the announced intention.

Certainly, Foucault himself was aware of these methodological difficulties. He is aware, for instance, that whereas in his masterful reading of Velasquez's *Las Meninas,* he instructs us to see that the one thing in the classical episteme that never gets represented is the act of representing itself, he too offers, in *The Order of Things,* a representation as if it were true. Foucault is aware, as well, that in constructing his epistemes in a manner that stressed that they should be understood strictly in terms of themselves, he attributed to them a significant degree of self-presence, so that the metaphysics which was pushed out one door reentered through another. Meanwhile, he tried, beginning with his essay "Nietzsche, Genealogy, History," to rectify these difficulties, to avoid "the metahistorical deployment of ideal significations and indefinite teleologies" through a pointed effort to "record the singularity of events outside any monotonous finality."[30] Still, the contradictions did not seem to go away. As Habermas has argued, Foucault "gives up the autonomy of the forms of knowledge in favor of their foundation within power technologies and *subordinates* the archaeology of knowledge to the genealogy that explains the emergence of knowledge from the practices of power,"[31] yet he cannot avoid writing a metanarrative.

The problem is that writing always entails an element of presence. "[F]ar from being some metaphysical trick foistered on language by philosophy," Robert Scholes observes, "it is the constitutive possibility of language itself,"[32] so that to seek to bracket presence or to project one's writing somehow beyond it, as Foucault does, is to proceed too much against the grain of the matter. Foucault's epistemic categories seem brilliant, and his insistence, in the genealogies, that History's monolithism needs subverting, seems ever necessary. Still, to substitute genealogies (i.e., small histories), which, like the Einsteinian event, move along no single time line, for History, does not do half of what Foucault promises, for his promises are utopian.

Thus in suggesting that we can write histories which can somehow evade authorial presence and some kind of teleological design, Foucault makes use of what his own formulations would deny. That is, unless one is misled, his own writings predicate both presence and design, and hence a metaphysics. To suggest otherwise seems more polemical than suasive; and Foucault's attachment to the possibility that metaphysics can be elided appears a mistake. Nor does the formulation (suggested by Foucault's work and most frequently identified with Lyotard's)[33] that would substitute *petites histoires* in the place of a grand narrative appear to obviate the need to posit a transcendental, or the need to posit a subject which should be more than a semantic marker. A subject need not be fully present to oneself (an impossible ambition) to write history, but there can be no history without this subject. Thus while there may be good reasons for critiquing the traditional subject (e.g., to critique its androcentricism), one still wants to retain the notion of the subject, possessed of a certain agency. We might say then that even the most accomplished critique of the subject or of metaphysics employs (knowingly or not) the very things—i.e., subjectivity and metaphysical discourse—which it sets out to question. As Derrida writes:

> There is no sense in doing without the concepts of metaphysics in order to shake metaphysics. We have no language—no syntax and no lexicon—which is foreign to this history; we can pronounce not a single destruc-

tive proposition which has not already had to slip into the form, the logic, and the implicit postulations of precisely what it seeks to contest.[34]

The critique of the subject and of presence (along with analogous concepts such as the referent, truth, history, periodization, etc.) by theorists such as Foucault, Barthes, Baudrillard, Jameson, et al., has been timely, if sometimes overstated. Instances of the latter should be, say, Baudrillard's self-contradictory statement that "the age of simulation thus begins with a liquidation of all referentials—worse: by their artificial resurrection in systems of signs, a more ductile material than meaning."[35] Or Barthes's, "'What takes place' in a narrative is from the referential (reality) point of view literally *nothing*; 'what happens' is language alone, the adventure of language, the unceasing celebration of its coming."[36] Still, these represent less the critique's substance than its excess. Meanwhile, the question for us is whether we can profitably make use of such concepts as the subject, meaning, history, periodization, truth, etc. I suggest we can, so long as we resist negation's obverse temptation, the desire to reify them. Rather, we must author history mindful of historicity; and author periods mindful of periodicity. The one (i.e., historicity, periodicity) does not replace the other (i.e., history, periods), though the first be irruptive and contestatory while the latter, in comparison, appears settled and paradigmatic. Instead, the two seemingly opposing terms complement one another, there being, for instance, no history without historicity, nor historicity without history. Hence history, so cogently arranged and ordered, is always more complicating and self-contradicting than it presents itself. Yet the complications which, if allowed, would disrupt history, are never one with themselves, so that any attention to their differences will result in the formation of a narrative, as one—a subject—tries to account for the fact of difference itself. Paradoxically, then, that which seemed to disrupt history—i.e., complications—also would appear to engender history, and, by analogy, periods.

Now periods—or the act of inscribing events in terms of periods—have, lately, met with a great deal of scrutiny and skepticism, in spite of—or more likely in response to—the fact that the urge to periodicize seems more and more manifest. De Man, perhaps our most forceful and persuasive critic of periodization, believes that literary histories work too hard to settle that which, by definition, is unsettleable: literature. The problem is that a literary history is, by definition, epistemological; it wishes to say something descriptively true about literary texts other than itself. As such, the literary history—or, more properly, the literary historian—attempts to systematize, by means of a grammar and a logic, that which somehow escapes total systematization. And it does so, says de Man, particularly due to the fact of the history's literariness, its rhetoric: "Rhetoric, by its actively negative relationship to grammar and to logic, certainly undoes the claims of the *trivium* (and by extension, of language) to be an epistemologically stable construct" (RT, 17).

If literary periodization strikes de Man "as a very unmodern, a very old-fashioned, conservative concept of history, where history is seen as a succession, so that the historical model that is being used at that moment is very dubious and, in a sense, naive, very simple" (RT, 120), it is for the reason that, in practice, literary history has tended to be synonymous with reification. It is certainly not for the reason that de Man rejects the epistemological project itself. Quite the contrary, for de Man's whole critical project revolves around the question of how this very project might be construed: "Aesthetics is not independent of epistemology. If there is a priority, that is if there has to be one, it certainly is epistemological. Any reading must include it."[37]

Yet if it is true that literature bespeaks an epistemological dimension, it is also true that this dimension is constantly frustrated as it, or its author, attempts to unite the signifier with the signified. And this, says de Man, is principally because of "the unreliability of rhetoric as a system of tropes which would be productive of a meaning. Meaning is always displaced with regard to the meaning ideally intended—that meaning is never reached" (RT, 23). And because he holds to this fact—i.e., that the epistemological object is infinitely deferred—as the most fundamental, de Man tends to devalue the writing of literary histories, thinking of them as one more field for frustration, though different from, say, the field of literature in that, for him, it seems not to demand doing. To write literary history is to show oneself insensitive to the fact that the most interesting difficulties which literature presents are not historical but "a-historical in the temporal sense of the term" (RT, 12); and rather than attempt to historicize literature (e.g., in terms of its genres, poetics, representations, themes, etc.) we should acknowledge all literature as essentially the working out of a romantic problematic (i.e., of subject and objects, and attempts at meaning). In this formulation, all literature desires to be something other than itself (i.e., to be one with the contemporary object, to be modern), yet finds this desire frustrated by its rhetorical nature:

> The continuous appeal of modernity, the desire to break out of literature toward the reality of the moment, prevails and, in its turn, folding back

upon itself, engenders the repetition and the continuation of literature. Thus modernity, which is fundamentally a falling away from literature and a rejection of history, also acts as the principle that gives literature duration and historical existence.[38]

That literature has a history is not denied; in fact, it is engendered by the repeated "folding back upon itself" movement. But this history is never so noteworthy a thing as the movement which precedes it. This movement, this assertion of literature's rhetoricity, is, in Hillis Miller's words, what is truly "inaugural in literature,"[39] and is what makes literature a more interesting thing than the history of literature, or than history itself. Reading Walter Benjamin's essay "The Task of the Translator," de Man makes it clear that, for him, history represents a structuring of a second order:

> [H]istory is not human, because it pertains strictly to the order of language; it is not natural, for the same reason; it is not phenomenal, in the sense that no cognition, no knowledge about man, can be derived from a history which as such is purely a linguistic complication; and it is not really temporal either, because the structure that animates it is not a temporal structure. Those disjunctions in language do get expressed by temporal metaphors, but they are only metaphors. (RT, 92)

De Man is one of our most profound critics, yet (as with Foucault) his structuralist inclinations sometimes demand a skeptical response. The difficulty is that, for de Man, one text often begins to look like another, as their differences are subordinated to the fact that they illustrate the epistemological problematic. This problematic I find (as the reader knows) most interesting, but I do not think it is the only problematic which literature ever foregrounds, nor do I think it manifests itself in the same way, or to the same degree, in all texts, no matter how they may be situated in terms of the determinants of class, culture, gender, race, history, etc. Yet for de Man, language operates as a kind of base structure, demanding that everything be converted into its terms. The difficulty with this is that language is also an extraordinary abstraction, and when the requisite conversion of differentiae is accomplished, a too apparent reduction seems the result. As Rodolphe Gasché argues, the shift in de Man's "focus to the autonomous potential of language, free of all relation to what is signified, causes language to turn opaque." He continues:

> [A] rhetorical reading of a text is not geared toward revealing anything regarding the meaning of that text. It is not *about* a text, and thus cannot be measured against it. For such a reading, all the distinctive discursive

moments and levels blend into one undifferentiated and nontransparent mass. But does this mass, therefore, correspond to that night of abstraction in which all cows are black?[40]

Gasché downplays the importance for de Man of the referent, and therefore his critique is perhaps too harsh. Yet another purpose is served by bringing it forward, and that is that it helps me, at least, escape a little bit from under the sway of de Man's authority, and to move in a direction—that of periodization—which (as I have made clear) must be judged as most un–de Manian. And yet, what, after all, is periodization but another act of reading? It is an act of interpretation, of making connections. It does not necessarily bespeak a faith in absolute origin, a faith that one's reading of literary history is identical to literary history. Yet it does acknowledge differences; it does take note of the fact that literature, like anything else, aside from remaining more or less true to itself, also changes—change itself perhaps being the defining determinant of history—and that these changes, whether they are the decline of the epic or the rise of the novel, are worth investigating and theorizing about. That is, if, again, one wishes not to live in that world where all cows are black.

Meanwhile, any author does well to believe that there is "something out there" which corresponds to his or her reading. Not to believe that he or she can present—as opposed to represent—this something, or that this something is, for us, ever equatable with an unconstructed real. Yet it is to believe that the indexical gesture may speak of that which is *more* than self-reflexive, and that this something is worthy of our attention. In this respect, I very much like Barbara Johnson's remarks, made in an interview, that aside from the urge to deconstruct the real, "there has to be an equal desire to reach something. You have to desire to get to meaning or to truth or to satisfaction, somewhere along the line, in order for the demystification to have an organic relation to anything other than your own narcissistic desire for it to be as complicated as possible."[41] One might make the further point that lacking this desire, everything should become one with itself.

One finds here no reason not to include the desire to periodize, the desire to say how literature appears to be constructed differently in one time and place, as opposed to another, all the while acknowledging that this "time and place" is already a metaphor, fraught with all kinds of axiological questions. Certainly, periodization is never value-free. The fact that we mark out a space called the Renaissance or the Modern already entails a judgment, though we frequently forget this. I say "we," but this is already assuming too much, for depending upon where one stands, this forgetting is, or is not, easier to do. Clearly, some groups benefit from conventional periodizations—as well as conventional definitions of literature—more than others, and this explains why the intersection of periodization and value has become a foregrounded problematic for those groups (e.g., women, blacks, Hispanics, gays, etc.) that have been marginalized by the same.[42]

Periodizations dictate what we do and do not see. They also mirror where we stand, "tend[ing] more or less silently to place uniquely high value on our own period, since it is on behalf of that period that the valuations are made."[43] Yet if, in the words of Heiner Mueller, "periodization is colonial politics,"[44] reflecting our mining of the past for what proves useful for us, it would also seem most necessary—necessary as a way of forging identity, of saying who we are, which always entails the saying of who we are not, the positing of an other. Identity can only come into existence via the means of comparison and contrast, and periodization foregrounds this desire. It makes manageable what would otherwise be unmanageable; and while it may, at times, appear corrupt, it need not be so.[45]

PERIODIZING (AMERICAN) LITERARY MODERNISM

How does one periodize American literary modernism? What criteria does one use? In part, it would seem that the answer depends on one's methodology and what it is designed to look (and not look) for. If one's interests are in gender issues—say, in the way the values of the "new woman" find themselves expressed in the writings of authors such as Alice James, Charlotte Perkins Gilman, Kate Chopin, Edith Wharton, or Willa Cather—then one's criteria are going to be rather different than those of one whose interests are in poetic experimentalism or in cultural crisis. Thus the author who is judged to be a "modernist" according to one set of criteria will find oneself displaced by that of another set, the way that Henry James, generally understood to be a modernist when the question concerns literary technique, appears something else when the question is one of the new woman.[46]

My own interest is in the question of epistemology, in the problematic of the author wishing to aesthetically appropriate the object. I am attracted to Paul Smith's argument that "an informing characteristic of modernism itself" is "that the object of knowledge is still fundamentally *there* and available for us, but that it is our means of apperception and explication which are problematic. . . . [T]he object of knowledge is still veiled by—rather than *produced* by—the discourse that trains its sight upon it."[47] Like the problematic of gender, this is not to say that the problematic of epistemology is not locatable in other epochs. Rather, it is to say that, as compared to other epochs, this problematic seems to be unusually foregrounded in the modernist epoch.

Thus one takes note of the example of the poets Wallace Stevens in "The Credences of Summer" ("Let's see the very thing and nothing else. / Let's see it with the hottest fire of sight"), Ezra Pound in "Approaches to Paris" ("It [imagist poetry] means constatation of fact. It presents. It does not comment. It is irrefutable because it does not present a personal predilection for any particular fraction of the truth") and Louis Zukofsky in *Prepositions* ("An Objective: [Optics]—The lens bringing the rays from an object to a focus. [Use extended to poetry]—Desire for what is objectively perfect, inextricably the direction of historic and contemporary particulars"), or the painter, Marsden Hartley ("the thing must be brought clearly to the surface in terms of itself, without cast or shade or the application of extraneous ideas"), the architect Louis Sullivan ("For words in themselves he had come to form a passing aversion, since he had noted their tendency to eclipse the vibrant values of immediate reality. Therefore, he preferred to think and contemplate without the use of words"), and the photographers Alfred Stieglitz ("There is a reality—so subtle that it becomes more real than reality. That's what I'm trying to get down in photography") and Edward Weston ("taking advantage of this [the camera's] lens power: recording with its one searching eye the very quintessence of thing itself rather than a mood of that thing").[48] In short, epistemology may be, as de Man would have it, a permanent category, but it is a permanent category with a history.

This said, how does epistemology's history relate to Stein, Hemingway, Williams, and Moore? It has been, of course, something of a commonplace that these four authors should be grouped in the vanguard of American modernist writers. Theirs is the work which is irruptive of that which was previously in place (i.e., Henry Wadsworth Longfellow, John Greenleaf Whittier, Edwin Arlington Robinson, et al.); theirs is the work which brings our literature into the twentieth century; theirs is the work which launched an experimentalism which is still very much part of our aesthetic ethos. All of this, assuming that one adequately defines one's terms, is fair enough. At the same time, I would like to argue that in addition to seeing Stein, Hemingway, Williams, and Moore in terms of things or movements new, we might also offer a construction which places them less at the beginning of a narrative than at its end. Thus the literary modernism of Stein's *Tender Buttons,* Hemingway's *In Our Time,* Williams's *Spring and All,* and Moore's *Observations* is as much the end of something as it is the beginning of something else. It is the end of a way of seeing, of thinking about the world as something out there, waiting to be interpreted, just as its interpretative frustrations signal the beginning of a way of being in the world in which the tension between mind and object is conceived less as oppositional than as interlaced.

Meanwhile, Stein, Hemingway, Williams, and Moore offer evidence of wishing to pursue epistemology to its utmost point, to the point where, if possible (and it is not), knowledge and its object are one. This is, in a sense, the end of the line for the Modern schema; here, the object has always been the final desideratum, the end of the quest. If it is realized, eureka!; if not, one must go at things in a different way. Yet in *Tender Buttons, In Our Time, Spring and All,* and *Observations,* the authors do not veer off in another direction; they pursue the cognitive object. The form of their works reflects this interest, for they are not painted on large canvases but are circumscribed in their attentions, like literary still lifes. In this manner, they offer less a megalography than a rhopography, less an attention to narrative replete with grand characters and action, than an attention to what is, or is thought to be, ordinary.[49] The artists themselves do not think that their objects are ordinary, however, and much of their project entails making us see just how much, in the course of things, is undervalued or overlooked. Here, "[t]he enemy is a mode of seeing which thinks it knows in advance what is worth looking at and what is not," an enemy against which the artist sets the image, designed so as to foster the sense "of things seen for the first time."[50] The image is not had for the asking, however; it represents, in Charles Altieri's words, the culmination of an intense struggle "to forget the old idealizations so that it can disclose energies and structures within the scene which compel the entire personality to subordinate its will to the authority which it comes to see."[51] In the subordination of the will to the autonomous thing resides the further ambition to see the thing as if transcendentally, free of context, isolated in a single "moment" of time. So, much like the painter Lily Briscoe in Virginia Woolf's *To the Lighthouse,* there is a side of Stein, Hemingway, Williams, and Moore which would like to attend to the world with such concentration, such intensity, that they might block out of view everything that is not the object of attention, all backdrop, all relations, every thing that is not included in the thing-itself, in the "ordinary experience." Or as Lily reflects to herself,

One must keep on looking without for a second relaxing the intensity of the emotion, the determination not to be put off, not to be bamboozled. One must hold the scene—so—in a vise and let nothing come in and spoil it. One wanted, she thought, dipping her brush deliberately, to be on a level with ordinary experience, to feel simply that's a chair, that's a table, and yet at the same time, It's a miracle, it's an ecstasy.[52]

Yet perhaps a more familiar analogy than the still life is the photograph. That is, if in these literary still lifes there is evident a willingness to conceive of language as transparent and neutral, as subordinated to the quest for the thing-itself, then might not the photograph, that ostensibly transparent and neutral artistry whose *"noeme,"* as Roland Barthes calls it, "is authentication itself," not "a 'copy' of reality, but . . . an emanation of *past reality: a magic,* not an art,"[53] be the fitting model for what these authors were doing? With the photograph, the thing-itself seems not so much represented as it is presented. Made possible less by an act of mind than by a chemical process, the photograph achieves an objectivity with respect to its referent that the literary artist can only aspire to, and not imitate. Whereas photography may be tendentious, it never deceives as to the thereness, the factness, of its object. Emphasizing the photograph's singularity this way, Barthes writes, "in Photography I can never deny that *the thing has been there.* There is a superimposition here: of reality and of the past. And since this constraint exists only for Photography, we must consider it, by reduction, as the very essence, the *noeme* of Photography."[54]

Of course, Barthes celebrates one side of photography's reception: innocent, apodictic vision. As in literary representation, such vision has always been more seductive than real. Walter Benjamin, for instance, noted how the camera with "its interruptions and isolations, its extensions and accelerations, its enlargements and reductions" engages in a technique of reproduction which "substitutes a plurality of copies for a unique existence."[55] Yet while Benjamin offered his critique in the 1930s, James Agee, as late as 1946, could sigh, "It is doubtful whether most people realize how extraordinarily slippery a liar the camera is."[56] The reason was that for the generation born in the last years of the nineteenth century and which came of age in the teens and twenties, the camera seemed a most propitious instrument for rendering the "objective" world. Its veracity was less questioned than celebrated. Lewis Mumford wrote that it restored "to the eye, otherwise so preoccupied with the abstractions of print, the stimulus of things roundly seen as things, shapes, colors, textures."[57] Edward Weston wrote that with it, "the physical quality of things can be rendered with utmost exactness: stone is hard, bark is rough, flesh is alive."[58] And Marianne Moore, late in her life, wrote:

> For anyone with "a passion for actuality," the camera often seems preferable to any other mechanism; or so I felt in 1896, enthralled by Lyman Travelogues at the Opera House in Carlisle, Pennsylvania. As sequel to lantern slides, cosmoscope, and stereopticon, Brooklyn Institute movies were an Aladdin's revel.[59]

What the camera did, then, was to help shift attention to the visible world. As a model, it did not make it any more possible for writers such as Stein, Hemingway, Williams, and Moore to aesthetically realize things as they are; yet it did serve as a model for seeing, and it did appear to promote the idea of a pure mode of seeing as a possibility. Thus we find Hemingway saying, "[I] put down what I see . . . in the best and simplest way I can,"[60] and Williams, "to see, see, see! and make the words speak of what I saw."[61] And we find Stein emphasizing the atomic, divisible momentariness of the visible world, and stating that it is her ambition not to render "things felt, not things remembered, not established in relations but things which are there, really everything a human being can know at each moment of his existence and not an assembling of all his experiences."[62]

And with this attention to the atomic, the moment, we see the climax of the Modern paradigm. For even as the Modern epoch understood reality under the aspect of time, as the succession of present moments which, once experienced, became part of the past (just as they were, before experienced, part of the future) so the age also understood reality as something capable of being reduced from a fluid succession of moments to but a single, individual moment.[63] And it is the search for this moment, for the ultimate foundation of cognition, that captures the imagination not only of late Modernist thinkers but, not surprisingly, also of its artists. Thus both Hart Crane and Paul Rosenfeld, directing their attention to how art (led by the camera) has become consumed by the moment, respectively write: "speed is at the bottom of it all [photography]—the hundredth of a second caught so precisely that the motion is continued from the picture infinitely: the moment made eternal."[64] "Never, indeed, has there been such an affirmation of the majesty of the moment. No doubt, such witness to the wonder of the here, the now, was what the impressionist painters were striving to bear, but their instrument was not sufficiently swift. For such an immediate response, a machine of the nature of the camera was required."[65]

Of course, what happens in this quest is that one comes to realize that the moment is not the ultimate foundation of cognition at all, but that the moment, standing solid and unrelated, is a fiction, that the spatial moment breaks down into an almost infinite number of smaller moments—i.e., things which help constitute the "moment": electrons, neutrons, protons, quarks, etc.—none of which are unrelated. Still, photography captures well that prior world, that world of concrete, visible facts in which every fact gives the appearance of being sharply defined and knowable. It is, in a sense, the mechanical equivalent of a Georges Seurat painting, in which all of the dots, the visible record of sensations, can be counted. Or as Susan Sontag writes,

> Through photographs, the world becomes a series of unrelated, free-standing particles; and history, past and present, a set of anecdotes and *faits divers*. The camera makes reality atomic, manageable, and opaque. It is a view of the world which denies interconnectedness, continuity, but which confers on each moment the character of mystery.[66]

The authors of *Tender Buttons, In Our Time, Spring and All,* and *Observations,* making use of what might be called a "technique of originality,"[67] attempt—sometimes with baffling results—to record the world in a manner not so unlike that of the camera. I say "not so unlike" on purpose, for it would be far too reductive to say that Stein, Hemingway, Williams, and Moore ever set out to offer literary photographs. They did not. They did, however, demonstrate an interest—an interest which does, in fact, link them with modernist photographers such as Stieglitz and Weston—in objects *qua* objects, as if these objects were the only things which, in a post-sacramental age, remained sacred. Meanwhile, whether the objects remained sacred or not, these artists were successful, vis-à-vis what the age demanded, to the extent that they were able to bring into their work what Sontag speaks of as "mystery," though what I might simply speak of as "celebration," in deference to modernism's agenda of demystification. Be it "mystery" or "celebration," however, the artistic effort will not, in their terms, redeem itself unless such is found therein. That is, if one does nothing but create an infinitude of images, one places oneself in danger of being swamped by the same, of living in a sea of images but of not being able to discriminate one image from another. The texts sometimes threaten to do this; still, when they are good, it is because they illustrate the nineteenth-century French historian Jules Michelet's conception of history as love's protest. They are, as such, wholehearted attempts to embrace the world, to clutch it so tightly that it can never escape from one's grasp.

There is, finally, a madness in all this. The world is in constant flux; it is not so respectful of one's desires as to be easily halted in its tracks. And yet these artists, confronted by such intractableness, give back tit for tat. They display in their turn an unyielding stubbornness, a David-like refusal to be put off by the world's thwarting immensity. That the world is large is understood, but their interest is less in the world than in the part, the particulars of the world that can be discovered at an arm's length. These they approach as if they were real, as if one's affection for, and attachment to, the world's objects might redeem all efforts and all things. That things sometimes, momentarily, fall out this way is a tribute both to their determination and talent.

★   ★   ★   ★   ★

In the chapter that follows, "Shifting Paradigms: Emerson, James, and Hulme," I wish to offer a narrative which moves from a discussion of Emerson's essay "Nature" through James's *Pragmatism* and Hulme's *Speculations* and ends with a general discussion of the epistemological assumptions which seem to have determined much of what Stein, Hemingway, Williams, and Moore did as artists. That is, I wish to examine *Tender Buttons, In Our Time, Spring and All,* and *Observations* as texts which are inscribed in a history, or better yet, a number of histories, even as I have the fortitude to follow up (and to construct) only one of these. Of course, texts are more than historically determined objects; they both disrupt and make history in their turn. And thus to write a history is to engage in an activity with a built-in default. This said, I should return to my immediate purpose, which is to direct the reader to what immediately follows: a history that charts the subtle transformations in the way the subject-object equation finds itself conceived, particularly in the literary domain, from the generation of Emerson to that of our four modernists. With this chapter, I hope to clarify better just why it is that I think these writers might be understood to represent the culmination of an episteme.

2
Shifting Paradigms:
Emerson, James, and Hulme

EMERSON'S "NATURE"

In his 1836 essay "Nature," Ralph Waldo Emerson proposes to "inquire, to what *end* is nature?"[1] To what or to whom, he wishes to know, can we attribute nature's ultimate meaning? To what purpose are the disparate particulars of our found reality gathered together? To what extent can we realize their transcendental significance? In short, Emerson proposes to inquire about nothing less than the Meaning of meanings, and the most surprising aspect of it all is that he means to get an answer. Perhaps this is because—buoyed by an unusual optimism and a trust in the world—he believes that the answer is already entailed in the question: "Undoubtedly, we have no questions to ask which are unanswerable. We must trust the perfection of the creation so far as to believe that whatever curiosity the order of things has awakened in our minds, the order of things can satisfy" (N, 7).

At the same time that his focus is upon ends, Emerson does not wish to be thought an enemy to nature's particulars. "I have no hostility to nature," he writes, "but a child's love of it. I expand and live in the warm days like corn and melon" (N, 38). He therefore speaks lovingly of the stars and woods, and even of "cities, ships, canals, [and] bridges" (N, 13). Here, nature is never an end in itself but something "mediate," something "made to serve" (N, 28). It exemplifies "the doctrine of Use," the principle which requires that everything works toward a larger end. Without this element of service, all natural events should be meaningless: "All the facts in natural history taken by themselves have no value, but are barren, like a single sex" (N, 21). Emerson may not deny difference. "Our dealings with sensible objects is a constant exercise in the necessary lessons of difference," he says, but these lessons are hierachically followed by those "of likeness, of order, of being and seeming, [and]

50

of progressive arrangement" (N, 26). Yet, difference, for him, is
subordinated to the more encompassing order of judgment. Nothing
has value unless it can be married "to human history" (N, 21) and
by extension, the divine. Neither the seashore nor the forest is beautiful unless it finds itself embedded in a host of relations and understood as exemplifying a divine or "universal grace":

> Nature is a sea of forms radically alike and even unique. A leaf, a land-
> scape, the ocean, make an analogous impression on the mind. What is
> common to them all,-that perfectness and harmony, is beauty. . . .
> Nothing is quite beautiful alone; Nothing but is beautiful in the whole.
> A single object is only so far beautiful as it suggests the universal grace.
> (N, 24)

Of course, the fact that comparisons can be made need not imply
a universal backdrop; it indicates only that there exists a faculty for
judging, a thinking subject. Still, it seemed clear to Emerson that
an explanation of how a person comes to make such judgments
could not stop here, with the human mind. One still needed to
explain how the mind came by its categories of judgment. The
choices here were few. One could side with the empiricists and argue
that disparate sensations, through a mere process of addition, were
able to organize themselves into mental categories. Or one could
side with the Kantians and argue that the forms of such categories
exist *a priori*. Emerson sided with the Kantians:

> [T]he Idealism of the present day acquired the name of Transcendentalism
> from the use of that term by Immanuel Kant, of Konigsberg, who replied
> to the skeptical philosophy of Locke, which insisted that there was noth-
> ing in the intellect which was not previously in the experiences of the
> senses, by showing that there was a very important class of ideas or
> imperatives, forms, which did not come by experience, but through
> which experience was acquired; that there were intuitions of the mind
> itself; and he denominated them *Transcendental* forms.[2]

At the time, Kant's argument seemed the more plausible one. The
empiricists who came before him, John Locke and David Hume,
were never successfully able to explain how the mind was able to
synthesize the discordant elements of experience if it began as a *tabula
rasa*. Kant wrote in the first chapter of the *Critique of Pure Reason:*
"Now it is clear that it cannot be sensation again through which
sensations are arranged and placed in certain forms. The matter only
of all phenomena is given us *a posteriori;* but their form must be
ready for them in the mind (*Gemuth*) *a priori,* and must therefore be
capable of being considered as separate from all sensations."[3]

Emerson also felt that Locke's and Hume's answers were faulty—e.g., "Hume's abstractions are not deep or wise"[4]—and chose to conceive the human intellect as an aspect of the Divine. Reality was dualistic; there was Matter and Mind, Nature and Soul, the NOT ME and the ME: "Strictly speaking, . . . all that is separate from us, all which Philosophy distinguishes as the NOT ME, that is, both nature and art, all other men and my own body, must be ranked under this name, NATURE" (80). That which was not separate was identified with the SOUL. Meanwhile, consciousness, an important aspect of this SOUL, was not something which could be understood in material terms. And though consciousness was the means by which the world was known, the fact that it was allied with Spirit meant that it should never know material things as "things-in-themselves." From first to last, these were conceptual things, known via the means of the mind's forms, the way in which, for instance, any one object, once known, should immediately find itself spatially and temporally framed: "Therefore is Space, and therefore Time, that man may know that things are not huddled and lumped, but sundered and individual" (27).[5] Things then were, at once, both discrete and not discrete, for their separateness and individuality were already conditioned by pre-existent noetic categories.

What this also meant, however, was that it became easier to doubt the substantive fact of the world:

> But whilst we acquiesce entirely in the permanence of natural laws, the question of the absolute existence of nature still remains open. It is the uniform effect of culture on the human mind . . . to lead us to regard nature as phenomenon, not a substance; to attribute necessary existence to spirit; to esteem nature as accident and an effect. (N, 33)

The stance has its dangers, for if we undermine our belief in the external world too much, we risk the danger that our mind might become our cell. Emerson himself admits the danger: "Yet if it [mind] only deny the existence of matter, it does not satisfy the demands of the spirit. . . . It leaves me in the splendid labyrinth of my perceptions, to wander without end" (N, 41). At the same time, he does not show himself prepared to tack another way, to show more than an attenuated interest in the world's materiality. He prefers the mind's labyrinth to the city's streets. And even when he finds himself in these streets, his gaze is upward, toward the heavens: "Seen in the streets of the cities, how great they [the stars] are!" (N, 9) Thus does every thing speak of the Sublime, of the Absolute.

For Emerson, the Absolute is where the "end" of nature is located, where all the diverse particulars are made one. "Man is conscious of a universal soul within or behind his individual life, wherein, as in a firmament, the nature of Justice, Truth, Love, Freedom, arise and shine" (N, 21). The Absolute both engenders and adjudicates, there being no material fact except as it originates here and no truth except as it also finds its measure here. Thus does all creation shadow forth the perfection and unity of the Absolute, of the Supreme Being: "that spirit, that is, the Supreme Being, does not build up nature around us, but puts it forth through us, as the life of the tree puts forth new branches and leaves through the pores of the old" (N, 41). It follows, then, that the worlds of the Finite and the Absolute are not altogether distinct. They interact, with the spirit manifesting itself in the concrete forms of the material, and with the material acquiring ideal identity in the Absolute: "There seems to be a necessity in spirit to manifest itself in material forms, and day and night, river and storm, beast and bird, acid and alkali, preexist in necessary Ideas in the mind of God, and are what they are by virtue of preceding affections in the world of spirit" (N, 25). Here, the finite plane seems then to serve as a palimpsest, readily made transparent, upon the absolute. All things in nature have their correspondence with spiritual events; all are symbols. Or as Sherman Paul writes, "Correspondence as a doctrine of expression was not, as Emerson called it, the assigning of symbolic value to an object. It was instead, the *perception* of the symbolic import of an object: a way to apprehend reality."[6]

For Emerson, nature exists as a metaphor for the Absolute, a fact which he finds reflected in our language. "Parts of speech are metaphors because the whole of nature is a metaphor" (N, 24). Language is symbolic because the world is symbolic: "Every natural fact is a symbol of some spiritual fact" and "[w]ords [themselves] are signs of natural facts" (N, 20). As such, language embodies a spiritual meaning which is inseparable from its sensuous expression, the two terms, sign and spiritual fact, being always interdependent. Hence, when there is no sign, there is no spiritual manifestation, and when there is no spiritual manifestation, there is no sign. Symbolism proves inescapable.

Meanwhile, aside from being symbolic, language for Emerson is also hypotactic; it mirrors the forms of the Absolute. It does this not in its parts, its words, but in its whole, its syntax:

> The central unity is still more conspicuous in actions. Words are finite organs of the infinite mind. They cannot cover the dimensions of what

is in truth. They break, chop, and impoverish it. An action is the perfection and publication of thought. (N, 30)

It is in the sentence, the "action," where synthesis takes place, where the disparate elements are gathered together to form a whole. This synthesis is most dramatically evinced in the copula, the relational word "is," which joins together subject and object. Here we find the universal order being mirrored. As Ernst Cassirer writes, "only by this 'is' do we posit a necessary *content* of our judgment, do we state that the representations in question necessarily belong to each other and are not merely connected by fortuitous, psychological associations."[7]

For Emerson, mind is an active agent. Upon it hangs almost everything, including how well we grasp the symbolism of natural events. There might be times, says Emerson, when we, inclining to a belief "in the absolute existence of nature," are unable to see past the thingness of reality, "to look beyond [our] sphere" (N, 33). Such states, however, are only temporary, or are expressive of an "unrenewed understanding." For we have only to call upon the faculty of our Reason (a faculty possessed by all) to see that nature is not solid and opaque, that through its veil can be seen the absolute vision which gives nature its "grace." With Reason, "[t]he first effort of thought tends to relax [the] . . . despotism of the sense which binds us to nature as if we were part of it, and shows us nature aloof, and, as it were, afloat" (N, 33). Further efforts lead to a state wherein "outlines and surfaces become transparent, and are no longer seen; causes and spirits are seen through them" (N, 33).

Reason reveals more than nature's imbuing grace; it also reveals nature's moral fibre: "The moral law lies at the center of nature and radiates to the circumference" (N, 29). All nature is permeated with a moral code. Thus the fisherman is able to learn strength from the presence of "sea-beaten rock" and tranquility from the "azure sky." "[E]very substance, every relation, and process" has its purpose; and no part of nature goes to waste or is exhausted by its use as a commodity. "[E]very globe in the remotest heaven, every chemical change from the rudest crystal up to the laws of life, every change of vegetation from the first principle of growth in the eye of a leaf, to the tropical forest and antediluvian coal-mine, every animal function from the sponge up to Hercules, shall," says Emerson, "hint or thunder man the laws of right and wrong, and echo the Ten Commandments" (N, 28). The moral purpose is really the end of nature; and all nature's particulars possess, in addition to their private functions, ethical, universal functions. "This ethical character so penetrates the bone and marrow of nature, as to seem the end for which it was made. Whatever private purpose is answered by any member or part, this is its public and universal function, and is never omitted" (N, 28).

Yet even as Nature permits itself to be read, to be the emblem of a higher end, it never ceases to be mysterious. Even "the wisest man" does not "extort her secret, and lose his curiosity by finding out all her perfection" (N, 9). Nature is not "a toy to a wise spirit" (N, 9) but "the Sphinx at the road-side" (N, 25) which reminds us "that a guess is often more fruitful than an indisputable affirmation, and that a dream may let us deeper into the secret of nature than a hundred concerted experiments" (N, 43). From this point of view, impudent knowingness disgusts and the most fitting response when face to face with the Universe's inscrutable mystery is silence. "That essence," says Emerson, "refuses to be recorded in propositions," and "he that thinks most, will say least" (N, 40). Or, as he says elsewhere, "No power of genius has ever yet had the smallest success in explaining existence. The perfect enigma remains."[8]

Shifting Paradigms

Emerson's "Nature" remains an extraordinary essay, and while the purpose of the prior summary is to help highlight, via contrast, the epistemic assumptions of the authors studied in subsequent chapters, I do not wish to suggest that I think his work fundamentally dated or that I necessarily conceive literature in teleological terms. Stein, Hemingway, Williams, and Moore may all write after Emerson, but they do not necessarily write better—i.e., demonstrate a greater knowingness about the world—than he. In fact, I might suggest the opposite to be the case. Still, my inquiry does not point this way, but rather toward wanting, as I say, to bring out certain assumptions in Emerson's work, including the acceptance of the following:

1. a universal order
2. a subject-object dualism paralleling a spirit-matter dualism
3. a universal symbolism
4. a hypotactic syntax
5. a moral world order
6. the world's ineffable mystery

Why I should want to accent these assumptions has to do with my sense that while they specifically follow from a reading of a single Emerson essay, they are nevertheless assumptions that seem to manifest themselves in any number of Emerson's Romantic contemporaries but then find themselves noticeably resignified by the time we reach the generation which includes Stein, Hemingway, Williams, and Moore. By "resignified," I mean to suggest less that the terms change—for I believe otherwise—than that they receive different accentuation. Accordingly, my attention is directed not to an epistemic "rupture" but to a "shift," or simply to a marked transformation in what qualities get foregrounded or understood as offering an accurate epistemological representation, literary or otherwise, of the real.

Meanwhile, though I wish neither to reduce the Renaissance authors (e.g., Emerson, Thoreau, Hawthorne, Alcott, Whitman, Melville) nor the Modernists to some unitary design, I think it possible to historicize some concerns to a point where certain assumptions would seem plausible to an artist working in the mid-nineteenth century and others would make sense to an artist working in the 1910s or 1920s. Here what I am particularly referring to is the mind/ sensations equation, and what this meant in terms of theories of artistic representation. The point is not that Emerson's Romanticism, or any other branch of American Romanticism, presented itself as the only frame through which an artist might work at this time, but rather that the times did make it a mode to be taken seriously. In other words, until theorists could explain some of the remaining mysteries surrounding natural phenomena, particularly until they could adequately explain how it was that a purely sensate mind was able to categorize other sensations outside itself, the spiritual (or Kantian) alternative, that which predicated all natural events upon a universal *a priori,* would remain a persuasive world view. Thus even while the scientific revolution and its practical offshoot, the Industrial Revolution, made great advances during the early decades of the nineteenth century, it was still not possible to disregard, or dismiss, the *a priori* solution to the problem of existence.

Of course, it remains neither necessary nor desireable to rule out such a solution. Yet the fact is that as the nineteenth century progressed, the *a priori* explanation of reality, put forth most strongly by Kant, began to be seriously reconsidered. As noted above, perhaps the central question was how the human mind ordered its perceptions. Not satisfied with Hume's description of consciousness, Kant had argued that the mind reflected the existence of *a priori* categories.[9] The universality of our ideas, Kant said, could be most clearly demonstrated in mathematics. Here we find propositions (i.e., $2+2=4$) which are synthetical *a priori;* their truth need never be tested in experience because their truth is established apart from experience, upon a universal plane.[10] So too must it be, Kant argued, with all synthetic mental operations. There seemed no other way of explaining their existence except by admitting an *a priori* reality. Certainly such operations could not be accounted for by the simple reception of sensations:

> The manifold of representations may be given in an intuition which is purely sensuous, that is, nothing but receptivity, and the form of that intuition may lie *a priori* in our faculty of representation, without being anything but the manner in which a subject is affected. But the connection . . . of anything manifold can never enter into us through the senses, and cannot be contained, therefore, already in the pure form of sensuous intuition, for it is a spontaneous act of the power of representation; and as, in order to distinguish this from sensibility, we must call it understanding, we see that all connecting, whether we connect the manifold of intuition or several concepts together, and again, whether that intuition be sensuous or not sensuous, is an act of understanding.[11]

Given the framework of knowledge at the time, Kant's statement was a more than persuasive description of things. As John Randall writes: "A [scientific] method developed to deal with billiard balls, and employing concepts quite adequate to that purpose, will not take you far in treating human life. Indeed, as Kant found, it stops short before the egg."[12] Still, important developments with respect to our understanding of the natural world were being made in the middle of the nineteenth century, developments which would ultimately undercut the suasiveness of Kant's *Critique*. The most noteworthy of these was the publication of Charles Darwin's *The Origin of Species* in 1859. What Darwin did, among other things, was to show how it was possible to give a physical explanation for such a complex phenomenon as human understanding. He did this by introducing a logical, causal explanation for evolution, an idea which had been circulating for some time, but always without a plausible explanation of how it worked.

At the base of Darwin's theory was the belief that all organisms must compete for a limited quantity of natural resources. Therefore any change, either through accident or mutation, which enabled an organism to compete better would eventually, through heredity, become a permanent part of that organism's makeup. Given long periods of time most species would, as their adaptive traits became more numerous, increase in complexity. Natural selection, Darwin wrote, "leads to the improvement of each creature in relation to its organic and inorganic conditions of life; and consequently, in most cases, to what must be regarded as an advance in organization."[13] Thus it was that natural selection could account for man's most complex features—emotions, moral sense and intelligence, all representing advances in man's physical makeup first acquired to further his adaptation to a changing environment.

Again, the suasiveness of Darwin's theory was completely predicated upon the nineteenth-century individual's conception of time. The theory itself would have been completely unthinkable in an earlier age, even Kant's eighteenth century, for the reason that, conceptually, there simply would not have been enough historical time for the theorized transmutations to have taken place. Yet in the nineteenth century, all this had changed, and as far as Darwin and his contemporaries were concerned, he (as theorist) had, in Stephen Kern's words, "time to burn":

> In 1654, when Bishop Ussher calculated the year of creation as 4004 B.C., he invited scientific challenge. In the 1770s the Comte de Buffon determined that the earth was at least 168,000 years old, and by 1830 Charles Lyell estimated it as "limitless," time enough for the geological formations to be created by gradual processes still in action. Lyell formulated his uniformitarian theory by substituting time for catastrophic upheavals, and in 1859 Darwin, working on the assumption that he had time to burn, stretched out his theory of ever so slight variations and estimated the age of one area that he studied at over 300 million years.[14]

The consequence of all this was that after the publication of *Origin of Species* it became less admissible for intellectuals to argue, as Kant had done, that the mind was a function of a universal spirit. Darwin and his adherents were too successful in demonstrating how mental activity came under the aegis of natural law. As for the mental functions which had baffled the empiricists and had inspired Kant, such operations now seemed more simply the culmination of a long history of evolutionary growth. Thus once one accepted that natural law propelled almost all organisms toward states of greater complexity and that the stage upon which this development unfolded extended over millions of years, it became much easier to comprehend how an organ so complex as the human brain could, after innumerable stages of adaptive development, evolve to its present state. In short, Darwin's work prepared the way for the acceptance of the human brain as an organ like any other organ, the corollary being that thought was nothing more than a very advanced animal instinct. As Bruce Kuklick writes, the theory's controversy concerned not so much the "link between the human organism and those of the lower animals but rather between human reason and animal instinct."[15]

In addition to paving the way for a fuller material explanation of human cognition, Darwin's theory also led intellectuals to rethink the matter of design. Fostered by the success of the Newtonian description, design was the philo-theological belief that nature was purposive, that each element, if traced back to its origins, would reveal a divine first cause, instilling it with spiritual significance. As John Dewey writes,

> The classical notion of species carried with it the idea of purpose. In all living forms, a specific type is presented directing the earlier stages of growth to the realization of its own perfection. Since this purposive regulative principle is not visible to the senses, it follows that it must be an ideal or rational force. Since, however, the perfect form is gradually approximated through the sensible changes, it also follows that in and through a sensible realm a rational ideal force is working out its ultimate manifestation.[16]

In the United States, the most active proponents of design were the Unitarians, among whose members were counted many of the leading New England Brahmins. Unlike the Transcendentalists, who refused to subordinate their religious beliefs to the facts of experience, the Unitarians genuinely sought to accommodate their beliefs to experience. They did this for two reasons: first, to insure that there was no contradiction between their beliefs and the already legitimized scientific world view; and second, to place greater distance between their beliefs and those of the Transcendentalists, whom Unitarians saw as unwisely promulgating a "romantic individualism and irrationalism."[17] Meanwhile, the accommodation of theology to experience, or design, worked so long as people continued to conceive the Newtonian description as reflective of a harmonious order, divinely inspired. Such an accommodation, however, became less attractive after the dissemination of Darwinism. For Darwin argued that nature was neither particularly frugal nor purposive, that in the innumerable variations and adaptations making up the evolutionary process, nature displayed a prolifigacy and a randomness not previously imagined. As one historian writes,

> [Darwin] postulated an incredibly wasteful process of random proliferation and ruthless extinction. In place of the benevolent harmony in which all nature conspires to the happiness of creation, Darwin presented "nature red in tooth and claw." If indeed order bespeaks an orderer, if like produces like, if natural law is but the mode of the divine action, if all

the effects are intended, what conclusion followed respecting a deity who would design the world on the model of a slaughterhouse where most perished horribly, where the "saving remnant" was saved by chance adaptation alone, and where the meek would never live to inherit anything? For those who had made the natural theology the foundation of their reconciliation of religion and science, the Darwinian theory suddenly opened the abyss beneath their feet.[18]

Darwinism persuasively undermined two of the previous century's most firmly rooted intellectual beliefs: immaterial "consciousness" and design. Spiritually based, these beliefs gave way to material explanations, demonstrations that matter, propelled by physical law, could accomplish everything that the beliefs were said to do. In effect, what Darwin did was to naturalize the world one last time; for not since Newton had anyone been able to plug so many of the existing gaps in humankind's factual understanding of its world. People now had to make adjustments in their beliefs and cosmologies; they had to make their beliefs compatible with their new understanding of natural events. Of course, there were some (e.g., Bernard Bosanquet and Josiah Royce) who continued to propose ideal interpretations of mind, interpretations which predicated all phenomena upon a universal plane; yet these philosophies seemed, in time, to find fewer and fewer adherents, and it was not long before they were being accused of side-stepping the real issues, of engaging in mere verbal solutions. Charles Peirce's reaction to the intangibility of idealist solutions was a common one:

> You only puzzle yourself by talking of this metaphysical "truth" and metaphysical "falsity," that you know nothing about. All you have got any dealings with are your doubts and beliefs, with the course of life that forces new beliefs upon you and gives you power to doubt old beliefs.[19]

The situation was, as Richard Rorty writes, one wherein

> the tradition of German idealism . . . declined in England and America— into what has been described as "a continuation of Protestantism by other means." The idealist purported to save the "spiritual values" which physicalism seemed to neglect by invoking Berkelian arguments to get rid of the individual ego (while resolutely ignoring Hegel's historicism). But few took these high-minded efforts seriously.[20]

In the United States, pragmatism was the most overt response to this new felt need to accommodate accepted truths to experience. Similar in many ways to European positivism, pragmatism was a philosophical and cultural movement which grew out of discussions entertained by the Metaphysical Club in Cambridge.[21] (The irony in the name was intentional.) The club's members included such thinkers as Nicholas Green, Oliver Wendell Holmes, Jr., William James, Charles Peirce, and Chauncey Wright. Initially, what tied these men together was their assent to the proposition put forth by the British psychologist Alexander Bain that a belief be equated with "that upon which a man is prepared to act."[22] According to Bain, a belief was less a metaphysical fact than it was a habitual mode of action, or behavior.

The pragmatic perspective was first given definition by Charles Peirce. He called it a "scientific method for distinguishing properly formulated questions from fictitious ones, valuable answers from unrewarding ones, real matters of controversy from purely verbal ones."[23] Such distinctions were made, said Peirce, by examining the practical effects of an idea, by seeing whether its adoption resulted in tangible consequences. If it did, the idea must be understood to possess real signification; if it did not, it should be thought otherwise. Peirce wrote, "Consider what effects, that might conceivably have practical bearings, we conceive the object of our conception to have. Then, our conception of these effects is the whole of our conception of the object."[24] Thus all our ideas are rooted in sense experience. There is no *a priori* bank from which the mind might draw a different perspective. "Our idea of anything," wrote Peirce, "*is* our idea of its sensible effects; and if we fancy that we have any other we deceive ourselves, and mistake a mere sensation accompanying the thought for the part of the thought itself."[25]

Passing beyond the assumption that our ideas are predicated not upon a universal plane but upon sense objects, it follows that the external world exists whether we accept it or not. The world is independent of our experience of it; it does not depend upon the mind to give it being. On the other hand, it is something, in the Modern view, that one can approach, that one can seek to know first hand. Articulating this view, Peirce (albeit a semiologist himself) writes,

There are real things, whose characters are entirely independent of our opinions about them; those realities affect our senses according to regular law and, though our sensations are as different as our relations to the objects, yet, by taking advantage of the laws of perception, we can ascertain by reasoning how things really are, and any man, if he has sufficient experience and reason enough about it, will be led to the one true conclusion.[26]

That one should contemplate the world this way—as "things really are"—is of course indicative of a radical turnabout in the way of seeing. Certainly, Emerson never contemplated that one could know the world as it is. Such "marriage," he said, "is impossible because of the inequality of subject and object."[27] Yet this question of equality or inequality between subject and object had very much changed. For if Emerson held that inequality was the case here for the reason that the "subject is the receiver of Godhead,"[28] is, in effect, spirit, pragmatists and other modernist thinkers were generally more suspicious. For them, as I have already suggested, humans are not all that corporeally different from their world; certainly, they would argue, we cannot see the relation of people to their world as anything so grandiose as spirit to matter. If anything, it is simply the relation of a highly advanced organism stationed before a full field of organic and inorganic matter. As Peirce writes, "The old dualistic notion of mind and matter, so prominent in Cartesianism, as two radically different kinds of substance will hardly find defenders today. Rejecting this, we are driven to some form of hylopathy, otherwise called monism."[29]

To the extent that dualism (be it Descartes's or Emerson's) predicated itself upon a spirit-matter split it found itself undermined. Nevertheless, dualism is not completely done away with here; it just assumes a new configuration. That is, even as those terms which governed the Renaissance (God-Human-Nature) and the Romantic (god/Human-Nature) appear to give way to a simpler two (Human-Nature) in the Modern perspective, there still remains an acknowledged divide between the Human and Nature. For even as the ability to think is credited less to God than to evolution, men and women are still conceived as thinking subjects. And since to think means, as it did for Emerson, to categorize experience, to see it in the context of space and time, the problem of subject and object remains. At the same time, men and women, subordinated to the level of experience even as they see themselves apart from it, have lost something of their grandeur. They find it more difficult to sustain the self-importance of their former state. And if Emerson, bolstered by a belief in his own god-like status vis-à-vis Nature, could deprivilege the world as "apparent, not substantial" facts, as things to be known phenomenally, it proved more difficult for those who came after not to show more respect for the facts of experience.

The point is that prior to the Industrial Revolution facts could be understood as relatively stable in number, analogically rooted as they were in a world not our own. After this revolution, facts seemed anything but stable; they multiplied at a prodigious rate, demanding not only acknowledgment but deference as well. In the subject-object tug of war, all these new facts pulled on the side of the object, giving the world of facts a solidity that it never had before. Now, everything appeared to be acquiescing to facts, mind included. Granted, the modern description offered a dualism that kept mind or language (mind's representative) apart from facts. Yet a dualism predicated simply on a duality of function without also being predicated on a duality of substance always stood in danger of being undermined. A sort of mythic parallel had to be constructed to keep the planes of language and facts both appositive and separate. This parallel, articulated most famously in the *Tractatus* by Wittgenstein (who later deemed it a fiction), was logical form, something which the reticulated plane of language and facts were both able to share without losing their individual identities.

Language, then, though it might not be identical to what it denoted, left us with every reason to believe that it represented the essence of what was pointed to. Looking ahead to the *Tractatus,* Peirce wrote, "the pragmatist grants that a proper name (although it is not customary to say it has *meaning*) has a certain denotative function peculiar, in each case, to that name and its equivalents; and that he grants that every assertion contains such a denotative or pointing-out function."[30] Added to which, "the very meaning of a word or significant object ought to be the very essence of reality of what it signifies."[31]

JAMES AND PRAGMATISM

Refused a position at Harvard, Peirce soon retired from the front lines of the philosophic movement after formulating his pragmatic stance. Formidable as Peirce's intellectual work is, it might have suffered an even greater eclipse than it did had not another member of the Metaphysical Club, William James, taken with the pragmatic perspective since its inception in the 1870s, resuscitated the philosophy in his famous 1907 volume *Pragmatism.* It was James who, in such texts as *Principles of Psychology, Essays in Radical Empiricism* and *A Pluralistic Universe,* did so much to make pragmatism a discernible philosophy, making the pragmatic idea the basis for the country's first philosophical formulation of experience. The time was ripe. The decades prior had witnessed a multitude of scientific advances— theoretical and practical—and people found themselves more predisposed to look to science for large scale explanations. As James wrote in the opening pages of *Pragmatism,* never before had so many people been of such a decided empirical temperament:

> For a hundred and fifty years past the progress of science has seemed to mean the enlargement of the material universe and the diminution of man's importance. The result is what one may call the growth of naturalistic or positivistic feeling. Man is no longer lawgiver to nature, he is an absorber. She it is who stands firm; he it is who must accommodate himself. Let him record truth, unhuman though it be, and submit to it![32]

James felt that people, in seeking knowledge, must learn to resign themselves to experience, to the facts of the natural world. The ways of abstraction and *a priori* reasoning could only lead to fragile irrelevancies, closed systems whose truth would shed little light upon the realities of the world. Rather than suffer such stale artificialities, one should substitute for them the lessons of everyday experience. Freshness would be one happy result. Thus the pragmatist

> turns away from abstractions and insufficiency, from verbal solutions, from bad *a priori* reasons, from fixed principles, closed systems, and pretended absolutes and origins. He turns towards concreteness and adequacy, towards facts, towards action, and towards power. That means the empiricist temper regnant and the rationalist temper sincerely given up. It means the open air and possibilities of nature, as against dogma, artificiality, and the pretense of finality in truth. (P, 31)

James's method of ferreting out a body of accepted truths is the same as Peirce's. Thus the test of any proposition is whether it can be said to have practical effect. Only those propositions that have such effect can be deemed serious, or worthy of attention: "Whenever a dispute is serious, we ought to be able to show some practical differences that must follow one side or the other's being right" (P, 28). Truth, then, is not to be understood as a quality found independent of experience, as a frozen universal. Rather, it is a process, a process of verification that has no definite culminating point: "Truth *happens* to an idea. It *becomes* true, is made true by events. Its verity *is* in fact an event, a process; the process namely of its verifying itself; its veri-*fication*. Its process is the process of valid-*ation*" (P, 97). There is nothing intrinsically true or false about an idea; such qualities can only be ascribed after a correspondence between the idea and external fact has been made. Once made, it is then possible to test the idea to see whether it does accord point for point with the external fact. If it does, the idea is true; if it does not, the idea is false. Thus for James, truth is nothing more than "the simple duplication by the mind of a ready-made and given reality" (P, 93). True ideas agree with natural facts:

> It is hard to find any one phase that characterizes these consequences (verification and validation) better than the ordinary agreement-formula—just such consequences being what we have in mind whenever we say that our ideas "agree" with reality. They lead us, namely, through the acts and ideas which they instigate, into, or up to, or towards, other parts of experience with which we feel all the while . . . that the original idea remains in agreement. (P, 97)

Truth is always a means and never an end. James adopted this view in recognition of the fact that we can never possess a complete knowledge of reality and that without such a knowledge there can be no meaningful discussion about truth's end. Framed by our experiences, truth is always a contingent, acceptable only so long as it satisfies our sense of reality; it does this by being verifiable, not only in terms of our own situation, but also in terms of others'. Truth "[i]s what gives us the maximum possible sum of satisfaction, taste included, but consistency both with previous truth and with novel fact is always the most important claimant."[33] In sum, truth is an expedient, an "instrumental," to be made use of while it works, and to be disposed of when it ceases to do so: "Any idea upon which we can ride, so to speak; any idea that can carry us prosperously from any one part of experience to any other part, linking things satisfactorily, working securely, simplifying, saving labor; is true in so far forth, true instrumentally" (P, 34).

James's is a pluralistic vision. Said to be only a "method"—which is not true, for it clearly constitutes an ideology as well—pragmatism leads necessarily to a heightened appreciation of particulars: "[O]ur pragmatism has forced us to be friendly to the pluralistic view" (P, 81). This view, which James, forced or not forced, readily espouses, emphasizes the importance of seeing particulars in and of themselves outside the context of large schemes. Wholes are not universals imposed upon particulars, but collections forged out of a host of similar particulars. As such, the whole is always secondary to the particular. "Empiricism . . . lays the explanatory stress upon the part, the element, the individual, and treats the whole as a collection and the universal as an abstraction. My description of things, accordingly, starts with the parts and makes the whole a bearing of the second order."[34] James thus emphasizes the disparateness of reality rather than its harmony. Connections are visible but are overshadowed by nature's infinite multiplicity, a situation which is in no way static. Reality is never "complete and ready-made"; it is always in a state of flux, changing and growing as its elements take on different and more numerous forms. Darwin, for one, had already claimed that this was the case. To argue otherwise, like the rationalists, insisting that finite particulars correspond to fixed universals, seemed to fly in the face of natural fact:

> Experience is in mutation, and our psychological ascertainments of truth are in mutation—so much rationalists will allow; but never that either reality itself or truth is mutable. Reality stands complete and ready-made from all eternity, rationalism insists, and the agreement of our ideas with it is that unique unanalyzable virtue in them which she has already told us. As that intrinsic excellence, their truth has nothing to do with our experience. (RE, 111)

Reality, James insisted, is much more "chaotic" than the rationalists will admit: "No single connection runs through all the experiences that compose it" (RE, 26). In fact, judging by experience, it seems that the most prevalent connection is simply that of conjunction, a connection which might even be without consequence: "It may be that some parts of the world are connected so loosely with other parts as to be strung along by nothing but the copula *and*. They might even come and go without those other parts suffering any internal change" (P, 81). If this is the case, then we would then have to view the constitution of the world as "additive," gaining and losing elements irrespective of any absolute connection. Taking account of both the connectiveness and disconnectiveness of experience, the radical empiricist's universe might be compared to

> one of those fried human heads with which the Dyaks of Borneo deck their lodges. The skull forms a solid nucleus; but the innumerable feathers, leaves, strings, beads and loose appendices of every description float and dangle from it, and, save that they terminate in it, seem to have nothing to do with one another. (RE, 5)

Beyond its pluralism—and its ethnocentricity—the empiricist's world is homogeneous, or composed of but a single substance. Thus, instead of being divided into matter and spirit, the world is solely composed of matter, or in James's phrase, "pure experience." Nothing can be granted reality unless it can be experienced by the senses: "Everything real must be experienceable somewhere, and every kind of thing experienced must somewhere be real."[35] The world, then, is both materially substantive and monistic; once we accept this fact we will have no difficulty in seeing that "knowing can easily be explained as a particular sort of relation towards one another into which portions of pure experience may enter" (RE, 5).

The question of the subject-object nexus, so central to the explanatory purposes of pre-Jamesian philosophy, now finds itself both downgraded and transformed. What has most changed is the way in which the subject, or the mind, is codified in a strictly materialist discourse. Mind and object, it is argued, partake of a single material substance, and therefore it should be a mistake to posit an absolute distinction between them. Rather, "[s]ubject and object are identical" (RE, 111). Hence the difference that we acknowledge when we speak of subject and object is one of kind, not quality; it is a difference in "relation and function." James says, "Thought and things are absolutely homogeneous as to their material, and their opposition is only one of relation and of function. There is no thought-stuff different from thing-stuff. . . ; but the same identical piece of 'pure experience' (which was the name I gave to the *materia prima* of everything) can stand alternately for a 'fact of consciousness' or for a physical reality, according as it is taken in one context or another" (RE, 72).

Thought and emotion are physiological processes. Consciousness, as a separate spiritual entity, does not exist. Instead, James writes, "It is made of sensations; it is something perceived. Its *esse* is *percipi,* and it and the image are generally homogeneous" (RE, 112). Before there is thought, there have to be sensations; and before there can be an experience of sensations, there has to be a nervous system capable of relaying sensations: "[A]ll our activity belongs at bottom to [a] type of reflex action, and . . . all our consciousness accompanies a chain of events of which the first was an incoming current in some sensory nerves and of which the last will be a discharge into some muscle, blood-vessel, or gland."[36] Our first perceptions as an infant are nothing more than pure sensation; only later do thoughts come.

That thoughts do eventually come is due to the complexity of the nervous system, a product of evolution. A less complex system would not have given men and women the ability to think, to get above their sensations. For thinking is not the simple additive combination of sensations that the early empiricists conceived it to be. Were this the case, there would be no explaining how our cognition differed from that of animals. But it is not the case, and we "ought not treat the perception as a sum of distinct psychic entities, the present sensation namely, plus a lot of images from the past all 'integrated' together in a way impossible to describe" (*Psych,* 79–80). The "notion of images flocking and fusing" is "mythological" (*Psych,* 103).

Our ability to think is predicated on the evolved nervous system and its malleability before sensations. Of this latter fact, James says, "Sensations, once experienced, modify the nervous organism, so that copies of them arise in the mind after the stimuli is gone" (*Psych*, 44). The repetition of particular sensations leads to the forging of paths in the nervous system, paths designed to facilitate the comprehension of the sensation vis-à-vis similar prior sensations: "The chief cerebral conditions of perception are the paths of association irradiating from the sense impressions, which may have already formed. If a certain sensation be strongly associated with the attributes of a certain thing, that thing is almost sure to be perceived when we get the sensation" (*Psych*, 82). Thought, then, equals a process of habitual association, the actual sensation recalling similar sensations already experienced. Our perception of a single sensation is accordingly not identical with the sensation itself but is understood against a backdrop of past experiences. Through purely empiric means, our minds order experiences, categorizing the chaotic sensations of immediate experience in terms of a larger whole:

> The process aroused in the sense-organ has shot into various paths which habit has already organized in the hemispheres, and . . . instead of our having the sort of consciousness which could be correlated with the single sensorial process, we have that which is correlated with this more complex process. This, as it turns out, is the consciousness of that more complex "object," the "whole thing," instead of being the consciousness of that more simple object, the few qualities or attributes which actually impress our peripheral nerves. (*Psych*, 79)

Finally, James argues that, like thought and language, emotions must be understood in physiological terms. In fact, emotions are nothing more than bodily changes brought on by set objects: "[T]he bodily changes follow directly the perception of the exciting fact, and that our feeling of the same changes as they occur is the emotion" (*Psych*, 449). Emotions and bodily changes are inseparable. If you try to imagine emotions divorced from bodily fact, you will find that you have "nothing left behind, no 'mind-stuff' out of which the emotion can be constituted and that a cold and neutral state of intellectual perception is all that remains" (*Psych*, 451). It would almost be more proper to say that we have emotions because we experience physiological changes than to say we have physiological changes because we experience emotions: "We feel sorry because we cry, angry because we strike, afraid because we tremble, and not that we cry, strike, or tremble, because we are sorry, angry, or fearful, as the case may be" (*Psych,* 451). Emotions, then, are clearly more than mental states; they are physical states as well.

James, we can see, stressed a materialistic explanation of the world. As opposed to Emerson's, James's world is one in which

1. universals become subordinated to particulars (there being no assumption that universals exist);
2. subject-object dualisms are reduced to monistic problems;
3. human response is understood in physiological terms;
4. natural facts lose their symbolic identity;
5. parataxis in language reflects a plurality in facts;
6. an absolute moral law is replaced by a pragmatic ethic; and
7. a world replete with mystery gives way to a world suspicious of the same.

This view strongly reflected scientific advances and the concomitant impulse of all modernists to naturalize further their own intellectual disciplines so they did not appear contrary to fact. Or, as James stated, it was the "*attitude of looking away from first things, principles, 'categories,' supposed necessities; and of looking towards last things, fruits, consequences, facts*" (P, 32). In the end, James presented himself as offering less an intellectual system than an empirical method, one which, before anything else, required that truths be harmonious with found experience. And while we ourselves should not so readily concur with the contention that "[a]ll these [ideas], you see, are anti–intellectualist tendencies" (P, 32), we note the shift in emphasis from what others had offered before.

THE MODERNIST IMAGINATION

What was the consequence of all this for the literary imagination? Well, in many instances it meant, in Lionel Trilling's words, an increased respect for the "object as object, as it exists apart from us."[37] That is, there followed for many a heightened modernist feeling both of one's separateness from, and of one's attachment to, things, with the latter sense being, in turn, enhanced precisely by a type of imagination which sought to bridge the gap between knower and object. For particular writers such as Stein, Hemingway, Williams, and Moore, it meant (as José Ortega y Gasset said of Proust's contribution) the invention of "'a new distance between ourselves and things'—a distance modified by attention and imagination, by love and desire."[38] Here the "attention and imagination" were not of a romantic order, if that meant an opposition to what James spoke of as the "enlargement of the material world." Rather, they were to be more likened to Wallace Stevens's conception of the mind as a special—even "metaphysical"—faculty in a wholly physical world:

> We feel, without being particularly intelligent about it, that the imagination as metaphysics will survive logical positivism unscathed. At the same time, we feel, and with the sharpest possible intelligence that it is not worthy to survive if it is to be identified with the romantic. The imagination is one of the great human powers. The romantic belittles it. The imagination is the liberty of the mind. The romantic is a failure of that liberty. It is to the imagination what sentimentality is to feeling. It is a failure of the imagination precisely as sentimentality is a failure of feeling. The imagination is the only genius. It is intrepid and eager and the extreme of its achievement lies in minor wish-fulfillments and it is incapable of abstraction.[39]

What had changed since, say, Emerson or even Whitman, was not so much the terms of invention—i.e., subject and object—so much as the weight given to the terms. The terms themselves are almost essential, that is if there is to be a language. Yet their use varies. Nineteenth-century Romantics not only celebrated the subject (e.g., Whitman's "I contain multitudes"), but they also frequently sought to transform everything into its terms. As Denis Donoghue writes respecting the romantic self: "The self refuses to recognize itself in any part of the universe until the entire universe is transformed into subjective terms, every apprehended object becoming subject."[40]

Of course, Stevens's practice is hardly different. Still, even in Stevens, whose Romantic antecedents are pronounced, one notes a greater tentativeness respecting claims for an imperial self. He polemicizes on behalf of the imagination—telling us that it will survive the age's positivism—yet there is a note of doubt here as well. He really is not so certain that the imagination will survive, and whether he is or is not, he is also mindful that the world is substantive as well as phenomenal. "Art must fit with other things; it must be part of the system of the world," he writes. "And if it finds a place in that system it will likewise find a ministry and relations that are its proper adjuncts."[41] Meanwhile, what was true for Stevens ("not ideas about the thing, but the thing itself")[42] was even more true for writers such as Stein, Hemingway, Williams, and Moore, writers more predisposed to heed T. E. Hulme's call "that after a hundred years of romanticism"[43] the artist should bear witness to the world as it is, as a place not only of continuities but of discontinuities as well. Shortly before his death in 1917, Hulme wrote,

> We constantly tend to think that the discontinuities in nature are only apparent, and that a fuller investigation would reveal the underlying continuity. This shrinking from a gap in nature has developed to a degree which paralyzes any objective perception, and prejudices our *seeing things as they really are*. For an objective view of reality we must make use both of the categories of continuity and discontinuity. Our principal concern then at the present moment should be the re-establishment of the temper or disposition of mind which can look at a gap or chasm without shuddering. (*Spec,* 3; emphasis added)

For Hulme, as for the Modernists in general, reality is something characterized by discreteness: there are things, which are marked by distinct boundaries and separateness, and there are the spaces between these things. Or rather, there is simply space itself, which constitutes the container-like frame for things. So, because things are conceived to be ultimately self-contained, there develops a consequent conception, and that is that these things might be known in their state of separation. That they are not already known this way has to do with the fact that while things are ultimately atomistic, they do not readily appear so. Instead, they appear as caught in webs of relations (Hulme's "continuities"), relations which hide their discreteness. Hence to know *things as they are* requires an exceptional determination, for they need to be sought beneath the surface welter of experience, and brought back to the surface as if they were some precious mineral discovered deep within the bowels of the earth. And here, for Hulme, the earth's surface might be thought of as a metaphor for language, for it is in the nature of language, says he, that it entraps and hides that which we would know, or re-cognize. For if "[t]he great aim" of this generation's artists "is accurate and definite description" (*Spec,* 132), then this ambition would appear frustrated by the abstractness of language: "[I]t expresses never the exact thing but a compromise—that which is common to you, me and everybody" (*Spec,* 132). It expresses not the particular thing but the generic. If we set out to express *the* table, we end up expressing only *a* table. The difficulty—if we construe it as such, and Hulme and a significant number of Modernists did—is that both mind and language work by means of classification. Perception is less a true, intuitive knowing than a kind of pigeonholing:

> I look, I listen, I hear, I think I am seeing, I think I am hearing everything, and when I examine myself I think I am examining my own mind.

But I am not.

What I see and hear is simply a selection made by my senses to serve as a light for my conduct. My senses and my consciousness give me no more than a practical simplification of reality. In the usual perception I have of reality all the differences useless to man have been suppressed. My perception runs in certain moulds. Things have been classified with a view I can make of them. It is this classification I perceive rather than the real shape of things. I hardly see an object, but merely notice what class it belongs to—what ticket I ought to apply to it. (*Spec,* 158)

Emerson, of course, might have said the same thing. Where Hulme and artists such as Stein, Hemingway, Williams, and Moore differ, however, from Emerson is in their conviction that one can transcend this situation, this difficulty. Hulme believes that while the ordinary course of both perception and language is one that caters to the habitual, it is possible, with a powerful degree of determination, not only to "see things as they really are" but also "to force the mechanism of expression out of the way in which it tends to go and into the way he wants" (*Spec,* 133, 160). To explain himself, Hulme offers the metaphor of the artist's (or, more accurately, the draftsman's) curve, that flat wooden or plastic tool which assists one in drawing curvilinear lines. This curve, says he, might be understood to stand for language; that is, while the world is replete with an infinite number of curving lines, all differing slightly from one another, the curve, or language, allows us only to express, or give voice to, a select few of the same. All the other curves are rendered not as they are but as they conform to one of the typic curves. Thus the vast multitude of curves—i.e., of sensations—are bent, or distorted, into shapes already recognizable.

So while convenience is one happy consequence of this curve, descriptive accuracy is not. The particular gives way to the general, and the general is always, to some extent, a falsification of its own differentiae. Still, most of us rarely take heed of this fact. The reason, says Hulme, is that the curve, or language, dictates just what it is that we are able to see. And, "[a]s we not only express ourselves in words, but for the most part think also in them, it comes about that not only do we not express more than the impersonal element of an emotion, but that we do not, as a matter of fact, perceive more" (*Spec,* 166). Rather, we both perceive and think, according to pre-established molds, molds which are firmly embodied in language itself.

That is, most of us behave this way. The artist, however—the genuine artist—is the exception, argues Hulme. Less dominated by the *"necessities of action"* than of *"perception,"* the artist is able to see the individual curve, to "perceive just for the sake of perceiving" (*Spec*, 166). The artist is able to do so because he or she both recognizes the falsity inherent in ordinary perception and expression and chooses to do something about it. Particularly, the artist chooses to exercise a strictness of attention in both perception and the expression of this perception. This means, first, that the artist seeks "*to see things as they really are*, and apart from the conventional ways in which [one has] been trained to see them" (*Spec*, 133; emphasis added). And second, that the artist seeks "the concentrated state of mind, the grip over oneself which is necessary in the actual expression of what one sees" (*Spec*, 133).

At this point, the artist is free to render freshly those things which without his or her attention would be otherwise lost. Art itself would be superfluous if we all experienced the things of the world as they are rather than as they are when rendered generic. For then, "[o]ur eyes . . . would carve out in space and fix in time the most inimitable of pictures. In the center of one's mind, we should hear constantly a certain music" (*Spec*, 147). Yet as we mostly do not experience the world this way—i.e., intuitively—it becomes the artist to create "not a counter language but a visual concrete one[,] . . . a compromise for a language of intuition which would hand over sensations bodily" (*Spec*, 134). When this language gives voice to emotions, it is, says Hulme, imagination; when it gives voice to things, it is fancy. In either case, it entails the invention of "fresh epithets and fresh metaphors, not so much because they are new, and we are tired of the old, but because the old cease to convey a physical thing and become abstract counters" (*Spec*, 134–35). The need is to return to the concrete, "to make you continuously see a physical thing" (*Spec*, 134). A physical thing as seen not so much in the context of other things but as it stands in itself, independent, less a means to an end than a bona fide end in itself. As such, one tries to see things not as past experience would insist that we should see them but as they exist in the immediate moment. Quoting Plato, Hulme writes, "The object of aesthetic contemplation is something framed apart by itself and regarded without memory or expectation, simply as being itself, as end not means, as individual not universal" (*Spec*, 136).

Believing then that it is the modern artist's purpose "to pierce through here and there, accidentally as it were, the veil placed between us and reality by the limitations of our perception engendered by action" (*Spec*, 147), Hulme celebrates the objects won in this wrestle with perception. "It must be," he says, "an intense zest which heightens a thing out of" its backdrop, which sees a thing as an individual thing, worthy of our attention (*Spec*, 136). It must be an expression of an affection, of a love which refuses to let things die, which refuses to let them be washed over by the sweeping currents of history. As such, "art must always be individual and springs from dissatisfaction with the generalized expressions of ordinary perception and ordinary language" (*Spec*, 153), expressions which defer "direct communication" with the thing-itself in favor of something not quite so interesting. Here, the best art, the best poetry, evinces a "kind of instinctive feeling which is conveyed over to one, that the poet is describing something which is actually present to him, which he realizes visually at first hand" (*Spec*, 167).

Stein, Hemingway, Williams, Moore, and the Technique of Originality

Today, Hulme's argument appears, perhaps, quaintly naive, yet it is my contention that Stein, Hemingway, Williams, Moore, and a fair number of other modernist artists did, in fact, believe that they were attending and giving voice to "something which is actually present." And while there would have been overstatements this way—as understanding got confused with polemics—the bias toward the autonomous object remains marked. For instance, in "Nuances of a Theme by Williams," Stevens admonishes the isolated star to "Shine alone, nakedly, shine like bronze, / that reflects neither my face nor any inner part / of my being, shine like fire, that mirrors nothing." Meanwhile, Williams himself made attention to the particular thing almost a requirement, arguing that the "four pinces of divers powder cleverly compounded to cure surely, safely, pleasantly a painful twitching of the imagination, makes logic a butterfly, offers a finality that sends us spinning through space, a fixity the mind could climb forever, a revolving mountain, a complexity with a surface of glass; the gist of poetry."[44]

Unlike Emerson, who chose to translate all experience first into consciousness and then, by extension, into divinity, the modernists spoken of here mostly tended to look outward, to the thing as it stood beyond the pale of mind's imprint. They also tended (to refer back to James) not to predicate a radical distinction (i.e., one of quality as opposed to kind) between subject and object and almost to proceed as if the opposition had ceased to be a problem. And all this was carried out in the spirit of Alfred North Whitehead's statement "[t]hat this dragging in of the mind as making additions of its own to the thing posited for knowledge by sense-awareness is merely a way of shirking the problem of natural philosophy. That problem is to discuss the relations *inter se* of things known, abstracted from the bare fact that they are known."[45]

In artistic terms, the consequence was the promotion of the belief that the external object could be rendered in language; that it could be presented in all its *thatness;* even to the point wherein the verbal object gave way completely to that other object, the referent. The way, these modernists said, was through a disciplined attention to the object. Thus Williams writes, "to see the thing itself without forethought or afterthought but with great intensity of attention,"[46] an attention that, in Stein's words, meant "the absolute refusal of never using a word that was not an exact word," the word that conveyed "the difference between what is and is not that" object.[47] Or as Pound put the matter: "Use no superfluous word, no adjective, which does not reveal something."[48]

At its most radical, the ambition seemed nothing less than to speak the object, to forge, in Stein's words, such a natural "relationship between the word and the thing seen" that, in one's best efforts, one achieved "something that was not the name of that thing but was in a way that actual thing."[49] Words and objects were more than akin, and if used properly the former, said Williams, should bespeak a "fidelity to the object, the thought around it and their passionate welding."[50] Or, according to Louis Zukofsky, should simply operate as pure or "absolute symbols," wherein there was no telling apart the word and the object: "The economy of presentation in writing is a reassertion of faith that the combined letters—the words— are absolute symbols for objects, states, acts, interrelationships, thoughts about them. If not, why use words—new or old?"[51] Meanwhile, if a number of the American Modernists leaned toward conflating language with its object, it probably had something to do with the epoch's celebration of the present moment. For these moderns, time itself was conceived as both fluid and atomistic; and life, in Williams's words, was "above all things else at any moment subversive of life as it was the moment before—always new, irregular."[52] Though in a way, Williams's conception was less subversive than paradigmatic, so predicated did it appear on a metaphor supplied by Newton several hundred years before. In 1687, Newton wrote: "Absolute, true, and mathematical time, of itself, and from its own nature, *flows* equally without relation to anything external."[53] Fluid, yet divisible, a fact which every tick-tock of the clock reminded people, at least, before the 1916 invention of the sweeping second hand. And for those who did not trust their clocks, there were the scientists (e.g., Wilhelm Wundt) who calculated the present moment to be between five and twelve seconds long. William James himself spoke of "the practically cognized present [as] no knife-edge, but a saddle-back, with a certain breadth of its own on which we sit perched, and from which we look in two directions into time."[54]

By the 1920s, of course, Einstein had completely called into question the prevailing metaphor of time as fluid and atomistic, yet it took a while for the significance of this change to register in any broad scale way. Meanwhile, reality was being more generally conceived as a singular succession of present moments—or *nows*—which, if one were a Marcel Proust or a Stephen Dedalus, could be held on to: "Hold to the now, the here, through which all future plunges to the past."[55] In this way, the divisible moment—James's "specious present," Proust's *moments bienheureux,* Woolf's "rings of light," Joyce's "epiphanies," Stein's "continuous present," etc.[56]—came to assume an importance which itself pressed the conception of time's continuity into shadow. Reality started to seem less a "successive but an immediate existing,"[57] as Stein claimed, and if this were so, it followed that one should use language somewhat differently than one's predecessors, the Romantics, who had both conceptually and linguistically preferred unity to separateness. For instance, the interest of a Carlyle or an Emerson in synthetical structures seemed to find itself mirrored in their individual syntaxes, the way that, for Romantics in general, one might, in Ernst Cassirer's words, say, "the true vehicle of linguistic meaning is never sought in the particular word, but only in the synthesis upon which all speech and all understanding are essentially based."[58] Yet for Stein, Hemingway, Williams, and Moore, things seem to stand otherwise. For them, the most veritable reality was the reality of the present moment, of the object in isolation. Things might be connected or stand in relation, but these qualities were thought subordinate to the fact that discrete objects exist at all, as things-in-themselves. Accordingly, the grammar of the Romantics, the grammar of the sentence, struck these authors as unsuitable to their actual needs. As Edmund Wilson noted, "A linguistic logic based upon laws of direct causality and linear time cannot authentically correspond to a universe of possibilities such as [William] James describes," a universe (to go directly back to James) in which "[t]he real world as it is given objectively at this moment is the sum total of all its being and events now."[59]

What these writers wanted, in a sense, was not a grammar of the sentence but a grammar of the word, of the moment, a grammar that would permit a Pound to write "In a Station of the Metro"—Pound: "In a poem of this sort one is trying to record the *precise instant* when a thing outward and objective transforms itself, or darts into a thing inward and subjective"[60]—or a Stein to write the *Portraits*—Stein: "In making these portraits I naturally made a continuous present an including everything and a beginning again and again within a very small thing."[61] If "reading word by word would make writing that is not anything be something,"[62] as Stein discovered, then writing word by word could make writing—the writing of these modernists—be something infinitely closer to the world of immediate experience, of the noumenon, than had been gotten in writing before. The need, said Williams, was to "breakaway from that paralyzing vulgarity of logic," to follow "some unapparent sequence quite apart from the usual syntactical one" and then

> to separate the words from the printed page, to take them up into the world where the words are no more than titles under the illustrations. It is an affirmation of the forever sought freedom of truth from usage. It is the modern world emerging among the living ancients by paying attention to the immediacy of its own contacts.[63]

Modernism, as conceived by the authors under discussion, meant paying attention to the immediacy of their own contacts. The real world was a physical place, made, as Hemingway wrote, of "wine, bread, oil, salt, vinegar, bed, early mornings, nights, days, the sea, men, women, dogs, beloved motor cars, bicycles, hills and valleys, the appearance and disappearance of trains on straight and curved tracks . . . cock grosse drumming on a basswood log, the smell of sweetgrass and fresh-smoked leather and Sicily."[64] One could abstract from this world, but one could not easily transmute it. The world was simply too busy being itself, something which in the main these authors appreciated. It was for this reason that they (in polemical fashion) tended to devalue metaphor, wary as they were of the tool which relocated their attention away from the immediate object. As Zukofsky wrote, "The disadvantages of strained metaphor is not that it is necessarily sentimental (the sentimental may at times have its positive personal qualities) but that it carries the mind to a diffuse everywhere and leaves it nowhere."[65]

Consequently, the thing-itself took precedence over the substitution; the sensual object was preferable to its symbols. The modern writer, Williams said, "does not translate the sensuality of his materials into symbols but deals with them directly."[66] And thereby he or she becomes, with Marianne Moore, "a literalist of the imagination,"[67] believing with Pound that "the natural object is always the adequate symbol."[68] Hence, in a way, the modernism as practiced by this group of writers is very much about the "reality" of objects, of reducing systems and ideas to their basic physical components. This held true not only with the movement's prevailing paradigm for artistic creation—the objective correlative—so visceral in its conception, but also with the larger matter of beliefs. These, the artists seemed to say, could not be deduced from above but only induced from below, from the ground of particular experience. As such, their work often became synonymous with the breaking down of past religious and spiritual beliefs, beliefs that had been predicated less upon experiential evidence—the new test of beliefs—as upon abstract principles. Thus Wallace Stevens, speaking for many moderns, could write, "Modern reality is a reality of decreation, in which our revelations are not the revelations of belief, but the precious portents of our own powers. The greatest truth we could hope to discover, in whatever field we discovered it, is that man's truth is the final resolution of everything."[69] For these moderns, then, truth seemed less and less like an absolute. It was, said Moore, "no Apollo / Belvedere, no formal thing."[70] It was, added Eliot, "a hypothetical limit of experience," one which he and his contemporaries found it neither necessary to accept or reject:

> But what we do know is that we are able to pass from one point of view to another, and that we are compelled to do so, and that different aspects more or less hang together. For rejecting a higher experience there may be no reason. But that this higher experience explains the lower is at least open to doubt.[71]

Nevertheless, as determined as Stein, Hemingway, Williams, or Moore were to front the world as it is, their quest for origin added up to less a genuine exercise in revelation than a modernist stylistics mimicking the same. In short, they invented, without really intending to, a *technique of originality,* wherein the "true" object was less presented than represented in a mode reflective of the times and its values. Characteristic of this technique were the following:

1. a heightened sensitivity to the particularity and disparateness of experience, as opposed to its continuity and universality;
2. a monistic conception of the epistemological problem of mind and matter;
3. a more paratactic language reflecting an increasingly pluralistic vision;
4. a notably descriptive language that privileges metonymy over metaphor;
5. a physiological conception of human response, notably mirrored in the objective correlative schema for artistic invention; and

6. a notion of "truth" that, while still hinged upon a theory of correspondence, appears strikingly constricted when compared to prior notions founded upon the acceptance of *a priori* principles.

Here, among artists such as Stein, Hemingway, Williams, and Moore, one finds little, if any, anxiety about a project that seems to demand a complete overhaul of all that we mean by representation, by imitation. That "[i]mitation does not correspond to its essence," in Jacques Derrida's words, "is not what it is—imitation—unless it is in some way at fault or rather in default,"[72] is not construed as a problem. The reason is that they still hold to the fiction that language, when freshly used, is more or less transparent. They also still hold to the fiction of a self willfully strong enough to bridge the chasm which separates it from the object. Finally, perhaps, we find a style wherein "[t]he work of art," to borrow Hans-Georg Gadamer's formulation, "is conceived as an ontological event and the abstraction to which aesthetic differentiation commits it is dissolved. A picture is an event of presentation."[73] The picture itself "is absolutely different from what it represents, but shares in the being of that[,]" so that, when the artistry is successful, "what is represented comes to itself in the picture. It experiences an increase in being."[74] As I say, I think this a fair description of what the said authors do. Though if it is, we need also to note how sacramental an aesthetics this is. For even while a Stein, a Hemingway, or a Williams might proclaim his or her materialism, the whole aesthetic project here, focused upon both the bridging of the space between subject and object as well as the energetic redemption of things, bespeaks a fundamental belief in the world's immanence.[75] It is a belief, which while either "explicit or suppressed, masked or avowed, substantive or imagined . . . [,]" underwrites the presumption of creativity, of signification in our encounters" with the world, and which is, ultimately, theological.[76] Therefore, if one, such as de Man, says that what we find here is more like a variation upon a theme—the theme of Romanticism, say—than something radically other, I would not protest. Still, neither an epoch nor an artist is ever completely identical to another— nor should we want them so—and if my discussion in the following chapters on Stein, Hemingway, Williams, and Moore focuses itself around the hitherto named epistemic formations, it is not with the design to repress these artists' individual differences as it is with the design to say something about the history of our literature, specifically of its poetics of representation.

3
Gertrude Stein and *Tender Buttons*

Monet, Stein, and the Innocent Eye

In his fine essay on Claude Monet's last canvases, Roger Shattuck concludes, "As I see it, Monet remained representational while becoming non-figurative."[1] That is, while the titles of Monet's paintings (i.e., *The Path through the Irises, Water Lilies—Reflections of the Willow, Water Lilies*) point to the representational nature of his compositions and secure their link to the visible world, his technique is more and more "non-figurative, rendering the vibrating field and raw retinal data rather than the conventional forms and figures (straight line, circle, angle, grid, etc.) of learned perception."[2] Shattuck's argument is that Monet "refused to take the final step into abstract art."[3] No matter how painterly his last canvases became—and they are very painterly—Monet always remained an artist whose roots were in the nineteenth century. Shattuck also argues, as do I with respect to Gertrude Stein, that the allegiance of Monet to the "innocent eye"—the allegiance to the artistic faith that allows one fully disciplined in his or her attentions to capture the world's impressions not as they make themselves known to the understanding but rather, and more impressively, as they make themselves felt as images upon the retina—ultimately led to something else entirely, to the complete overturning of the trope of the innocent eye itself.

With the hindsight of the historian I would like to argue that one of the ways in which the paradigm of the innocent eye—of "naive realism"—was undermined was by passing through it, by pressing its logic to its extremity. Thus if a late-nineteenth-century painter such as Monet, or an early-twentieth-century writer such as Stein stood convinced that a "world" existed outside cognition, only waiting to be the object of his or her knowledge and not as an integrated aspect of that knowledge but as a *ding an sich,* then perhaps the most expeditious exit from the formula was to simply act upon it, to seek out the thing-in-itself. Not that either Monet or Stein sought such an exit; rather, they moved in this direction (of "exit") truly trusting,

80

I believe, in the representational logic in which they began. Yet the quest was always a quixotic one, and as it was practiced with words (as in *Tender Buttons)* rather than with paint (as in the *Water Lillies* series) it seemed more likely to have its failure appear marked. Paint used in a nonrepresentative manner seemed to admit of interpretative possibilities (e.g., those of abstract art) not shared with words, though recently proponents of literary postmodernism and *écriture féminine* have recuperated Stein's word paintings in a way which a half century ago few would have anticipated.

Of course, the classificatory questions I raise are not interdependent of what we know about, or how we interpret, authorial intention. As I said in chapter 1, it would be unwise to press the relation of intention and work too far, but they are nevertheless related, and our understanding of the former plays a determining role in what we make of the latter. However, I do not mean to suggest that intention and work are related to the extent that the intentionalists Steven Knapp and William Benn Michaels, in their controversial essay, "Against Theory," would have us believe. There they write: "The mistake made by theorists has been to imagine the possibility or desirability of moving from one term (the author's intended meaning) to a second term (the text's meaning), when actually the two terms are the same. One can neither succeed nor fail in deriving one term from the other, since to have one is to have them both."[4] Rather, one might argue, along with William C. Dowling, that "to say that either of two terms—here, intention and meaning—is entailed by the other is not, surely, to say that one is identical with the other, and in all sorts of cases the distinction turns out to be logically significant."[5]

With Stein, the distinction is also "logically significant." Like Monet, she sets out to do the impossible: to see the things of this world with such concentration, such intensity, that she would block out everything that is not the object of attention, all backdrop, all relations, everything that is not included in the thing-itself. Her titles— "A Shawl," "A Table," "A Book,"—are often the only clues regarding the representational nature of her pieces. Still they, along with everything else we know about Stein's artistic intentions, are clues enough to warrant our relating the Stein of *Tender Buttons* and the early portraits with the Monet of the last canvases. If, as Shattuck argues, Monet never really broke through into the world of full-fledged abstraction, an abstraction that is nonrepresentational even while it is figurative ("At this crucial juncture in European painting, Kandinsky and Mondrian and Malevich were becoming non-representational while remaining emphatically figurative"),[6] one may also say much the same about Stein—that her work remains, more or less, grounded in an aesthetics of representation. This is not to deny the almost opaque nature of her verbal constructions; rather, it is to say that the abstractness of Stein's work follows more from an intention to offer "an exact reproduction of either an outer or an inner reality" than from an interest in abstraction itself.[7] And it is to factor in this intention as a legitimate point of discussion.[8]

Thus I locate Stein's work in the tradition of an innocent eye aesthetic. This tradition, as Shattuck and E. H. Gombrich, among others, have pointed out,[9] had many advocates during the nineteenth century. The phrase itself was coined by Ruskin:

> The perception of solid Form is entirely a matter of experience. We *see* nothing but flat colours; and it is only by a series of experiments that we find out that a stain of black or grey indicates the dark side of a solid substance, or that a faint hue indicates that the object in which it appears is far away. The whole technical power of painting depends on our recovery of what may be called the *innocence of the eye;* that is to say, of a sort of childish perception of these flat stains of colour, merely as such, without consciousness of what they signify,—as a blind man would see them if suddenly gifted with sight.[10]

Other advocates of the "innocent eye" included Jules Laforgue, Henri Bergson, Roger Fry, T. E. Hulme, and, closer to home, William James in his *Principles of Psychology*. James's views deserve quotation, not only because they so nicely articulate both the concept of the "innocent eye" and the nineteenth-century psychological notions underlying it, but also because James (who, early on, aspired to be a painter) had an immediate influence upon Stein herself:

> The whole education of the artist consists in his learning to see the presented sign as well as the represented things. No matter what the field of visions *means,* he sees it also as it *feels*—that is, as a collection of patches of color bounded by lines—the whole forming an optional diagram whose intrinsic proportions one who is not an artist has hardly a conscious inkling. The ordinary man's attention passes *over* them to their import; the artist turns back and dwells *upon* them for their own sake. "Don't draw the thing as it *is,* but as it *looks*" is the endless advice of every teacher to his pupil; forgetting that what it "is" is what it would also "look" provided it were placed in what we have called the "normal" situation for vision. In this situation the sensation as "sign" and the sensation as "object" coalesce into one, and there is no contrast between them.[11]

Yet if my thesis is that Stein pursued an "innocent eye" aesthetic, an aesthetic in which "the sensation as 'sign' and the sensation as 'object' coalesce into one," then it would perhaps be wise, before examining Stein's artistic application of this aesthetic, to explore her intellectual and artistic beginnings so as better to understand her later assumptions.

STEIN'S EARLY TYPOLOGIES

"I belong to the generation who born in the nineteenth century spent all the early part of my life escaping from it,"[12] Gertrude Stein once said. Whether she ever did escape from the influence of the nineteenth century is debatable. Certainly her beginnings are here—here being a century or zeitgeist that gave unusual prominence to the scientist's description of things, which meant of course giving prominence to description itself, along with its adjunct, categorization. Both as a young woman and later as a mature artist, Stein subscribed to this sense of things, a statement evidenced by the centrality which, in her 1937 memoir *Everybody's Autobiography,* she gave to William James's entry into her life: "[T]hen William James came that is I came to him and he said science is not a solution and not a problem it is a statement of the observation of things observed and perhaps therefore not interesting perhaps therefore only abjectly true."[13]

Elsewhere, Stein also refers to the importance which James placed upon scientific description and the influence which this view had upon her:

> When I was working with William James I completely learned one thing, that science is continuously busy with the complete description of something, with ultimately the complete description of everything. If this can really be done the complete description of every thing then what else is there to do. We may well say nothing, but and this is the thing that makes every thing continue to be anything, that after all what does happen is that as relatively few people spend all their time describing anything and they stop and so in the meantime as everything goes on somebody else can always commence and go on. And so description is really unending.[14]

The statement is telling; it gives evidence, as the work itself gives evidence, that Stein's original aesthetic—an aesthetic which throughout her career did, with respect to intention, not so much change as intensify itself—was grounded in the epistemology of science. Her first mature work as a thinker—the published product of her experiments with Leon M. Solomon, not to mention her studies in psychology at Harvard and in medicine at Johns Hopkins—was not in literature at all, but in science. What particularly interested her were the twin concerns of description and categorization. This is most clearly noted in the second article she wrote for the *Psychological Review* in 1898, an article she authored alone. Here, broadening the range of the first experiments, Stein sought "to examine the phenomena of normal automatism by a study of normal individuals, both in regard to the variations in this capacity found in a large number of subjects, and also in regard to the types of character that accompany a greater or lesser tendency of automatic action."[15] To this end, she found that people, with respect to their subconscious responsiveness, generally break down into two groups. Respecting the typology of the first group, Stein writes,

> This consists mostly of girls who are found naturally in literature courses and men who are going in for law. The type is nervous, high-strung, very imaginative, has the capacity to be easily roused and intensely interested. Their attention is strongly and easily held by something that interests them, even to the extent quite commonly expressed of being oblivious to everything else. But, on the other hand, they find it hard to concentrate on anything that does not catch the attention and hold the interest.[16]

This is a rather crude scientism, on a par with that of Stein's contemporary Frank Norris. What we see here, as we see in Norris, is less an attention to things as they are than to something else: things caught up in a whole host of preconceptions. Yet this scientism which could, in the name of science, stereotypically speak of "the habit of self-repression, the intense self-consciousness, the morbid fear of 'letting one's self go,' that is so prominent an element in the New England character,"[17] was to be a major constituent of Stein's own aesthetic efforts as well.

Typology itself is most evident in the first fictions: *Fernhurst, Q.E.D.* and *The Making of Americans* (the composition of which, according to Leon Katz, was commenced much earlier, in 1903, than was once thought, even prior to the composition of *Q.E.D.*).[18] For instance, *Fernhurst,* subtitled "The History of Philip Redburn[,] A Student of the Nature of Woman," is the story of a man, again like a character out of a Norris novel, whose "instincts gave the lie to his ideals and his ideals to his instincts" (47) and two women, "[t]he one practical worldly with noble aspirations, a mystic's ecstasy and the power of always adapting the means to a specific end and the other with a mind of a philosopher, a spirit exquisitely sensitive to beauty and a dreamy detached nature with an aspiration for the

common lot and a strange incapacity to touch the lives of others"
(20). Meanwhile, *Q.E.D.*, the story of a female ménage à trois, sets
in opposition Mabel Neathe, "an Italian type" whose "long angular
body" nevertheless "betrayed her New England origins," and Adele,
whose "instincts . . . have always been opposed to the indulgence
of any feeling of passion . . . due to the Calvinistic influence that
dominates American training and has interfered with [her] natural
temperament" (103) over the affection of Helen Thomas, "the
American version of the English handsome girl"—"a blooming
Anglo-Saxon" (54, 80). The other characters, like the passengers
aboard the steamer that first carries Adele to Europe, are "mere
wooden objects . . . sure to be of some abjectly familiar type that
one knew so well that there would be no need of recognizing their
existence" (53).

In *Three Lives* and *The Making of Americans*, typology also remains
a major concern even as Stein's artistic attention is beginning to take
her elsewhere, notably toward the creating of a continuous present.
Still typology is most evident here, particularly in the way Stein
characterizes blacks—"Rose Johnson was a real black, tall, well built,
sullen, stupid, childlike"[19]—who, in the case of Rose and Sam, are
incapable of feeling anything more than a momentary sadness upon
the death of their own baby: "Rose Johnson had liked the baby well
enough and perhaps she just forgot it for awhile, anyway the child
was dead and Rose and Sam her husband were very sorry but then
these things came so often in the negro world in Bridgepoint, that
they neither of them thought about it very long" (85). One might
think that the "earth-born, boundless joy of negroes" (86) would
help explain Rose and Sam's disposition not to grieve, yet unfortunately, Rose, untrue to her race, "had not the wide, abandoned
laughter that makes the warm broad glow of negro sunshine" (86).
Hers is simply a more selfish and sullen type, which once understood
works as a key to explain nearly everything about her.

Similarly, the other central characters in *Three Lives*—Anna, Melanctha, Jefferson, Lena—are all walking types. Thus once one
understands that Anna's type is to be always scolding the servants
beneath her and to be adoring, admonishing, and protecting her
employer Miss Mathilda; that Melanctha's type is to be caught up
in her blueness, "sudden and impulsive and unbounded in some
faith" (89); that Jefferson's type is to be "a serious, earnest, good
young joyous doctor" liking "to take care of everybody" and loving
"his own colored people" (110) but also distrustful of Melanctha's
kind of "real courage," the kind that, in Jefferson's words, "makes
all kind of trouble, for them who ain't so noble with their courage"

(167); and that Lena's type is to be "patient, gentle, sweet and german" (239), one really understands everything there is to know about these characters. This typology given, they will not now turn around and surprise the reader by acting out of character.

As for *The Making of Americans,* this novel, as Stein tells us in *How Writing is Written,* was first conceived as an attempt to embody all the fruits of her studies in human typology, going back to her experiments under the tutelage of James and Munsterberg at Harvard. From these studies she "found out a great deal about how people act"—she "found there a certain kind of human being who acted in another kind of way, and their resemblances and differences."[20] And this led her to wonder whether "if you could make a history of the whole world, their slight resemblances and lack of resemblances" (HWW, 156). To this end, she began, in *The Making of Americans,* her effort to chart the whole of human typology:

> I made enormous charts, and I tried to carry these charts out. You start in and you take everyone that you know, and then when you see anybody who has a certain expression or turn of the face that reminds you of some one, you find out where he agrees or disagrees with the character, until you build up the whole scheme. I got to the place where I didn't know whether I knew people or not. I made so many charts that when I used to go down the streets of Paris I wondered whether they were people I knew or ones I didn't. This is what *The Making of Americans* was intended to be. I was to make a description of every kind of human being until I could know by these variations how everybody was to be known. (HWW, 156)

That the ambition was beyond her, beyond anyone, is implicitly admitted, even as it is overtly denied: "Then I got very much interested in this thing and I wrote about nine hundred pages, and I came to a logical conclusion that this thing could be done. . . . [W]hen I found it could be done, I lost interest in it" (HWW, 156). That she maintained her interest for so long (for 925 pages) is perhaps the most amazing thing. Few readers have been able to follow her this far with anything more than a forced enthusiasm. One problem is the reductiveness of the typology itself. It is difficult to see the advantage gained by the insight—if it is an insight—that all of human nature can be reduced to "two kinds of being, independent dependent, dependent independent."[21] Granted, Stein both extends these descriptions—"Those . . . who have in them dependent independent being as the bottom of them have resisting in them as their natural way of fighting" (275–76)—and suggests variables within them: "Resisting fighting is for those then who have dependent independent being in them not their only way of winning. They can have yielding and sensitive being and instrument being in them, sometimes for winning, just to keep going, sometimes for winning to subdue some one near them" (276). Still, one suspects that these extensions and variations prove, for most readers, hardly more enlightening than the original schema.

The problem is that Stein is less interested in description than in essences, in each individual's fundamental type or "bottom nature." There is a Platonic simplicity about her intent, her ambition being not only to reduce all difference to a basic binary opposition (independent-dependent || dependent-independent) but also to ground all character in a single nature: "Men and women have in them many ways of living,—their ways of eating, their ways of drinking, their ways of thinking, their ways of working, their ways of sleeping, in most men and many women go with the way of loving, come from the bottom nature in them" (154). Again, this "bottom nature" is subject to intermixture with other natures— "Many men and many women have their way of loving and their way of thinking and their way of working come from the mixture in them of other nature or natures with the bottom nature in them" (154). Still, the permutations are not so many so as to obscure the sense that personalities are grounded in a handful of determinable natures. Thus it is that Mabel Linker "had escaping being in her" (235); Mary Maxworthing "had in her a little impatient feeling, she had a pleasant gayety in her" (215); Mr. David Hersland "had a mixture in him" (155), a mixture that included "a feeling of beginning, of fighting of brushing people away from him" (157); and Mrs. Hersland and Madeleine Wyman who "both had in them dependent independent being, [even though] it was in them in different fashion, Madeleine ha[ving] in her instrument being, Mrs. Hersland ha[ving] not in her such being, she ha[ving] yielding in her but that was to loving in marrying, yielding in her to the being that was part of her as in her children and her sisters and her brothers and her mother and her father" (277).[22]

Stein acknowledges that people change character—"In every one there is changing" (215)—but the tenor of the novel remains utterly deterministic. As Stein says at the beginning: "It is hard living down the tempers we are born with" (3).

THREE LIVES, THE MAKING OF AMERICANS,
AND THE PRESENT MOMENT

In *Three Lives* and *The Making of Americans,* one notices a shift in Stein's artistic intention. This shift is not a new interest in typology;

that interest could be found in the earlier texts *Fernhurst* and *Q.E.D.*, albeit not as advanced as it is in the later texts. Rather, the new interest lies in Stein's interest in the moment of present immediacy, a focus which would govern so much of what she did artistically afterwards. In *Three Lives,* Stein began to think of time and narration not as something broken up into past, present, and future, but rather as a prolonged or continuous present always at the point of beginning again. As Stein herself later wrote,

> In beginning writing I wrote a book called *Three Lives* this was written in 1905. I wrote a negro story called *Melanctha.* In that there was a constant recurring and beginning there was a marked direction in the direction of being in the present although naturally I had been accustomed to past present and future, and why, because the composition forming around me was a prolonged present. A composition of a prolonged present is a natural composition in the world as it has been these thirty years it was more and more a prolonged present.[23]

The concept was not necessarily out of keeping with the spirit of Modernism; in fact, to the extent that it celebrated the present materiality of all reality, it seemed to exemplify such. The past was an abstraction, a memory. The future was also an abstraction, an anticipation, but the present moment differed from both the past and the future in that it afforded Stein and her contemporaries a possible exit out of abstraction. It offered, or it teasingly seemed to offer, a pathway to reality itself, the hard, measurable substance which one—say, a turn-of-the-century Dr. Johnson—might stub a toe against. It offered, in short, an opportunity to cognize the thing itself—if one could get around the Kantian objections, perhaps by suspending one's belief in transcendental categories and by reducing all knowledge to that of sensations.

At first, in writing *Three Lives,* Stein imagined no conflict between the rendering of the prolonged present and memory. That the latter might color the former did not become a consideration until she was well into the composition of *The Making of Americans.* Rather, in *Three Lives* Stein expressed more interest in the psychology of consciousness, in its duration and its quality of being present to itself. Later, in an effort not so unlike Edmund Husserl's attempt to distinguish perception from the representation of such by grounding the former in its own self-evidence, she would seek that origin (the thing-in-itself) which occasioned the now of consciousness. But in *Three Lives* and *The Making of Americans* she was content to work with narratives and a more simple concept of presentness.

Meanwhile, Stein's aesthetic rendering of presentness took two basic forms, the prolonged present and the continuous present, with the latter representing an extension of the former. In *Three Lives* Stein first began to experiment with the idea of a prolonged present. Essentially what this meant, as the critic Donald Sutherland explains, was that a "prolonged present asserts a theme and then proceeds to complicate and elaborate it, in the manner of a fugal theme in Bach, so that the presence of the original theme, no matter how elaborately overlaid with variations, is maintained or prolonged as a going existence in each present passage or moment."[24] Examining *Three Lives,* then, one finds a style heavily reliant upon: (1) the present participle and the gerund, intended to accent the nowness of narrative events; and (2) multiple forms of repetition, intended to accent the connectiveness of each narrative moment with those that came before and those that come after. For instance, in the following passage, one notes the frequent use of both the present participle and the gerund as well as the repetition of key words such as "doubting," "loving," "feeling," "always," "real," and "now," the last three words also used to reinforce the idea of the narrative events' present solidity:

> *Always now* Jeff had to go so much faster than was *real* with his *feeling.* Yet *always* Jeff knew *now* he had a right, strong *feeling. Always now* when Jeff was *wondering,* it was Melanctha he was *doubting,* in the *loving. Now* he would ask her, was she *real now* to him, in her *loving.* He would ask her often, *feeling* something queer about it all inside him, though yet he was never *really* strong in his *doubting,* and *always* Melanctha would answer to him, "Yes Jeff, sure, you know it, *always,*" and *always,* Jeff felt a *doubt now,* in her *loving.*
> *Always now* Jeff felt in himself, deep *loving. Always now* he did not know *really,* if Melanctha was true in her *loving.*
> All these days Jeff was uncertain in him, and he was uneasy about which way he should act so as not to be wrong and put them both into bad trouble. *Always now* he was, as if he must *feel* deep into Melanctha to see if it was *real loving* he would find she *now* had in her, and *always* he would stop himself, with her, for *always* he was afraid *now* that he might badly hurt her. (165; emphasis added)

Sometimes Stein's use of repetition goes beyond that of a word or short phrase to include that of a sentence, as in "Melanctha always loved to be with horses," first found on page 91 and then later (with a slight variation) on page 217. Even entire passages are repeated in this way, such as the one first found on page 85, in the novella's opening, and then later on page 225, in its closing:

The child though it was healthy after it was born, did not live long. Rose Johnson was careless and negligent and selfish, and when Melanctha had to leave for a few days, the baby died. Rose Johnson had liked the baby well enough and perhaps she just forgot it for awhile, anyway the child was dead and Rose and Sam her husband were very sorry but then these things came so often in the negro world in Bridgepoint, that they neither of them thought about it very long.

Such repetitions work not so much to stop the narrative as to slow it down, to expand the sense of present time and to emphasize the continuity and contiguousness of the narrative events.

Later, in *The Making of Americans*, Stein tried to go further, using the technique of the continuous present to forge the impression that narrative events transpire upon an apparently seamless strip of present moments. As Stein later said, she was most impressed by the "present immediacy" of experience and wanted to find a technique for its communication. The technique of the continuous present, which developed from the prolonged present, was most notable for its cinematic quality. Even more so than in *Three Lives* the intent was to capture the feel and weight of duration. (Here one thinks of both Henri Bergson and William James. The latter, for instance, writes: "We are constantly conscious of a certain duration—the specious present—varying in length from a few seconds to probably not more than a minute, and . . . this duration [with its content perceived as having one part earlier and the other part later] is the original intuition of time.")[25] As such, Stein pushes harder on the techniques—the uses of the gerund, the present participle, and repetition—developed in the earlier novel, wanting as she does to offer an art that imitates the almost breathless stream of successive present moments. Repetition is most important here because each present moment is, while not a repeat of the prior moment, very close to being a repeat, carrying with it something of the prior moment even as it is itself quite different and as such new. Explaining her use of repetition in *The Making of Americans*, Stein writes:

The question of repetition is very important. It is important because there is no such thing as repetition. . . . There is always a slight variation. Somebody comes in and you tell the story over again. Every time you tell the story it is told slightly differently. All my early work was a careful listening to all the people telling their story, and I conceived the idea which is, funnily enough, the same as the idea of the cinema. The cinema goes on the same principle: each picture is just that infinitesimally different from the one before. If you listen carefully, you say something, the other person says something; but each time it changes just a little. . . . And in *The Making of Americans* I did this thing. (HWW, 158–59)

There are two things to take notice of here in Stein's explanation. One is the already mentioned emphasis upon repetition and variation therein. The second is the emphasis that Stein places upon her own "careful listening." The point is that this lengthy "record of a decent family progress respectably lived by us and our fathers and our mothers, and our grand-fathers and grandmothers,"[26] is, as Stein's use of first-person pronouns suggests, a very personal and subjective book. It "hasten[s] slowly forward" partly for the reason that Stein finds herself emotionally caught up in the story, ever reliving and relearning. Perhaps, she is not so much relearning as simply learning, learning about the people who surrounded her during her growing up. In any case, the point of view is emphatically her own. Hence, even as she tries for a present immediacy, the reiteration of the authorial "I" offers the ostensibly objective phenomenon a subjective character. The following passage illustrates both the cinematic repetition and the self-mirroring:

> I am writing everything as I am learning anything. I am writing everything as I am learning anything. I am writing everything as I am learning anything, as I am feeling anything in any one as being, as I am having a realization of any one, I am saying everything then as I am full up then with a thing, with anything of any one. I am certain that some are sometimes whole ones to me, that some are sometimes a piece of their kind of them in me, always I am certain each one is existing, they are themselves inside them, sometime mostly every one is a whole one to my feeling, very often before then very often after then that one is not a whole one in my feeling, that one is a piece of the kind of being that is the being they are of in being.[27]

As personal and romantic a novel as *The Making of Americans* is, Stein nevertheless felt (though not without some expressions of self-doubt) that she had accomplished what she had set out to do—to offer both "a description of every kind of human being that existed" (HWW, 156) and a present immediacy in which memory did not play a part. The ambition was interesting, but the truth is that she accomplished (if techniques simulating such are set aside) neither.

With respect to her ambition to describe every individual, though Stein claimed success in this venture and even wrote another book, *A Long Gay Book,* with much the same design, the operation was doomed from the start. As Stein herself foresaw, the task was beyond the doing by any one person. The whole assumption upon which it rested—that of a finite typology—was most dubious. The problem was, as Hayden White (in another context) writes, that "when the list of things resembling one another reached a certain limit, the whole operation would break down; and the fact of the apparent differentness of all things from all other things would assume the status of a primary datum of perception."[28] It appears that Stein, who wanted "to find out if you could make a history of the whole world, if you could know the whole life history of everyone in the world, their slight resemblances and lack of resemblances" (LIA, 153), found in the writing of *The Making of Americans* and *A Long Gay Book* that a complete typology was not to be had, not by her and not by anyone else, no matter how hard one tried. She did not simply "los[e] interest in it" after having "found [that] it could be done" (HWW, 156); she wisely gave it up.

Meanwhile, in the second instance, regarding the ambition to offer a present immediacy outside of memory, Stein again takes on a challenge which seems almost by definition impossible. How, that is, does one escape memory without escaping temporal and spatial relations? For Stein, the putative answer was to remain always in the present moment, as if *that moment* existed free of relation. Hence, she posited the technique of the continuous present, the cinematic technique which postulated that all existence was no more than a present existing located on the point of an atomistic moment, a moment that was ever gliding from one successive point to the next but which, if one were strict enough in one's attention, one could remain present in, thereby escaping memory through escaping both temporal and spatial relations. As Stein wrote, "By a continuously moving picture of any one there is no memory of any other thing and there is that thing existing" (LIA, 176).

In *The Making of Americans, A Long Gay Book,* and the early portraits, the cinematic technique was most characterized, in Stein's own terminology, by the qualities of "listening" and "talking." These qualities, said Stein, were instrumental in keeping "remembering" out of her work. Remembering itself was dependent upon repetition, and while it figured frequently in those texts employing the continuous present, this repetition was always repetition with a difference, something Stein referred to as "insistence" to differentiate it from repetition per se. Meanwhile, "listening" and "talking" constituted present actions not requiring repetition and therefore existing outside of remembering or memory. As Stein said, "remembering is repetition and confusion, and being existing that is listening and talking is action and not repetition" (LIA, 180).

Stein's program for realizing unmediated knowledge was ingenious, yet flawed. By "listening" and "talking" one does not avoid repetition or resemblance any more than one avoids memory. One creates a technique for simulating a stream of unrelated present moments, yet the technique always remains just that: a simulation. The transcendental object remains uncaptured.

Stein knew in those moments when she was most honest with herself that her quest had fallen short. For instance, in referring to *The Making of Americans,* she wrote: "I found out this question of resemblances, and I found in making these analyses that the resemblances were not of memory. I had to remember what person looked like the other person. Then I found this contradiction: that the resemblances were a matter of memory" (HWW, 156). And elsewhere she wrote:

> As I say I had the habit of conceiving myself as completely talking and listening, listening was talking and talking was listening and in so doing I conceived what I at that time called the rhythm of anybody's personality. If listening was talking and talking was listening then and at the same time *any little movement any little expression was a resemblance, and a resemblance was something that presupposed a remembering.*
>
> Listening and talking did not presuppose resemblance and as they do not presuppose resemblance, they do not necessitate remembering. Already then as you see there was a complication which was a bother to me in my conception of the rhythm of a personality. I have for so many years tried to get the better of this bother. (LIA, 174–75; emphasis added)

Mostly, though, Stein was not one to admit defeat, and successes were claimed for ambitions that were neither realized nor realizable. For instance, as late as *The Geographical History of America* (1936), Stein is still claiming that she has a bona fide program for eluding memory. This later program, she tells us, rests upon a somewhat Cartesian discrimination between the way of human nature and the way of the human mind. In the first case, the way of human nature, perception is always colored by human identity and human memory. The object of perception is never exactly the object as it is. And, given Stein's epistemological ambitions, human nature is not the privileged mode: "Human nature is what any human being will do,"[29] or, less flatteringly, "Human nature is animal nature" (GHA, 117). Instead, the privileged mode is that of the human mind. For if human nature is to be identified with the retrogressive "[t]hey" of the statement, "They used to think the world was there as we see it," the human mind finds itself identified with the statement's subsequent truth: "[B]ut this is not so the world is there as it is" (GHA, 82). That is, the "[h]uman mind exists absolutely in the immediate," knowing "what it knows when it knows it."[30] It knows nothing that is not apprehended in the present moment; it engages in no relations other than those with the thing-in-itself. Denuded as it is, "[t]he human mind has neither identity nor time and when it sees anything has to look flat" (GHA, 183). As such, it does not impose itself upon the object; it simply tells what it (the object) is: "The human mind has to say anything is now" (GHA, 173).

That this ambition was quixotic I have already said. However, Stein, not perfectly happy with the results of *The Making of Americans* (suggesting, without actually saying so, that a narrative of its length was not the best way to escape memory), felt that she might succeed with the same ambition in a more circumscribed format; hence she began writing her portraits. *The Making of Americans,* though a novel, was in a sense not that structurally different from the early portraits, for in both instances the major formal force was located in the paragraph. That is, Stein was governed by the principle that wholes are slowly come by through the assemblage of their parts:

> So you see what I mean about those early portraits and the middle part of The Making of Americans. I built them up little by little each time I said it it changed just a little and then when I was completely emptied of knowing that the one of whom I was making a portrait existed I had made a portrait of that one. (GHA, 179)

If *The Making of Americans* was structurally akin to the early portraits, it did present a problem of length that (more clearly than in the early portraits) also translated itself into a problem of memory. Thus, while *The Making of Americans,* so emphatically attentive to present existing, was by no means a traditional novel, it nevertheless had sufficient enough narrative elements to make the whole matter of escaping memory significantly problematical even for Stein. For if the first ambition was to describe people as they were—essentially—this ambition appeared frustrated by the form: story. Stein writes,

> When I first began writing although I felt very strongly that something that made that some one be some one was something that I must use as being them, I naturally began to describe them as they were doing anything. In short, I wrote a story as a story, that is the way I began, and slowly I realized this confusion, a real confusion, that in writing a story one had to be remembering, and that novels are soothing because so many people one may say everybody can remember almost anything. (GHA, 181)

That essences might, paradoxically, be only apprehensible via the means of narrative was not seriously considered. Consequently, the early portraits were begun with the hope of avoiding the difficulties (particularly the difficulties of resemblance and memory) inherent in narrative form. What she would now do, Stein reasoned, would be dramatically to localize the area of attention. Instead of chronicling a whole family saga, her original ambition in *The Making of Americans,* Stein would make word portraits of individuals, mostly one per portrait, though sometimes two or more. The idea was inspired by portrait painting, and it was even in Stein's mind that she might use words the way a painter uses colors, less to delineate the contours of her subject than to bring out its essence:

> And so I am trying to tell you what doing portraits meant to me, I had to find out what it was inside any one, and by any one I mean every one I had to find out inside every one what was in them that was intrinsically exciting and I had to find out not by what they said not by what they did not by how much or how little they resembled any other one but I had to find out by the intensity of movement that there was inside in any one of them. (GHA, 183)

In the early portraits (i.e., "Ada," Matisse," "Picasso," etc.), the technique remains very much what it was in *The Making of Americans.* It is cinematic, once again making use of those qualities of present existing that Stein labeled "listening" and "talking." It is also insistent, moving in a manner more circular than linear, as Stein plays not so much, as she claims, with repetition, as with variations upon a theme—in this case the subject's essence. For instance, in her 1909 portrait of Matisse, Stein circles around what, she feels, is the "intrinsically exciting" thing about the artist—the uncertainty of his talent:

> He certainly very clearly expressed something. Some said that he did not clearly express anything. Some were certain that he expressed something very clearly and some of such of them said that he would have been a greater one if he had not been one so clearly expressing what he was expressing. Some said he was not clearly expressing what he was expressing and some of such of them said that the greatness of struggling which was not clear expression made of him one being a completely great one.[31]

The problems that arose with this type of portraiture were not that different from those Stein confronted in *The Making of Americans.* She had given up the novel for the portrait because she was tired of typology and resemblance: "It [resemblance] was not a thing that was any longer an important thing, I knew completely how any one looked like any other one and that became then only a practical matter, a thing one might know as what any one was liable to do, but this to me then was no longer interesting. And so I went on with portrait writing" (GHA, 182). Yet, the old problems (those connected with narrative, resemblance, remembering) continued to crop up. Thus if the technique of the early portraits was similar to that of *The Making of Americans,* so were the difficulties. For one, her portraits were, like the novels, interpretative acts. She might wish, as in the Matisse portrait, to objectify her subject's essence, but the result itself clearly reflected her opinions about the man; that is, it was both ambivalent and patronizing. For another, despite the effort to circumscribe the area of her attention, narrative and memory still seemed to intrude themselves. In fact, remembering seemed something like a nemesis from which she could not escape.[32]

This problem of memory led Stein to turn from the style of the early portraits—that of listening and talking—to the style of *Tender Buttons,* that of looking. Though she set out in her portraits to engage only in listening and in talking, Stein found that she was also very much "looking." "Then slowly once more I got bothered, after all I listened and talked but that was not all I did in knowing at any present time when I was stating anything what anything was. I was also looking, and that could not be entirely left out" (GHA, 188). The problem with "looking," Stein said, "was that *in regard to human beings* looking inevitably carried in its train realizing movements and expression and as such forced me into recognizing resemblances, and so forced remembering and in forcing remembering caused confusion of present with past and future time" (GHA, 188). Which was to say that all her portrait subjects, being drawn from her own coterie of friends, naturally stirred up emotional responses, making it impossible to avoid resemblance and remembering. These responses might have been avoided had she been able, Stein said, to stay strictly within the boundaries of listening and talking—that is, of present existing. Yet she was unable to do this, and gave in to looking and thus to remembering.

Frustrated, Stein again altered the technique with the hope of making it a more accurate presentation of "things as they are." Not happy with the cinematic technique and all its problems, she wanted "to tear it down[,] . . . to attack[ ] the problem from another way" (HWW, 159). Now she would use "three or four words instead of making a cinema of it" (GHA, 159), but she would not reject "looking" itself, even as it was identified with the early portraits' failure. Rather, she would suppress both listening and talking in favor of looking not at human beings but at things, hoping that the latter should present fewer problems of resemblance and remembering. It was time to confront the problem head on:

> I began to make portraits of things and enclosures that is room and places because I needed to completely face the difficulty of how to include what is seen with hearing and listening and at first if I were to include a complicated listening and talking it would be too difficult to do. That is why painters paint still lives. You do see why they do.
>
> So I began to do this thing, I tried to include color and movement and what I did is . . . a volume called *Tender Buttons*. (GHA, 189)

Tender Buttons

Tender Buttons (1914) is Stein's attempt "to express the rhythm of the visible world" (ABT, 112). For a long while, she "had been interested only in the insides of people, their character and what went on inside of them" (ABT, 112). However, troubled by the nagging sense that "after all the human being essentially is not paintable" (ABT, 112), she felt it best to turn her attention to still lifes so as to get a better hold on both her world and art. She wanted to concentrate upon the simple description of things—domestic things—and "to live in looking" (GHA, 189). Accordingly, sight is the principle faculty in *Tender Buttons,* and while it has probably been so in any age, one still finds real affinities between Stein's project here and that of Michel Foucault's Classical episteme. (Foucault: "sight [has] an almost exclusive privilege, being the sense by which we perceive extent and establish proof, and, in consequence, the means to an analysis *partes extra partes* acceptable to everyone.")[33] Repeatedly, Stein here speaks of things as being seen. For example, in "A Piece of Coffee," she writes, "The *sight* of a reason, the same *sight* slighter, the *sight* of a simpler negative answer, the same sore sounder, the intention to wishing, the same splendor, the same furniture."[34] And in "A Box": "A box is made sometimes and them *to see to see* to it neatly and to have the holes stopped up makes it necessary to use paper" (14; emphasis added). As Stein herself says elsewhere, "you see I feel with my eyes" (ABT, 65).

One consequence of Stein's privileging of sight or "looking" in *Tender Buttons* is the special status now bestowed upon both appearance and color. In the first instance, the problematic of appearance might be set in the terms that Heidegger used in *Being and Time,* though Heidegger and Stein would clearly differ about the possibilities of approaching that which does not show itself. "Appearance, as the appearance of something," Heidegger writes, "does *not* mean that something shows itself; rather, it means that something makes itself known which does not show itself. It makes itself known through something that does show itself. Appearing is a *not showing itself*."[35] However, unlike Heidegger, Stein would like to think that essences, things-in-themselves, are captured and revealed in her still lifes. The names affixed to each (i.e., "A Chair," "A Cutlet," "Water Raining," etc.) offer us the ostensible object of attention, the appearance, even while we wait for the more essential thing-in-itself to be evinced. Again and again we find Stein using the word favored in the Heidegger passage, "show," to suggest that a real essence is making itself known. As for example in "A Mounted Umbrella":

> What was the use of not leaving it there where it would hang what was the use if there was no chance of ever seeing it come there and *show* that it was handsome and right in the way it *showed* it. The lesson is to learn that it does *show* it and that nothing, that there is nothing, that there is no more to do about it and just so much more is there plenty of reason for making an exchange. (20; emphasis added)

If appearances do not yield up essences in *Tender Buttons*—and I do not think they do—Stein's objects are nevertheless quite sensuously considered, particularly in terms of color. Everywhere one looks, one finds things being described not by their color but by an emotional relation which Stein discovers between the object and the spoken color. For instance, in "A Long Dress," several colors are needed to simulate not the appearance of the dress but its essence, its inner "intensity of movement": "Where is the serene length, it is there and a *dark* place is not a *dark* place, only a *white* and *red* are *black,* only a *yellow* and *green* are *blue,* a *pink* is *scarlet,* a bow is every *color*" (17; emphasis added). The same is true of the the unnamed substance in "A Substance In A Cushion":

> A closet, a closet does not connect under the bed. The band if it is *white* and *black,* the band has a *green* string. A sight a whole sight and a little groan grinding makes a trimming such a sweet singing trimming and a *red* thing not a round thing but a *white* thing, a *red* thing and a *white* thing. (11; emphasis added)

Stein's interest in color, like her interest in sound, related back not, she said, to her emotions (though I read her interest in colors back this way) but to her strong desire to know just what was any object's thingness.[36] "I began to wonder," she wrote, "at about this time just what one saw when one looked at anything really looked at anything. Did one see sound, and what was the relation between color and sound, did it make itself by description by a word that meant it or did it make itself by a word in itself" (GHA, 191). For Stein, an object clearly is something solid and sensuous, to be best understood through such physical qualities as sound and color. Here, one is reminded of Wittgenstein's statement in the *Tractatus*—a text which, in its ambitions, is remarkably similar to *Tender Buttons*—that

> A speck in the visual field, though it need not be red, must have some colour: it is, so to speak, surrounded by color-space. Notes must have *some* pitch, objects of the sense of touch *some* degree of hardness, and so on.[37]

In like manner, one is also reminded again of Heidegger and his elevation of the truth of *aisthesis,* "the straightforward sensuous perception of something":

> To the extent that an *aisthesis* aims at its *idia* [what is its own]—the beings genuinely accessible only *through* it and *for* it, for example, *looking* at colors—perception is always true. This means that looking always discovers color, hearing always discovers tones. What is in the purest and most original sense "true"—that is, what only discovers in such a way that it can never cover up anything—is pure *noein,* straight forwardly observant apprehension of the simplest determinations of the Being of beings as such.[38]

Stein would probably feel uncomfortable with the metaphysical cast of Heidegger's language, yet her own intentions—governed as they are by her pursuit of things-in-themselves, of essences—are also decidedly metaphysical, as she seeks, in her own way, the Heideggerean Being of beings. Still, at the same time, Stein is a firmly committed realist—"I am essentially a realist"[39]—ever wishing to accent the solidity of things. In *Tender Buttons,* she repeatedly speaks of things not only in terms of their apparent qualities, color and sound, but also in terms of their more material qualities: number, measure, weight, difference. As for example in "A Box":

> A custom which is necessary when a box is used and taken is that a *larger part* of the time there are *three* which have *different* connections. The *one* is on the table. The *two* are on the table. The *three* are on the table. The *one, one* is the same *length* as is shown by the cover being *longer.* The other is *different* there is more cover that shows it. The other is *different* and that makes the corners have the same shade the *eight* are in *singular* arrangement to make *four* necessary. (14; emphasis added)

Here, Stein would suggest, to borrow Wittgenstein's phrasing, that "the world divides into facts,"[40] and that these facts, while tenuously connected, are more interesting in their isolation than in their connectiveness. This is a significant departure from her early work in which Stein celebrated not difference but resemblance. The two interests, difference and resemblance, need not be contradictory. One can have difference within resemblance, and resemblance within difference, and the sense is that these two alternatives operate within a single, more inclusive scheme, one that Stein herself does not reject. As she says elsewhere, "Everything being alike everything naturally everything is different simply different naturally simply different."[41] Yet at the same time, if Stein's categories presuppose the acceptance of a metaphysics, her movement in the direction of difference is in itself a celebration of physics. While it really does not yet push her to "Act so that there is no use in a centre" (63), it does eventually do so. That is, if in *Tender Buttons* Stein is writing mostly within a traditional conception of metaphysics, it appears by the end of this work, and in much of the work (say, for example, *Four Saints in Three Acts*) which postdates the text, that she moves away from a traditional metaphysics and begins to find, upon reflection, that, in Derrida's words, "there was no center, that the center could not be thought in the form of a present-being, that the center had no natural site, that it was not a fixed locus but a function, a sort of nonlocus in which an infinite number of sign-substitutes came into play."[42] This is not to escape metaphysics per se, so much as to deflect it through a radical accentuation of difference. In any case, such inventions make themselves felt, I think, somewhat later in Stein's career.

Meanwhile, in *Tender Buttons* Stein appears more taken with an atomistic conception of things. Her whole sense both of time and of space is that of measurements ingrained with clear-cut delineations. Even as time and space are forms of objects, they contain within themselves separation, gaps between one moment in time and the next, between one point in space and another. For example, in "Roastbeef," both time and space are spoken of as being divided:

> All the time that there is use there is use and any time there is a surface there is a surface, and every time there is an exception there is an exception and every time there is a division there is a dividing. Any time there is a surface there is a surface and every time there is a suggestion there is a suggestion and every time there is silence there is silence and every time that is languid there is that there then and not oftener, not always, not particular, tender and changing and external and central and surrounded and singular and simple and the same. (33–34)

Stein is obsessed with questions of definition, of defining what is and what is not an object. *Tender Buttons* is nothing if it is not first an exercise in definition, Stein's ambition being to translate into one language that which is found in another. Stein might not be happy with the term "translate," thinking of herself more as a presenter of realities; still, the ubiquitousness of the verb "to be," repeatedly used here to describe one thing in terms of another, makes the term warrantable. For example, in "A Piano" Stein uses the verb "to be" to establish a host of relations that are quite syllogistic:

> If the speed *is* open, if the color *is* careless, if the selection of a strong scent *is* not awkward, if the button holder *is* held by all the wavering color and there *is* no color, not any color. If there *is* no dirt in a pin and there can be none scarely, if there *is* not then the place *is* the same as up standing. (18; emphasis added)

Consequent with definition and the use of the copula is, of course, meaning, itself being a statement of a correspondent relation. This same meaning, like definition and copulative syntax, might further be said to be dependent upon perception, upon the interpretative act that first recognizes things in relation. As Heidegger writes, "Perception is consummated when one *addresses* onself to something as something and *discusses* it as such. This amounts to *interpretation* in the broadest sense; and on the basis of such interpretation, perception becomes an act of *making determinate*."[43] And Gadamer: "Perception always includes meaning."[44] In *Tender Buttons,* certainly, Stein "somehow manage[s] . . . to endow all phenomena with meaning"[45]—"somehow manages" because she is always attending to objects: to what they are and what they mean. In "Rooms," for example, meaning is repeatedly spoken of and repeatedly added to: "This *means* clearness it *means* a regular notion of exercise, it *means* more than that, it *means* liking counting, it *means* more than that, it does not *mean* exchanging a line" (77; emphasis added). The same is true in "A Table," though here the spoken of meanings seem less additive than synonymous:

> A table *means* does it not my dear it *means* a whole steadiness. Is it likely that a change.
> A table *means* more than a glass even a looking glass is tall. A table *means* necessary places and a revision a revision of a little thing it *means* it does *mean* that there has been a stand, a stand where it did shake. (26; emphasis added)

As things in *Tender Buttons* are solid and admit of definition and meaning, they also bespeak the classical (in the sense of physics) qualities of change, use, and necessity. In the first instance, while it is understood that objects are solid and stable, it is also understood that they are always caught up in a larger process of change. As Wittgenstein writes, "Objects are what is unalterable and subsistent; their configuration is what is changing and unstable."[46] Change is the law that governs all things. So it is, in *Tender Buttons,* that the "cloud does *change* with the movements of the moon and the narrow quite narrow suggestion of the building" (75); that "[l]ight blue and the same red with purple makes a *change*" (10); and that "[a] *change,* a final *change* includes potatoes" (41).

Meanwhile, in the second instance, everything must have a "use" if it is to have a meaning, which is to say if it is to be perceived and understood to exist. Stein's sensibility, in this respect, is a pragmatic one. One measures things by their practical effects: "What was the *use* of not leaving it [an umbrella] there where it would hang what was the *use* if there was no chance of ever seeing it come there and show that it was handsome and right in the way it showed it" (20; emphasis added). If a thing has no practical effect, what difference does it make whether it exists or not? The presumption is that it does not. One of course thinks back to James, as well as Peirce, who wrote, "Consider what effects, that might conceivably have practical bearings, we conceive the object of our conception to have. Then, our conception of these effects is the whole of our conception of the object."[47]

Not surprisingly, practical effects are to be found everywhere in *Tender Buttons.* Thus "back books are *used* to secure tears and church [and] . . . are even *used* to exchange black slippers" (77; emphasis added); "[t]he *use* of [a seltzer bottle] is manifold" (16; emphasis added); and "[t]he one way to *use* custom is to *use* soap and silk for cleaning" (12; emphasis added). There is even "some *use,*" it seems, "in not mentioning changing and in establishing the temperature" (69; emphasis added).

And just as change and use have their important roles to play in *Tender Buttons,* so too does necessity. By necessity here is meant, in Wittgenstein's words, that "objects stand in a determinate relation to one another."[48] Given the logic of experience, which exists prior to experience, things could not stand other than as they do. "[T]he only necessity that exists is *logical* necessity,"[49] and while this might strike us, as it did Paul de Man, as "an unwarranted reversal of cause and effect,"[50] it was for Stein a controlling metaphor, albeit not recognized as such. Thus necessity may be discovered in every relation, just as the language of necessity, in *Tender Buttons,* may be discovered on virtually every page. Thus, "[a] large box is handily made of what is *necessary* to replace any substance" (14; emphasis added); "[a] mind under is exact and so it is *necessary* to have a mouth and eye glasses" (45; emphasis added); and "[a] hurt mended stick, a hurt mended cup, a hurt mended article of exceptional relaxation and annoyance, a hurt mended, hurt and mended is so *necessary* that no mistake is intended" (43; emphasis added).

When one understands that Stein, amidst all the playfulness, still conceives things as being both necessary and determinate, it is easier to understand what she wants her language to do vis-à-vis its referent—that is, to "create a word relationship between the word and the things seen."[51] For what Stein desires most is an almost mathematical exactitude between sign and referent: "While I was writing I didn't want, when I used one word, to make it carry with it too many associations. I wanted as far as possible to make it exact, as exact as mathematics; that is to say, for example, if one and one make two, I wanted to get words to have as much exactness as that" (HWW, 157). For this, Stein needed to believe that sense was determinate, that the planes of objects and of language had a commensurate logic, guaranteeing that if she held, as she said she did in *Tender Buttons,* "to the absolute refusal of never using a word that was not an exact word," and "that the word or words that make what [she] looked at be itself [would] always [be the] words that . . . very exactly related themselves to that thing at which [she] was looking" (LIA, 196–97; 191). This did not mean that Stein knew the exact nature or location of this commensurate logic; it only meant that she recognized its existence. Again, to go back to the *Tractatus:*

> The propositions of logic describe the scaffolding of the world, or rather they represent it. They have no "subject-matter." They presuppose that names have meaning and elementary propositions sense; and that is their connexion with the world. (63)

Yet while Stein felt that language and reality shared the same logic, she showed more frustration than did Wittgenstein concerning the consequences. That is, if Wittgenstein, conceiving such a logic as a transcendental, believed that "[o]bjects can only be *named*[,]" not "*put . . . into words,*"[52] the Stein of *Tender Buttons* desired more than representation, even one grounded in a commensurate logic and possessing the exactitude of mathematics. She yearned to "put [things] into words," to go beyond simply naming. Stein now felt little more than indifference for names: "The name of a thing might be something in itself if it could come to be real enough but just as a name it was not enough something" (LIA, 242). The problem was that a name was something too static; it was not quick enough to capture the moment to moment quality of anything's existing:

> We that is any human being existing, has inevitably to feel the thing anything being existing, but the name of that thing of that anything is no longer anything to thrill any one except children. So as everybody has to be a poet, what was there to do. This that I have just described, the creating it without naming it . . . (LIA, 237)

Stein began to ask herself whether "there [was] not a way of naming things that would not invent names, but mean names without naming them," if there was not a way of "looking at anything until something that was not the name of that thing but was in a way that actual thing would come to be written" (LIA, 236). Not surprisingly, Stein felt there was a way—a way first to entrap and then to unfold the noumenon of reality upon the flypaper of language. In fact, doing so did not even require a whole new language: "Of course you might say why not invent new names new languages but that cannot be done" (LIA, 237). And so, she spoke of Shakespeare and the forest of Arden as illustrative of some special sort of evocation that did not entail naming:

> Shakespeare in the forest of Arden had created a forest without mentioning the things that make a forest. You feel it all but he does not name its names.
> Now that was a thing that I too felt in me the need of making it be a thing that could be named without using its name. After all one had known its name anything's name for so long, and so the name was not new but the thing being alive was always new. (LIA, 236)

Here, Stein argued, the trick was not to focus one's attention upon the name but upon the thing-in-itself. Discovering this (the thing-in-itself), its name, its essential thisness, would soon follow. As Stein, discussing *Tender Buttons,* writes: "I began to discover the name of things, that is not to discover the names but discover the things to see the things to look at and in doing so I had of course to name them not to give them new names but to see that I could find out how to know that they were there by their names or by replacing their names" (LIA, 235). In the process, Stein found herself surprised to discover that the words used to bring the thing-in-itself forward were not those usually associated with the object, that as often as not they had "nothing whatever to do with what words would do that described that thing" (LIA, 191).

It would appear, then, that much of the difficulty of Stein's language and of *Tender Buttons* in particular follows from this ambition to name things as they are found in their singular states of existing. That is, if we accept Stein's description, the difficulty follows not from a deficiency of exactitude but from its overabundance. "Every word" may well have "the same passionate exactness of meaning that it is supposed to have,"[53] yet now it is put to a wholly different purpose: to transcribe the ever fluid conditions of things, something which words, traditionally conceived, simply do not express. What Stein argues is that things are actions, that their unchangingness is merely apparent, not actual. The problem though is how to present things in flux when the available language allies itself with the stable and the abstract.

There is no easy answer to such a problem, and Stein's solutions are not always the happiest. In *Tender Buttons,* more and more anxious to realize the essence of a "thing's being existing," Stein turns away from the cinematic model of *The Making of Americans* and the early portraits and toward a concentrated attention encapsulated in phrases that are at once less attentuated and more enigmatical. All along, she aims to pass through the obstacle of a thing's name so as to know and feel the thing in its immediacy:

> As I say a noun is a name of a thing, and therefore slowly if you feel what is inside that thing you do not call it by the name by which it is known. Everybody knows that by the way they do when they are in love and a writer should always have that intensity of emotion about whatever is the object about which he writes. (LIA, 210)

Here, knowing and feeling are not the same, for the first is both subordinated to and embodied in the second. That is, to feel something is to know it, to know it in the best and most immediate way possible. Knowledge, Stein felt, always presented the problems of memory and resemblance. Feeling, in contrast, did not. As such, particularly in *Tender Buttons,* it became Stein's aim to push language as close to the object-in-itself as possible. Later, in the *Tractatus,* Wittgenstein himself wrote that "a picture is attached to reality; it reaches out to it"; and that within its relations there were to be found correlations with things, correlations that act as the picture's "feelers, . . . with which the picture touches reality" (9). Yet even this formulation, had it been available, would not have suited Stein, so serious was she about trying to "completely replace . . . the noun by the thing in itself" (LIA, 245).

Maybe it would be better to say that the formulation would *not entirely* suit Stein, for while she is dedicated to writing the sign and referent, she still clearly holds by the dualism. One sees evidence of this both in practice and in theory. At the same time, Stein is beginning to conceive of language in a different way, not in the way of correspondence within which the planes of language and things stand parallel, but rather, in the way of language as an enveloping net faithfully contouring the ever various and lumpish matter of reality. Language, unbuttressed, is allowed to collapse in upon the object, even as the latter remains in motion.

By way of illustration, let us examine the still life "A Little Bit Of A Tumbler," from the section "Objects":

> A shining indication of yellow consists in their having been more of the same color than could have been expected when all four were bought. This was the hope which made the six and seven have no use for any more places and this necessarily spread into nothing. Spread into nothing. (23)

Here, Stein takes an object, a tumbler, and avoiding all mention of its name (title excepted) tries to duplicate it in a word picture, a picture that is all along dictated by the need to see the object in its moment to moment existing, or, as Stein herself writes, to see it in "a space that is filled with moving, a space of time that is filled always filled with moving" (LIA, 161). To allow description here to stop with the name "tumbler," Stein thinks not enough. The name is too static; it does not begin to suggest just how alive with movement the object actually is. Better and more realistic than this kind of naming is to describe the object "by suggestion the way a painter" does, mindful at each moment of the need "to get the picture of it clear and separate in . . . [the] mind and create a word relationship between the word and the things seen."[54] Explicating her own still life, Stein writes:

> "A shining indication of yellow . . ." suggests a tumbler and something in it. " . . . when all four of them were bought" suggests there were four of them. I try to call to the eye the way it appears by suggestion the way a painter can do it. This is difficult and takes a lot of work and concentration to do it. I want to indicate it without calling in other things. "This was the hope which made the six and seven have no use for any more places . . ." Places bring up a reality. " . . . and this necessarily spread into nothing," which does broken tumbler which is the end of the story.[55]

Stein's own explication tells us what we perhaps already knew: that she really does not do what she set out to, which is to make the word be the thing; that she, while hesitant to admit it, is much more engaged in the making of metaphors, of substitutions, than she is in the making of non-linguistic things. "To write," Derrida says, "is to have the passion of the origin,"[56] and Stein more than any other writer has this passion. Yet even this will not produce the thing-in-itself, will not produce an imitation that stops being an imitation, that is something other than what is imitated. Again, as Derrida writes, "Imitation does not correspond to its essence, is not what it is—imitation—unless it is in some way at fault or rather in default. It is bad by nature. It is only good insofar as it is bad. Since (de)fault is inscribed within it, it has no nature; nothing is properly its own."[57]

Stein offers in *Tender Buttons* a technique of originality which, despite the self-promotion, remains but a technique—a simulation of the thing-in-itself. The technique is clever and imaginative and to be valued for these reasons. But one makes a mistake, as Stein's close friend Mabel Dodge made a mistake, to claim too much for these still lifes, to claim, as Dodge herself did in a letter to Stein, that they represent the "'noumenon' captured": "There are things hammered out of consciousness into black & white that have never been expressed before—so far as I know. States of being put into words the 'noumenon' captured—as few have done it."[58] Dodge's claim seems more wishful than true. And when she argues (in the same letter) that Stein's efforts "help us get at Truth instead of away from it as 'literature' so sadly does," what we find is one more attempt to circumvent the rhetorical dimension of the *trivium* (logic, grammar, rhetoric), an attempt which, while characteristic of this generation's authors, nevertheless always fails. As Derrida reminds us, "the thing itself is a sign."[59]

Meanwhile, claims such as Dodge's are telling; they remind us of just how slanted the contemporary aesthetic was toward epistemology, and they also particularly remind us of the force which the "innocent eye" still carried. Again, what one finds here is a tradition which, paralleling the growth of classical science, stressed the absolute thereness of reality and the possibility, given enough concentration, of knowing it. Stein is both a major and a culminating figure in this tradition. Few others take the assumptions of the innocent eye, both in practice and theory, to the point that she does. They take her to a place quite different from where she began. Her latter work is so non-referential and playful that it seems almost to have no connection to the classical aesthetic of correspondence upon which so much of the significant work (i.e., *Three Lives, The Making of Americans, Tender Buttons,* etc.) is, surprisingly, predicated. However, even later, in the theoretical work, Stein never really does reject the classical aesthetic of the innocent eye.

PICASSO

One later work which we might briefly examine is *Picasso*. First published in 1938 and ostensibly a study of the painter, it is a classic formulation of the innocent eye aesthetic. *Picasso* is, in fact, much more a defense of the author's own work, a defense bolstered by Stein's identification of her own aesthetic practice with that of the painter's: "I was alone at this time in understanding him, perhaps because I was expressing the same thing in literature" (Pic, 16). Here, assuming that things are unconnected and disparate, Stein once again speaks of "the struggle to express . . . the things seen without association but simply as things seen" (Pic, 35). The struggle is made more difficult by Stein's celebrating the thing-in-itself and then making this the only thing worthy of artistic attention: "Related things are things remembered and for a creator . . . remembered things are not things seen, therefore they are not things known" (Pic, 35).

Wishing then "to express not things felt, not things remembered, not established in relations but things which are there, really everything a human being can know at each moment of his existence and not an assembling of all his experiences" (Pic, 35), Stein embraces a second fiction: the child's innocent vision. It is, of course, a familiar Romantic conceit, demonstrating the continuity between a nineteenth- and twentieth-century aesthetic. Stein, however, appropriates it for Picasso and herself, and she offers it as evidence of their modernity, of the fact that like the child unencumbered by memory they too are able to see the world as it is—in its parts rather than as a series of wholes:

> A child sees the face of its mother, it sees it in a completely different way than other people see it, I am not speaking of the spirit of the mother but of the features and the whole face, the child sees it from very near, it is a large face for the eyes of the small one, it is certain the child for a little while only sees a part of the face of its mother, it knows one feature and not another, one side and not the other. (Pic, 14–15)

While it is doubtful that a child sees things exactly in this manner, the beauty of it, for Stein, lies in its presumed fidelity to reality. It communicates a sense "not of things seen but of things that exist" (Pic, 19), adding nothing to the perceived object. Read this way, the child's vision represents sight in its most elemental and absolute terms, anything over and above it representing not an improvement in vision but a reconstruction in memory. And if a child can see this way, the question becomes why not simply mimic the model, particularly if it affords a more honest presentation of the object. Thus does the artist imitate the child, forgetting that even one's understanding of the child's manner of perception is already a representation, a copy. Yet for Stein and (she says) for Picasso, the innocent eye aesthetic remained a workable formula:

> Really most of the time one sees only a feature of a person with whom one is, the other features are covered by a hat, by the light, by clothes for sport and every body is accustomed to complete the whole entirely from their knowledge, but for Picasso when he saw an eye, the other did not exist for him and as a painter . . . he was right, one sees what one sees, the rest is reconstruction from memory and painters have nothing to do with memory, they concern themselves only with visible things and the result was disconcerting for him and others, but what else could he do, a creator can only continue, that is all he can do. (Pic, 15)

Mostly, Stein felt, people did not understand that our picture of the world is, in James's words, "in abridgement, a foreshortened bird's eye view of the perspective of events."[60] And because no one understood this, no one tried to give it artistic expression, "to express things seen not as one knows them but as they are when one sees them without remembering having looked at them" (Pic, 15). For artists and laypeople alike, fresh seeing is continually interfered with by habitual modes of seeing and living. "Everything," says Stein, "prevents one, habits, schools, daily life, reason, necessities of daily life, indolence, everything prevents one" (Pic, 43) from realizing a direct vision of things. Yet at the same time, Stein argues, it can be done if one struggles hard enough, if one gears all one's attention to the present, isolated moment. Picasso was proof that such purity of perception could be had. He showed that it was possible "to express heads and bodies not like every one could see them, which was the problem of other painters, but as he saw them, as one could see them when one has not the habit of knowing what one is looking at" (Pic, 18). Other artists might satisfy "themselves with the appearance and always the appearance, which was not at all what they knew was there" (Pic, 19), but Picasso always revealed "the things seen without association but simply as things seen" (Pic, 35). Here, in a Picasso canvas, "the features seen separately existed separately and at the same time it was all a picture" (Pic, 25), a

picture that, while appearing ugly and unreal to the mind conditioned by traditional aesthetic values, constituted a much more accurate representation of reality. Said Stein, "The things that Picasso
could see were the things which had their own reality, reality not
of things seen but of things that exist" (Pic, 42).

As Stein describes it, Picasso's innocent eye aesthetic is remarkably
similar to her own. In fact, it is her own. And it is, of course, this
same aesthetic which, two decades earlier, informed *Tender Buttons*.
Like her supposed Picasso, Stein felt that no one in their time "had
really been able to tell anything without anything but just telling
that thing."[61] In *Tender Buttons* she would, however, "try to simply
tell some thing,"[62] try to block out all perceptions which were not
precisely of the thing-in-itself. As she later said, thinking back to
what she had tried to do:

> You must remember each time I took something, I said, I have got to
> satisfy each realistic thing about it. Looking at your shoe, for instance,
> I would try to make a complete realistic picture of your shoe. It is
> devilish difficult and needs perfect concentration, you have to refuse so
> much and so much intrudes itself upon you that you do not want it, it
> is exhausting work.[63]

CELEBRATING THE PATIENT PARTICULARS

Of course, all this looking, all this attention to things existing, had
a celebratory quality about it. It spoke of art not only as something
epistemological but also as something—and this was not really intended—spiritual. That is, to think of things-in-themselves as possessing their own inherent worth is, in effect, to think of them as
holy, as requiring respect and attention. And this, conjoined with
the faith that language and world are necessarily linked, makes for
a suggestion that the cosmos does bespeak a transcendent unity, or
godhead. Thus does the art of presentation become synonymous, in
one sense, with a species of ontological argument, though again,
Stein would be quick to deny this. She may write, "Blessed are the
patient particulars," yet her intention appears less holy than secular.[64]

Still, Stein celebrates things, believing them somehow graced with
prior importance, even if this importance should only be attested to
by their singularity, by their strangeness. In "A Box," she suggests
the need to acknowledge "the strange*ness* in the strangeness"—that
is, the fact that things exist at all, that there is something rather than
nothing: "[I]t is so rudimentary to be analysed and see a fine sub-

stance strangely, it is so earnest to have a green point not to red but to point again" (11). And in "Sausages," she tells us, "any extra leaf is so strange and singular a red breast" (52).

The result is that feelings of wonder and joy are frequent in *Tender Buttons*. Words and phrases such as "astonishment," "cheerfulness," "enthusiastic," "pleasure," "splendor," "spectacle," "violent kind of delightfulness," etc. describe Stein's own delight in "being living," her own affection for the "stouter symmetry":

> Lovely snipe and tender turn, excellent vapor and slender butter, all the splinter and the trunk, all the poisonous darkening drunk, all the joy in weak success, all the joyful tenderness, all the section and the tea, all the stouter symmetry. (35)

Meanwhile, that Stein should not only explore the genre of the still life but also work to see its domestic things as pleasurable in themselves suggest purposes that relate not only to epistemology but also to gender. My examination has concentrated upon the former, for this is the problematic which most interests me. Yet most problems admit of a multitude of solutions, and Stein's *Tender Buttons* appears not to be the exception. And here, rather than recapitulate the interesting argument which sees Stein's writing as exemplifying an *écriture féminine*,[65] I should like briefly to refer to Norman Bryson's equally interesting observations about the gendered history of the still life. The genre itself, as Bryson explains, has always been looked at somewhat askance by the art community, for the reason that it was less abstract (and hence "masculine") than descriptive (and hence "feminine"). If it were commonly believed (as it seems to have been) that, in Joshua Reynolds's words, "[t]he value and rank of every art is in proportion to the mental labour employed in it, or the mental pleasure produced by it," and that all great art aspires to the level of "general ideas," then it should not surprise that the still life, so generally rhopographic in its values, was not more highly esteemed as a genre.[66] Or that when it was, it was for the reasons that the values of the table were converted into "higher" values, allying the canvas with the megalographic: "And for as long as painting's mode of vision would be constructed by men, the space in which women were obliged to lead their lives would be taken from them and imagined through values of the 'greater' existence from which they were excluded."[67]

In *Tender Buttons*, meanwhile, Stein's handling of the domestic scene appears radically rhopographic, so resistant does she seem to the "higher" values. She might celebrate the holiness of things, yet she does so from a most secular and materialistic point of view, which either refuses to locate or despairs of locating meaning outside of human experience. Certainly, despair is the note struck in the line from "Food," "Why is there so much useless suffering" (77). Stein herself does not know the answer; and though she is ever engaged in creating meanings in *Tender Buttons,* Stein seems to place little faith in their permanency. This sense of things is perhaps only implicit here; however, it is made more explicit elsewhere. For example, on the point of transcendental meaning, Stein, believing that the world does "not mean much," writes that "[t]he meaningless of why makes all the nothingness so real."[68]And on the point of heaven, Stein, affirming its demise, writes: "Certainly it lasted heaven a very little time all things considered that is considered as long as anything is" (GHA, 159).

The ideas of heaven and the soul might once have been "interesting," yet they are no longer. The earth and the body now prove the more fascinating realities. As Stein writes, respecting the latter, "Why interest one's self in the souls of people when the faces, the head, the body can tell everything" (P, 47). Why interest oneself in the spiritual when everything can be understood in terms of the physical? Similarly, why feel any anxiety about eternity (cf. Pascal: "The eternal silence of these infinite spaces frightens me.") when it either exists here and now or it does not exist at all. "[E]ternity is not all troubling any one because every one knows that here on this earth are the only men and everybody knows all there is on this earth and everybody knows that there is all there is to it."[69] And if this were not the case, Stein wonders, would it make any difference? Would the spiritual not simply be another variation upon the physical?

> I never did take on spirits either then or later they had nothing to do with the problems of everlasting not for me, because anybody can know that the earth is covered all over with people and if the air is too what is the difference to any one there are an awful lot of them anyway and in a way I really am only interested in what a genius can say the rest is just there anyway.[70]

As witnessed here, Stein's interest in people and things was not unflagging. It just seemed that way, given the enormous engagement that such texts as *The Making of Americans, Tender Buttons,* and the portraits demanded. Yet Stein could tire of people ("there are an awful lot of them") and things; and while her work almost presents itself as a constant effort to redeem people and things from the hell of oblivion, there is no extraordinary importance apparently attributed to them. "Human beings have no meaning," and left "alone to live and die," they appear fragile and small before the universe's immensity, no different from any other animal: "[T]here are men only upon this earth and anything like anybody does it what is the difference between eternity and anything."[71]

Stein confesses that at first she found the idea of our insignificance frightening: "It was frightening when the first comet I saw made it real that the stars were worlds and the earth only one of them."[72] And unreal: "There is no realism now, life is not real it is earnest, it is strange."[73] Still, she grew accepting of the idea, to the point where she could turn around and take pleasure in her world: "we are on the earth and we have to live on it and there is beyond all there it is and here we are, and we are always here and we are always there and any little while it is a pleasure, and a pleasure is a pleasure as yes it is a pleasure as a treasure."[74] Which, in a sense, is what *Tender Buttons* and all of Stein's work amounts to: a pleasure in the "being living," in the moment to moment feel of experience.

STEIN AND THE POSTMODERN

Perhaps it is Gertrude Stein's love of pleasure and of play that ultimately transforms both her ambition and her work. For if Stein's work begins within an episteme which privileges analysis and discrimination and in which space is conceived as three-dimensional, time as linear, and language as artificial yet determinately connected with the parallel plane of "reality," it is nevertheless recognized that her work, particularly in and after *Tender Buttons,* moves somewhere else. If *Tender Buttons* begins as a quest for origin, for the thing-in-itself, this quest begins to find itself undermined by another interest, that of pleasure, of joy in the "being living," and of joy in the sensuousness of words themselves.

Writing in the thirties, Ortega y Gasset, in *The Dehumanization of Art,* spoke of the qualities of "play" and "delightful fraud" as characterizing a new modern sensibility, one which turned its attention away from problems of reference and human narrative, and back toward its own plasticity. Art here is autotelic; it serves its own ends. Delight follows not upon the mirroring of the "real world" but rather upon the creating of a new, self-reflexive and self-existent mini-world. In one of her later lectures Stein comments upon the independence of the art object (in this instance an oil painting) from reference:

I think the annoyance comes from the fact that the oil painting exists by reason of these things the oil painting represents in the oil painting, and profoundly it should not do so, so thinks the oil painting, so sometimes thinks the painter of the oil painting, so instinctively feels the person looking at the oil painting. Really in everybody's heart there is a feeling of annoyance at the inevitable existence of an oil painting in relation to what it has painted people, objects and landscapes. And indeed and of course as I have already made you realize that is not what an oil painting is an oil painting is an oil painting. (LIA, 84)

Though Stein speaks of different intentions, this same interest in play, in language as language, is at work in *Tender Buttons*. In a sense, of course, it could not be different, for no sooner does a sign emerge then "it begins," in Derrida's words, "by repeating itself,"[75] by calling attention to itself as sign. This is true of any language, though it is more obvious when an author foregoes "ordinary language"— that is, the technique, so identified with classical rationalism, which simulates language's transparency—and chooses instead to foreground a text's literariness. In *Tender Buttons* Stein often seems to work at cross purposes, on the one hand accentuating the materiality of her language and on the other hand seeking to employ language as pure sign, pure presence. Of the latter aim we have said enough, whereas of the former we might simply point to "A Red Hat" as being not atypical of Stein's delight in repetition and figure in her own language's rhetorical flourishes:

A dark grey, a very dark grey, a quite dark grey is monstrous ordinarily, it is so monstrous because there is no red in it. If red is in everything it is not necessary. Is that not an argument for any use of it and even so is there any place that is better, is there any place that has so much stretched out. (17)

In pointing to "A Red Hat" as exemplifying Stein's very real dependence upon schemes and tropes, we might also note that while *Tender Buttons* is, in David Lodge's words, "clearly a type of metaphysical writing based on a radical substitution (or replacement) of referential nouns"[76]—that is, a giant metaphor—its main trope is really not metaphor so much as it is metonymy (the use of attributive or suggestive words for what is actually meant). That is, while definitions of metonymy still seem somewhat wanting and while its identification, by Jakobson, Lodge, and others, with realism is not above questioning, it does appear that the "attributive or suggestive word" is really Stein's main technique here—that "dark grey" and "red" are synecdochical references to a hat or hats, just as "green," "straw color," and "chain" are synecdochical references to a purse or to others not it in "A Purse":

> A purse was not green, it was not straw color, it was hardly seen and it had a use a long use and the chain, the chain was never missing, it was not misplaced, it showed that it was open, that is all that it showed. (19)

This brings me back to Jakobson's point that a given language generally moves either to the pole of metonymy, which is identified with prose and realism, or to the pole of metaphor, which is identified with poetry and romanticism. "In normal verbal behavior, both processes are continually operative, but . . . under the influence of a cultural pattern, personality and verbal style, preference is given to one of the two processes over the other."[77] In *Tender Buttons* preference is given to one pole, the metonymic with its consequent suggestion of contiguity and realism, over the other. Yet, at the same time, with Jakobson, one recognizes that "both processes are continually operative"; and that Lodge, who argues that *Tender Buttons* "does not confine itself to merely changing the relationship of contiguous planes and of parts to wholes as they are in nature . . . but presents an object in terms of other objects often as far removed from it and from each other in context,"[78] is certainly not incorrect. The overarching point is that just as Stein in *Tender Buttons* tries, at the same time, to sketch things in terms of their realistic attributes and in terms of their metaphysical essences, so too does she employ a language that is both metonymic and metaphoric, both realistic and romantic. The contradiction, which is really not such, is inherent in the work and not to be resolved. So it is that if, in Jakobson's words, "no feeling is so pure as to be free from contamination by its opposite feeling,"[79] no technique is so pure as to be free from contamination by its opposite technique.

The same thing might also be said respecting another matter of technique in *Tender Buttons*—that is, synthesis versus analysis, or the copulative versus the paratactical. In *Tender Buttons* Stein is most interested in the question of definition and frequently makes use of the verb "to be" as a way of equating one thing with another. At the same time, however, she is very much interested in analysis, in the thing-itself standing separate from other such things. In terms of technique, the consequence of Stein's interest is that her language is also quite paratactic; it places one thing next to another without forging a hierarchy of value. This, of course, holds true in the text's general arrangement, with the still-life "Orange" following, without discernible patterning or prioritizing, those of "Salad," "Sauce," and

"Salmon" in the section "Food" just as "A Long Dress" follows "A Box," "A Plate," and "A Seltzer Bottle" in the section "Objects." It also holds true within the still lifes themselves. For instance, note the first paragraph of "Apple":

> Apple plum, carpet steak, seed clam, colored wine, calm seen, cold cream, best shake, potato, potato and no no gold work with pet, a green seen is called bake and change sweet is bready, a little piece a little piece please. (48)

Finally, then, *Tender Buttons* is a text embodying remarkable contradictions, both in intention and in fact. On the one side, Stein intends it to be the world; on the other, she intends it to be its own world. On the one side, she intends to know the essence of things-in-themselves; on the other, she intends to do so by dwelling on the appearance of things. On the one side, it is emphatically concrete and figurative; on the other, it is emphatically abstract and nonfigurative. On the one side, it is realistic; on the other, it is romantic.

The contradictions do not go away. Yet even as they do not go away, my own sense is that in *Tender Buttons* Stein, like the late Monet, does stand, facing forward, in the pass between one reality and another, one episteme and another. Of course, this judgment entails its own frame of reference, classifying texts according to the differing weights which they attach to the components of the *trivium*. Thus understood, I argue that Stein never really escapes the said pass, never really embraces a postmodernism (if it can be identified as a skepticism toward the epistemological project) that is not demarked by assumptions utterly modern (including epistemological), just as *Tender Buttons* never actually exemplifies a postmodernism that is not also demarked by the modern quest for the thing-itself. The quest was doomed from the start. Language simply does not work this way. As necessary as its relation to the signified object might be, it never relinquishes its function as sign to assume the role of the thing-itself. And yet even as *Tender Buttons* represents a failed quest, it is not without interest; and even as it represents, in this framing, the culmination of the modernist episteme, it is not without a relevance to our understanding of the postmodern.

4

Ernest Hemingway and *In Our Time*

THE INFLUENCE OF STEIN

Writing in the latter part of his life to the art historian Bernard Berenson, Ernest Hemingway reflected upon how when he reread his earlier fiction it would often seem as if it were not quite his own. "It always reads to me," he wrote, "when it's very good as though I must have stolen it from somebody else." Being the person he was, Hemingway was of course quick to withdraw the suggestion, finishing his own statement with the reassuring conceit "and then I think and remember that nobody else knew about it and that it never really happened and so I must have invented it and I feel very happy."[1] He was, we know, obsessed with the question of his own originality. He wanted as much as possible to disclaim his forebears ("No I don't think 'My Old Man' derives from Anderson" [SL, 105]) even as he wanted to claim his own progeny ("I'd like to have it ["Up In Michigan"] published so people could see Morley [Callaghan]'s source book" (SL, 327). Nevertheless, Hemingway had good reason to suspect (even if it were but an unwelcome intuition) the purity of his own originality, for as his critics have observed, his literary influences were many, including Kipling, Lardner, Maupassant, Anderson, Pound, Joyce, Tolstoy, and Turgenev.[2] In *In Our Time,* for example, the focal text of this chapter, one readily notes the influence of the story-telling technique that Conrad employed in the Marlow tales in "On the Quai at Smyrna"; the colloquial language of Twain's *Huck Finn* in "My Old Man"; and the wasteland imagery of Eliot in "Big Two-Hearted River."[3] One also notes the pervasive influence of Stein's syntax upon Hemingway's overall style.

The young Hemingway—the youth who called himself "Hemingstein" or "Stein," for short—took a liking to Gertrude Stein that the older Hemingway—the artist who either openly or covertly begrudged all literary rivals—might only acknowledge with embarrassment. For if the older Hemingway reduced the rival artist to a

"lazy" "[l]esbian [b]itch" who "was nice until she had the meno-
pause" (SL, 736, 423, 696), the younger Hemingway, Hemingstein,
conceived her in several different lights, all favorable. For the young
Stein, Gertrude Stein was a sibling ("Gertrude Stein and me are just
like brothers" [SL, 62]); a scowling parent ("I like to have Gertrude
bawl me out because it keeps one['s] opinion of oneself down" [SL,
310]); an oedipal lover ("I used to listen and learn and I always
wanted to fuck her" [SL, 650]); a godmother for his child and a
more general relative who could depend upon the allegiance of the
family ("It is up to us, i.e. Alice Toklas, Me, Hadley, John Hadley
Nicanor and other good men to get it [Stein's *The Making of Americans*] published" [SL, 118]); a mentor ("I've thought a lot about the
things you said about working and am starting that way at the beginning" [SL, 79]); a literary genius ("Her Making of Americans is one
of the very greatest books I've ever read" [SL, 206]); and a rival
lover (to the point, wrote Hemingway, that Toklas said to Stein,
"You [Gertrude] give up the friendship of Hemingstein or you give
up me" [SL, 795]). Aside from his wife, Hadley, she was the person
during the formative Paris years to whom he was most attached—
and it shows in his writing.

Stein helped Hemingway to begin to think of himself as an artist.
In gratitude, in the fall of 1923, he wrote her: "I am going to chuck
journalism I think. You ruined me as a journalist last winter. Have
been no good since. Like a bull, or a novillo [i.e., a fighting bull
under the age of three] rather, well stuck but taking a long while to
go down" (SL, 101). And Stein helped him not only to think of
himself as an artist but also to think like an artist. She made him
sensitive to method, particularly to her own. As Hemingway wrote
at this same time (November 1923) to Edmund Wilson: "Her
method is invaluable for analysing anything or making notes on a
person or a place" (SL, 105). Hemingway appears to have been referring to her use of frequent repetitions, "-ing" verbals and staccato-
like prose rhythms, all of which he transferred into his own work,
as for example in "Mr. and Mrs. Elliot":

> Mr. and *Mrs. Elliot tried very* hard to have a baby. *They tried* as often
> as *Mrs. Elliot* could stand it. *They tried* in Boston after they were married
> and *they tried* com*ing* over on the boat. *They* did not *try very* often on
> the boat because *Mrs. Elliot* was quite *sick*. *She was sick* and when *she was*
> *sick she was sick* as *Southern women* are *sick*. That is *women* from the
> *Southern* part of the United States. Like all *Southern women* Mrs. *Elliot*
> disintegrated *very* quickly under sea *sickness,* travell*ing* at night, and get-
> t*ing* up too early for *Elliot's* mother. (85; emphasis added)

In this passage, Hemingway adopts Steinian technique for Steinian reasons: to give a transpiring and full sense of the presence of events, and thus to make these same events obtrude their beingness upon our consciousness. The technique is purposeful, even if Hemingway has not yet appropriated it to his own interests, has not yet made it *his* technique. Eventually he did, yet even late in his career, such as in the 1958 George Plimpton interview, one can find him, in an almost ventriloquistic manner, employing Stein's voice to explain his own work: "Everything changes as it moves. That is what makes the movement which makes the story. Sometimes the movement is so slow it does not seem to be moving. But there is always change and always movement."[4]

Stein herself took note of Hemingway's borrowing, and in her disguised memoir *The Autobiography of Alice B. Toklas* made it clear that Hemingway was the student and she the teacher.[5] As she explains it, Stein taught him the value of seeing and concentrating. She told him that unless he gave up journalism, he would "only see words and that will not do" (ABT, 213). She found that she liked his poems, for "they were direct, Kiplingesque" (ABT, 213), but she found the early prose "wanting." There was, she told him, "a great deal of description in" it "and not particularly good description" (ABT, 213). Thus, he should "[b]egin over and concentrate" (ABT, 213). Her advice, she said, followed from her decision to comment only upon another writer's "way of seeing what the writer chooses to see, and the relation between that vision and the way it gets down" (ABT, 214).

If her advice directly led, as she tells the story, to the collection of *In Our Time*—"It was at this time that Hemingway began the short things that afterwards were printed in a volume called *In Our Time*" (ABT, 214)—its pedagogical value was also supplemented by Hemingway's reading of her work. Here, the most extraordinary influence was *The Making of Americans,* which the young writer transcribed and proofed so that it might be published in Ford Madox Ford's *Transatlantic Review*. In doing so, Hemingway "learn[ed] the value of [the] thing as no reading suffices to teach it to you" (ABT, 217). He thus made an excellent student, something that she could joke about with Sherwood Anderson:

And then they [Stein and Anderson] agreed that they have a weakness for Hemingway because he is such a good pupil. He is a rotten pupil, I [Toklas] protested. You don't understand, they both said, it is so flattering to have a pupil who does it without understanding it, in other words he takes training and anybody who takes training is a favorite pupil. . . . Gertrude Stein added further, you see he is like Derain. You remember Monsieur de Tuille said, when I did not understand why Derain was having the success he was having that it was because he looks like a modern and he smells of the museums. And that is Hemingway, he looks like a modern and he smells of the museums. (ABT, 216)

Meanwhile, in 1925, when Stein's influence was measured as a gain, bolstering his confidence, Hemingway wrote boldly back to reassure his editor, Horace Liveright, that his use of repetitions was deliberate: "There is nothing in the book [*In Our Time*] that has not a definite place in its organization and if I at any time seem to repeat myself I have a good reason for doing so" (SL, 154). Undoubtedly, he did. At the same time, we also find evidence, as in the story "Mr. and Mrs. Elliot," that the reason could reflect less an aesthetic or an epistemological necessity than a stylistic choice, a choice reflecting Stein's influence. Thus "Mr. and Mrs. Elliot" seems quite analogous to one of Stein's portraits wherein linear narrative is subordinated to a kind of circling description designed to reveal a character's essence rather than his or her history. Certainly, the story never moves beyond a reiteration of the theme introduced in the first paragraph—that of sterility. Hence at its conclusion, Mrs. Elliot sits with her female friend and bedmate, summoned from abroad, alongside but apart from her husband: "In the evening they all sat at dinner together in the garden under a plane tree and the hot evening wind blew and Elliot drank white wine and Mrs. Elliot and the girl friend made conversation and they were all quite happy" (88).

Hemingway himself acknowledged Stein's influence upon his work. Even later in his career when such acknowledgments were only grudgingly given—perhaps understandably, given Stein's couched accusations in *The Autobiography of Alice B. Toklas*—he spoke, as in *A Moveable Feast,* of her importance with regard to his prose rhythms: "She had . . . discovered many truths about rhythms and the use of words in repetition that were valid and valuable and she talked well about them."[6] And elsewhere: "I learned the wonderful rhythms in prose from her" (SL, 649). In fact, the influence had been a dramatic one. For instance, if one studies the very early prose (the high school juvenilia, the *Kansas City Star* reporting, the *Toronto Star* features, etc.), one finds a prose that is discursive in a rather traditional way, aspiring to tell a good story but not technically innovative. It is not a bad prose, yet it does not call attention to itself the way that Hemingway's later prose does, beginning with "Up In Michigan." In that story, which Hemingway spoke of as "an important story in my work" and "the beginning of all the naturalness I ever got" (SL, 468), we see him for the first time applying Stein's lessons and writing a prose that has a more than ordinary quality of self-conscious artistry about it, the kind that Ezra Pound adversely critiqued as too "licherary": "these short repeating sentences, TOO DAMN IMPRESSIVE. You'd git the sak for telegraphing in that manner."[7]

To illustrate just how much Hemingway actually took away from Stein's rue de Fleurus classroom—Stein herself said, "Hemingway learned a great deal and he admired all that he learned" (ABT, 217)— we would do well to place the opening passage of "Up in Michigan" after a passage of equal length drawn from *Three Lives:*

> Jane Harden always had a little money and she had a room in the lower part of the town. Jane had once taught in a colored school. She had had to leave that too on account of her bad conduct. It was her drinking that always made all the trouble for her, for that can never be really covered over.[8]

> Jim Gilmore came to Horton Bays from Canada. He bought the blacksmith shop from old man Horton. Jim was short and dark with big mustaches and big hands. He was a good horseshoer and did not look much like a blacksmith even with his leather apron on. He lived upstairs above the blacksmith shop and took his meals at A. J. Smith's.[9]

Both passages are syntactically quite simple with a subject-verb-object order constituting the controlling pattern. There is no inverting of this pattern and very little subordination, sentence variety being introduced by extending the sentence with coordinated elements and prepositional phrases. Modifiers and tropes are also kept to a minimum. The one Hemingway simile ("did not look much like a blacksmith") is negative, reminding us of Hemingway's later statement that "similes . . . are like defective ammunition" (SL, 809). Whether Hemingway recognized the irony of this statement is unknown. What is clear, however, is that *Three Lives* was an important book for Hemingway, a fact which Edmund Wilson noted in his October 1924 review of *In Our Time* for the *Dial:* Hemingway is "the American writer but one—Mr. Sherwood Anderson—who has felt the genius of Gertrude Stein's *Three Lives* and has evidently been influenced by it. Indeed, Miss Stein, Mr. Anderson and Mr. Hemingway may now be said to form a school by themselves."[10] Wilson's judgment was not without its own sources, for the year before Hemingway had written Wilson not only that he had recently "read a lot of her [Stein's] new stuff," but also that he wished "to write a review of an old book of hers sometimes" (SL, 105). That "old book" was the same one that earlier in the year (March 5, 1923), when reviewing Stein's *Geography and Plays,* Hemingway had told readers of the European edition of the *Chicago Tribune* they must read: "[Y]ou ought to read her Three Lives. The Melanctha story in Three Lives is one of the best short stories in English."[11] This injunction followed from his conviction that most all other writers were skirting the boundaries of "literature," and not really offering enough in the way of technical instruction:

> Gertrude Stein is a sort of gauge of civilization. If you think Mr. Sinclair Lewis is a great writer and Babbitt a great book you probably won't like Gertrude Stein. If you think Mr. Lewis is doing the best he can employing a *Saturday Evening Post* technique to prove an H. L. Mencken theory with masses of detail and occasional interjected shots of BEAUTY, or if you hold any other theory about Lewis that you have thought up for yourself—and if somebody ever lends you a copy of Geography and Plays, or if you buy one, you will be very happy for a number of hours. You will also be very disturbed. You will also learn something, if you happen to be a writer—or a reader.
> Gertrude Stein is probably the most first rate intelligence employed in writing today. If you are tired of Mr. D. H. Lawrence who writes extremely well with the intelligence of a head waiter or Mr. Wells who is believed to be intelligent because of a capacity for sustained marathon thinking or the unbelievably stupid but thoroughly conscientious young men who compile the Dial you ought to read Gertrude Stein.[12]

Despite the young Hemingstein's rashness, he was learning much from Stein, and learning it amazingly quickly. As the *Tribune* passage suggests, he was thinking not only about prose rhythms but also about the need for composition, the need to do more than pile up "masses of detail." Stein, who in her review of *Three Stories and Ten Poems* had urged that "Hemingway should stick to poetry and intelligence and eschew the hotter emotions and the more turgid vision,"[13] had herself learnt a great deal about composition, beforehand, from Cézanne. "Everything I have done has been influenced by . . . Cézanne and this gave me a new feeling about composition."[14] From the study of his canvases, particularly that of Madame Cézanne (which hung in her flat), she learnt the importance of concentration. Not surprisingly, then, she found the inspiration for her first successful literary work—*Three Lives*—by repeatedly gazing up at the Cézanne canvas: "She had begun not long before as an exercise in literature to translate Flaubert's Trois Contes and then she had this Cézanne and she looked at it and under its stimulus she wrote Three Lives" (ABT, 34). And what she learned here, early in the century, she was happy to share with Hemingway two decades later.

For his part, the young Hemingway seems to have been quite taken by Stein's references to Cézanne, and soon embarked upon his own attempt to compose stories in a manner analogous to Cézanne's canvas technique. Or, perhaps one should say that he set out to compose stories in a manner which Stein assured him bore a resemblance to Cézanne's, for at this point the young artist must have taken it somewhat on faith that a writer could appropriate a painter's technique.[15] Still, this is not to question the project, for there are some things about Hemingway's prose which are, in fact, very much reminiscent of Cézanne. Particularly what they have in common is a stance, vis-à-vis things themselves, which seeks, "from the depth of their silence, . . . to bring [them] to expression."[16] Yet there are smaller resemblances as well, such as the description of the "underbrush in the island of pine trees" in "Big Two-Hearted River: Part I," which, with its patient and uncluttered attention to the way that the planes of the trees parallel one another, or the way in which this parallel is occasionally broken by the diagonal of a slanted tree, reminds one of the way that Cézanne would pictorially handle a forest:

> The trunks of the trees went straight up or slanted toward each other. The trunks were straight and brown without branches. The branches were high above. Some interlocked to make a solid shadow on the brown forest floor. (137)

This sense is enhanced by Hemingway's attention to the way that the trees filter the sunlight: "The trees had grown tall and the branches moved high, leaving in the sun this bare space they had once covered with shadow" (137).

Nevertheless, one wants to stress that painterly techniques are often difficult to transfer to the page (e.g., think of the efforts to write a cubistic prose) and that while other authors, such as Rilke and Williams, also drew technical inspiration from Cézanne, Hemingway's initial understanding came filtered through Stein, a fact which, in the summer of 1924, he acknowledged in a letter to his mentor:

> I have finished two long short stories, one of them not much good and finished the long one I worked on before I went to Spain ["Big Two-Hearted River"] where I'm trying to do the country like Cézanne and having a hell of a time and sometimes getting it a little bit. It is about 100 pages long and nothing happens and the country is swell, I made it all up, so I see it all and part of it comes out the way it ought to, it is swell about the fish, but isn't writing a hard job though? It used to be

easy before I met you. Certainly was bad, Gosh, I'm awfully bad now but it's a different kind of bad. (SL, 122)

In short, Hemingway learned a great deal from Stein, and it was she who both introduced him to a Cézannean aesthetic and helped him to hone his own version. Later, in the Plimpton interview, he would "thank Gertrude for everything I learned about the abstract relationship of words" (227), and, also later, he would think back upon this time as the point when he "started to break down all [his] writing" so as to "get rid of all facility" (MF, 154) as well as took note of how the "piled on detail" of a Zola, or any other author, "is as dead and unconvincing as a steel engraving."[17] With Cézanne as his model, he would move toward a more austere aesthetic, wherein a selective description entailed as much the evocation of what was not seen as what was. Because this aesthetic would become synonymous with his credo, we can, in retrospect, see these first years in Paris as representing more than a start; for here, with Stein's help, Hemingway found a technique which would serve him well, particularly in the first half of his career, wherein his work is strongest.

OMISSION AS A FORM OF APOPHASIS

Hemingway first experimented with his newly inherited technique in "Out of Season": "It was a very simple story called 'Out of Season' and I had omitted the real end of it which was that the old man hanged himself. This was omitted on my new theory that you could omit anything if you knew that you omitted and the omitted part would strengthen the story and make people feel something more than they understood" (MF, 75). Hemingway later told F. Scott Fitzgerald that

> I meant it to be a tragic about the drunk of a guide because I reported him to the hotel owner . . . and he fired him and as that was the last job he had in town and he was quite drunk and very desperate, hanged himself in the stable. At that time I was writing the In Our Time chapters and I wanted to write a tragic story *without* violence. So I didnt put in the hanging. Maybe that sounds silly. I didn't think the story needed it. (SL, 180–81)

It is difficult to say just how accurate Hemingway's recall was, two and a half years later, of the incident that crystallized into "Out of Season." Certainly, the cause-and-effect relation which connects Hemingway's complaint against the guide and the guide's subsequent suicide seems, without further testimony, suspect. What is most interesting here (at least for us) is not the matter respecting the guide's fate but that Hemingway saw this story as his first attempt to write a fiction of suggestion rather than accumulation. The story thus bears as prominent a place in the Hemingway canon as does "Up in Michigan," the first story to evince a Steinian touch. What Hemingway seems to have learned about composition from Cézanne (through Stein) was something that he would appropriate so successfully and so fully that he himself, along with his readers and critics, came almost to forget that "natural" as his work might seem, it was nevertheless something quite artistic, something quite bound up with a technique borrowed from others.[18] Or as Hemingway, in the voice of Nick Adams, wrote in the deleted (because too autobiographical) section of "Big Two-Hearted River":

> He wanted to write like Cézanne painted.
> Cézanne started with all the tricks. Then he broke the whole thing down and built the real thing. It was hell to do. He was the greatest. The greatest for always. It wasn't a cult. He, Nick, wanted to write about country so it would be there like Cézanne had done it in painting. You had to do it from inside yourself. There wasn't any trick. Nobody had ever written about country like that. He felt almost holy about it. It was deadly serious. You could do it if you would fight it out. *If you'd lived right with your eyes.*[19]

Again, the passage is telling: on the one hand, it speaks of the "innocent eye" desire to live right with one's eyes, yet at the same time, it acknowledges that the "your" of "your eyes" refers in a very significant way to Cézanne. Hemingway's Nick wishes to live right with Cézanne's eyes; he wants to see his world—i.e., Upper Michigan—through the eyes of the Provençal painter. That Hemingway/ Nick would wish to inflect his vision this way does not surprise us; that he would think that this makes the country more "there" does. Meanwhile, to return to "Out of Season," what Hemingway first sought to do here and then later in subsequent stories was to write a dramatized fiction that worked by way of indirection. "I try," he said, "always to do the thing by three cushion shots rather than by words or direct statement" (SL, 301). Later, after the *Paris Review* interview, the technique would become recognized as Hemingway's "iceberg" theory, following from his understanding that the dignity of good fiction might be likened to the dignity of the iceberg: "I always try to write on the principle of the iceberg. There is seven-eighths of it underwater for every part that shows. Anything you know you can eliminate and it only strengthens your iceberg. It is the part that doesn't show."[20]

Of course, one might wonder whether an author, any author, does well to "eliminate" from his work that which he or she knows. Eliminate this and one eliminates all reason for the common reader to take an interest in the work. But here, as opposed to what he actually says, we should take Hemingway to mean not that he wishes to "eliminate" from his work that which he knows, but that he wishes to find a fuller way to articulate that which he knows, including finding a way to make an apparent absence double as a presence. That is, there is a sense in which all that we say and do finds itself determined by forces that are, for all extensive purposes, invisible. Certainly part of Hemingway's genius as a writer was to acknowledge these forces—to understand that there are things (à la Heidegger's concept of Being) which make themselves known without exactly showing themselves.

Meanwhile, as I say, "Out of Season" is a nice example of Hemingway's technique of suggestion. Everything that we know about its composition—from its 1923 date of origin to Hemingway's recollection that it was the place of some of his first experiments in self-conscious literary technique—would lead us to think it an apprenticeship story. Yet it is not, for Hemingway's handling of the technique of suggestion, the technique that, in Henry James's words, would "convert[. . .] the very pulse of the air into revelations," is here quite deft. To say this, however, is not altogether to acquiesce to Hemingway's own reading, is not to see the story as that of a poor man's suicide, "a tragic story *without violence*." There are many things which remain nicely understated here, including the tension between the husband and wife, but the suicidal violence is not one of these. There is simply not enough evidence, suggestive or otherwise, to make the poor man's (Peduzzi's) suicide plausible.

We are, of course, under no compulsion to accept Hemingway's reading. We know that literary meaning is not altogether determinate, and we are prepared to be suspicious of any reading which presents itself as definitive or final. And this seems an appropriate stance, particularly with regard to this story. For if "Out of Season" seems less successful as a tragic story, it does seem remarkably successful as one which thematizes misunderstanding itself. Again and again, one finds gaps in understanding, aporetic instances wherein what is said in words and gestures is completely lost in the receiving. This holds true in almost every interchange, be it between foreigner and native:

"There," said Peduzzi, pointing to a girl in the doorway of a house they passed. "My daughter."

"His doctor," the wife said, "has he got to show us his doctor?"

"He said his daughter," said the young gentleman. (100)

Native and native:

Everybody they met walking the main street of the town Peduzzi greeted elaborately, "Buon' di, Arturo!" Tipping his hat. The bank clerk stared at him from the door of the Fascist cafe. Groups of three and four people standing in front of the shops stared at the three. The workmen in their stone-powdered jackets working on the foundations of the new hotel looked up as they passed. Nobody spoke or gave any sign to them except the town beggar, lean and old, with a spittle-thickened beard, who lifted his hat as they passed. (98)

Or husband and wife:

"I'm sorry you feel so rotten, Tiny," he said. "I'm sorry I talked the way I did at lunch. We were both getting at the same thing from different angles."

"It doesn't make any difference," she said. "None of it makes any difference."

"Are you too cold?" he asked. "I wish you'd worn another sweater."

"I've got on three sweaters." (99)

This, as I say, seems nicely done. Yet this brings me to another point: despite Hemingway's extraordinary sensitivity to language's ambiguity and the constancy with which we miss the signs and misinterpret meaning in the process, he tends, when he turns to a discussion of theory, to be less keenly sensitive to these same problems of meaning. He shows no special sensitivity to the contingency of aesthetic value. Rather, he idealizes such value, conceiving of it as something independent of both history and place. Certainly, for instance, the theory of suggestion seems a little too idealized. Thus, like T. S. Eliot with his kindred theory of the objective correlative, Hemingway appears to ground his theory of suggestion in some essentialist definition of the human. He assumes too readily that his reader is like himself and that if "he" (the reader) searches back and discovers those "unnoticed things that made emotions" in himself, "he" will, through recalling these "things," produce the same emotions in his reader. "Remember," he told one aspiring author, "what the noises were and what was said. Find what gave you the emotion; what the action was that gave you the excitement. Then, write it down, making it clear *so the reader will see it too and have the same feeling* that you had."[21]

Yet Hemingway's reader is perforce different from himself, and is unlikely to experience the very "same feeling." Meanwhile, if this reader happens to be, say, female, or black, or Jewish, or gay, chances are that his or her response to the remembered things which made for the author's emotions will be quite different from those anticipated. Although Hemingway's fiction has a wide appeal, the appeal is not universal. Hemingway's theory of suggestion, in its logic, is also not universal, for this is a contingency whose persuasiveness depends upon shared assumptions. To claim, as Hemingway does, that if one experiences one sensation, followed by another, followed by a third, one will eventually experience a single emotion allies his psychology with nineteenth-century determinisms, something a present-day reader finds hard to accept.

This said, I should like to briefly return to the matter of this iceberg principle, or theory of omission. Susan F. Beegel has written that "Hemingway did not evolve his craft of omission in an historic vacuum, and his iceberg theory seems to encompass types of omission practiced by his literary mentors and contemporaries."[22] I agree, though for different reasons. That is, if Beegel sees Hemingway's practice of omission as primarily a technique of revision, "of discovering the story in the stream of consciousness, and eliminating the personal material leading to and sometimes from it,"[23] I would rather see the practice as one reflective of a peculiar modernist desire to talk about something by *not* talking about *it,* by not naming *it.* That is, I should argue that apophasis—the trope wherein one denies that one will speak of something even as everything one says makes reference to the denied object—seems to hold an unusual appeal for the moderns. Notice, for instance, the similarity between Hemingway's "principle of the iceberg" statement and statements by Wittgenstein, Stein, Cézanne, and Heidegger:

[Wittgenstein:] My work consists of two parts: the one presented here plus all that I have *not* written. And it is precisely this second part that is important to one. . . . In short, . . . I have managed in my book [the *Tractatus*] to put everything firmly into place by being silent about it.

[Stein:] She wondered whether "there [was] not a way of naming things that would not invent names, *but mean names without naming them,*" if there was a way of "looking at anything until that something that was not the name of that thing but was in a way that actual thing would come to be written" [emphasis added].

[Cézanne:] Now being old, nearly seventy, the sensations of colour which give the light are for me the reason for the abstractions which do not allow for me to cover my canvas entirely nor to pursue the delimitations of objects where their points of contact are fine and delicate; from which it results that my image or picture is incomplete.

[Heidegger:] Appearance, as the appearance of something, does *not* mean that something shows itself; rather, it means that something makes itself known which does not show itself. It makes itself known through something that does show itself. Appearing is a *not showing itself.*[24]

What we find here, I believe, is an almost overpowering sense that reality hides more than it shows—that while what we see gives evidence (for those who have eyes to see; i.e., artists and other co-religious) for what we do not see, it is the latter which gives shape to the former. This is much in the manner of *The Garden of Eden's* David Bourne's conviction that "the form came by what he would choose to leave out,"[25] or in the manner of the astronomical theory of the black hole, whereby that which is not seen—i.e., the black hole—can only be recognized by its effect, its gravity. We are, then, back in that paradoxical bind so beautifully exemplified by Wittgenstein's efforts in the *Tractatus.* On the one hand, we speculate about the invisible—about the seventh-eighths of the iceberg—and in a mood of somber resignation, we adopt the stance of reticence, even of silence. We propose to say nothing that does not carry with it its own self-evidence, e.g., Hemingway's "All you have to do is write one true sentence" (MF, 12). And yet, on the other hand, even as we, like Wittgenstein, propose "[t]o say nothing except what can be said,"[26] there still remains the desire to talk, to voice what is. There still remains the Cézannean urge to make the representation the thing: "A minute in the world's life passes! To paint it in its reality, and forget everything for that! To become that minute, to be the sensitive plate . . . give the image of what we see, forgetting everything that has appeared before our time."[27]

What we find here then are two, seemingly conflicting, gestures: one draws back, the other reaches out. Yet the first means to perform the function of the second: to name the world without naming it, the way that the blank spaces of a late Cézanne canvas speak of something ("that," in Hemingway's words, "always absent something else") rather than nothing.[28] And if the first gesture, of reticence, seems to work in the manner of the second, there is also the sense that the second gesture works in the manner of the first. By this, I mean that the gesture of reaching out always entails a collapsing back inward, a movement usually accompanied by the acknowledgment that, in Hemingway's words, "the real thing . . . always was beyond" one's reach. Or as Wittgenstein wrote in the preface to the *Tractatus,* "Here I am conscious that I have fallen far short of the possible" (T, 29).

Thus even if one could reach out surreptiously—"to do the thing by three cushion shots rather than by words or direct statement"—one is still eventually forced to concede a kind of defeat, the kind allegorized, in Wittgenstein's letter to a friend, by the track which leads nowhere:

> What happens, I believe, is this: we do not advance towards our goals by the direct road—for this we (or at any rate I) have not got the strength. Instead we walk up all sorts of tracks and byways, and so long as we are making some headway we are in reasonably good shape. But whenever such a track comes to an end we are up against it; only then do we realize that we are not at all where we ought to be.[29]

Of course, Wittgenstein eventually turned this frustration to another purpose, proposing in *The Philosophical Investigations* a philosophy wherein "nothing is hidden,"[30] wherein he stresses the dead-endedness of any attempt "to describe phenomena that are hard to get hold of, the present experience that slips quickly by, or something of the kind."[31] Hemingway did not, holding to a lifelong committment to move, sentence by sentence, toward the world as it is. Part of the irony, however, is that while Hemingway started off by dedicating himself to the principle of the iceberg, to the principle of apophasis, at his death he left close to 20,000 pages (published and unpublished) of manuscript. He simply wrote too much, blackening up the "bare space" which meant more than all the subsequent ink could say.

I do not mean to suggest that I find, as Hemingway wrote Liveright in 1925, the early "stories written so tight and so hard that the alteration of a word can throw an entire story out of key" (SL, 154).[32] Again, with the later Wittgenstein, we should be suspicious of claims to have bridged the linguistic to the non-linguistic, claims which, invoking necessity, take the form of "[s]uch and such is the case" (T, 103). We are too sensitive to the way that language always get things wrong—the way that it wishes to say one thing and ends up saying another. And yet, if a linguistic asceticism offers no truer representation than any other statement of what *is,* one does not want to be blind to its value, particularly in the hands of a master. Yes, it too gets things wrong, but it also does something beyond (mis)speaking: it listens; it creates a space wherein that which is not reducible to the linguistic may be heard. It admits of a mystery, even as it shows itself too respectful to try to say exactly what this mystery is. And in this sense it differs from that praxis which assumes that all is linguistic, that "nothing is hidden."

Of course, we do not often identify Hemingway as one ordinarily respectful of mystery. His prose seems to speak of the clear light of day, wherein everything finds itself delineated and observed. He likens it, as we have seen, to the observable eighth of the iceberg rather than to its subaqueous seven-eighths, and though he is capable of saying that "there are many mysteries" (DIA, 54), he is also capable, as in "A Clean Well Lighted Place," of seeing, with Stevens, the "[n]othing that is not there and the nothing that is" ("The Snow Man"): "Hail nothing, full of nothing, nothing is with thee."[33] And yet, as with Wittgenstein's understanding that with the *Tractatus* there existed two texts, one written, the other unwritten, with the latter being the more important of the two, so, too, might it be said that Hemingway's work consists of two parts, the part which is written (the visible eighth of the iceberg) and the part which is not (the hidden seven-eighths), and that of the two, it is the latter which is also more important.

"Big Two-Hearted River" offers Hemingway's most memorable display of apophasis. A story of a fishing trip by a lone young man in Upper Michigan, circa 1920, it has frequently been read allegorically as Nick Adams's therapeutic journey to displace his war memories, even though mention is neither made to the war nor to Nick's part in it. As Kenneth Lynn, debunking the long standing interpretation, writes, "Not a single reference to war appears in the story, and it is highly doubtful, furthermore, judging by what can be observed of Nick's behavior, that panic is the feeling that he is fending off."[34] Why then should the story have been read so often as this allegory? The answer, thinks Lynn, has much to do with the prominence and sway of two early readers, Edmund Wilson (in "Ernest Hemingway: Bourdon Gauge of Morale" [1939]) and Malcom Cowley (in his 1944 introduction to the Viking *Portable Hemingway*), both of whom saw Nick as psychically wounded by the war.[35] The popularity of this interpretation, in turn, came full circle, says Lynn, with Hemingway, in *A Moveable Feast* (circa late 1950s) and elsewhere (e.g., "The Art of the Short Story"),[36] making the claim that Nick's war experience was what he had deliberately omitted, again on the principle of the iceberg:

The test of any story is how very good the stuff is that you, not your editors, omit. A story in this book called "Big Two-Hearted River" is about a boy coming home beat to the wide from a war. Beat to the wide was an earlier and possibly more severe form of beat, since those who had it were unable to comment on this condition and could not suffer that it be mentioned in their presence. So the war, all mention of the war, anything about the war, is omitted.[37]

I suspect that Lynn is, more or less, right, that the story was not originally intended as a war story. It is odd, however, that after critiquing the traditional interpretation as lacking in textual evidence, he should seem so ready to put into its place a reading which is equally short on textual evidence: "Perhaps . . . the 'other needs' Nick feels he has put behind him include a need to please his mother, while his talk of his tent as his home may represent a reaction to being thrown out of his parents' summer cottage."[38] Rather than dismissing the story as an allegory of Nick's war experience, however, one might do better to investigate the degree to which the unsayable informs all utterances. That is, all does not reduce to language, yet there is also a way in which language seems to speak of that which is unsaid. Sometimes, this entails a determined unsaying (apophasis). My argument here is that many of the modernists were so determined, whether for the reason that the pulse of materialism made them uncomfortable with a more articulated metaphysics or for the reason that, as Susan Sontag argued in "The Aesthetics of Silence," the Enlightenment had led to "an almost insupportable burden of self-consciousness," wherein it remained "scarely possible for the artist to write a word (or render an image or make a gesture) that doesn't remind him of something already achieved."[39] In either case, apophasis seems to constitute a major modernist trope.

Meanwhile, "Big Two-Hearted River" remains a masterful story, whether it refers to the war or not, notable for the expression of loss, which, though hinted at via the means of language, is ultimately not reducible to language. Technically, the expression seems to depend upon two means: one, the oblique reference to something anterior: "He felt he had left everything behind, the need for thinking, the need to write, other needs. It was all back of him" (134). And two, an extraordinarily austere prose, which repeatedly seems to hint at, and to require, "that always absent something else" (DIA, 139). For example, note the following lines, speaking of a satisfying experience, yet hinting at something more threatening:

Nick looked down into the pool from the bridge. It was a hot day. A kingfisher flew up the stream. It was a long time since Nick had looked into a stream and seen trout. They were satisfactory. (134)

The result is that, again, we have two books, the one which is present and the one which is nominally absent; and whereas the first speaks of the therapeutic need to look, through an attention to details, beyond loss, the second, speaks of a loss that will not fully acquiesce to the requirements of language.

ADJUDICATING AESTHETIC VALUE

I would like to return to the question of aesthetic value and how it is adjudicated. My prior argument about Hemingway's tendency to idealize value—e.g., in the theory of suggestion, which takes for granted an undifferentiated human psychology—might have struck some readers as too severe. Surely, Hemingway was not the only one of his generation to idealize either aesthetic value or human psychology. (Respecting the latter, one need only think of Freud's work, so presumptive as it is of a unitary psyche.) Yet whether Hemingway's idealizations were singular or representative, this line of discussion strikes me as one worth pursuing. Ironically, it might help us to further understand the vagaries of Hemingway's own popularity and critical reception. For now, when it is increasingly difficult to esteem Hemingway's work without making a series of concessions—that is, without some appeal to the contingencies (e.g., historical, cultural, gendered, etc.) of value—it is illuminating, though disheartening, to find the author so convinced of art's universal stature, so convinced that "[t]he laws of prose writing are as immutable as those of flight, of mathematics, [and] of physics" (SL, 594). Thus for Hemingway, who claimed to think only "about writing truly" (SL, 698), good prose was a thing of beauty that kept both its mystery and its validity forever: "In truly good writing no matter how many times you read it you do not know how it is done. That is because there is a mystery in all great writing and that mystery does not dis-sect out. It continues and it is always valid" (SL, 770).

As I have said, I am sympathetic to the view which does not require everything to announce itself, and which leaves room for the inexpressible. I like, for instance, Cézanne's statement to J. Gasquet, "What I am trying [in my painting] to translate to you is more mysterious; it is entwined in the very roots of being, in the impalpable source of sensations,"[40] and should, with reason, read the statement back into Hemingway's own efforts. At the same time, it is better not to see matters fudged, or questions too patently begged. And here, with the combined appeal to immutable aesthetic laws, "truly good writing," and "mystery that does not not dis-sect out," Hemingway, like so many revered aestheticians, from Plato down through Hume, Kant, and F. R. Leavis, displays a special knack for begging the question, for making "be be finale of seem." Some might argue the point, however, that what remains indisputable is Hemingway's belief that "literature . . . is always literature" (SL, 418), and that "[a] true work of art endures forever; no matter what its politics" (SL, 419). Great art is unrestrained by contingencies; it is held down neither by time—"I don't think that good writing or good poetry has anything to do with our age at all" (SL, 189)—nor politics: "There is no left and right in writing. There is only good and bad writing" (SL, 363). However, as used here, good and bad writing are rather absolute terms, and Hemingway appears unmindful that in idealizing art, in unfastening its ties to both time and place, he might be giving away more than he gets, might be eviscerating art altogether. As the critic Barbara Herrnstein Smith observes:

> The recurrent impulse or effort to define aesthetic value by contradistinction to all forms of utility or as the negation of all other nameable sources of interest or forms of value—hedonic, practical, sentimental, ornamental, historical, ideological, and so forth—is, in effect, to define it out of existence; for when all such particular utilities, interests, and sources of value have been subtracted, nothing remains. Or, to put this in other terms: the "essential value" of an artwork consists of everything from which it is usually distinguished.[41]

This is not to argue that Hemingway's fiction is unlocatable in either time or place. In fact, few writers have been so successful in evoking either than Hemingway. His descriptions of Upper Michigan, Northern Italy, Twenties Paris, etc. are more than memorable. Yet the point is they *are* memorable; they *are* particularly locatable and are better for being so. However, they are so sometimes more in spite of the theory than because of it, for the theory, again, appears to go the other way. For instance, observe Hemingway's reference to "a sort of hidden legal metre (100 centimetres) somewhere within" himself, by which he, "without pleasure in trying to attain it but only a sense that you must" (SL, 301), sets out to measure his own prose. This is not a bad formulation in itself; it simply speaks, in the language of the categorical imperative, of the need to recognize a law more encompassing than one's own will, and as such strikes me as required. At the same time, if this acknowledgment is not balanced with a respect for a host of more immediate contingencies, it can easily lead one astray, as I think it does Hemingway. One might even say that he was too anxious to achieve literary immortality, and thereby put the cart before the horse. So, yes, "writing is something that you can never do as well as it can be done" (SL, 419), and yes, writing "under the strictest rules" gains a certain immortality for the work and its author. "[T]he immortality that I believe in is the immortality of what you write," he states (SL, 432). But no, if by this it is concluded that the standard of good writing, of that which is true, never changes:

> To me it's not a question of Keats and Shelley having been great and we having changed since then and needing another kind of greatness. I could never read Swinburne, Keats or Shelley. I tried it when I was a kid and simply felt embarrassed by their elaborate falseness. But of real poetry, true poetry, there has always been rymed and unrymed, a very little in all ages and all countries. (SL, 190)

For Hemingway, Keats, Shelley, and Swinburne might be excluded from the Pantheon of Great Writers due to their "elaborate falseness," but the Pantheon itself remained secure. And its most prominent members, admitted on the basis of their allegiance to a single standard, had no reason to fear for their tenancies. Cervantes, de Maupassant, James, Shakespeare, Tolstoy, Turgenev were all safely ensconced in this literary paradise and all, vis-à-vis one another, were forever ranked. The only thing that might upset the rankings would be the introduction of a new member, say, an upstart such as Hemingway:

> For your [Charles Scribner's] information I started out trying to beat the dead writers that I knew how good they were. (Excuse vernacular) I tried for Mr. Turgenieff first and it wasn't too hard. Tried for Mr. Maupassant (won't concede him the de) and it took four of the best stories to beat him. He's beaten and if he was around he would know it. Then I tried for another guy (am getting embarrassed or embare-assed now from bragging; or stateing) and I think I fought a draw with him. This other dead character.
>   Mr. Henry James I would thumb him once the first time he grabbed and then hit him once where he had no balls and ask the referee to stop it.
>   There are some guys nobody could ever beat like Mr. Shakespeare (The Champion) and Mr. Anonymous. But would be glad any time, if in training, to go twenty with Mr. Cervantes in his own home town (Alcala de Henares) and beat the shit out of him. Although Mr. C. very smart and would be learning all the time and would probably beat you in a return match. The *third* fight people would pay to see. Plenty people. (SL, 673)

Overlooking the passage's crudity, one notes here an institutional-like conception of literature remarkably similar to that expressed by

Eliot in "Tradition and the Individual Talent." In both instances, literature appears as something monolithic, something which either does or does not do justice to an external Truth. Yet this said, Eliot's formulation should be conceded as the more subtle. For Eliot, tradition involves a humbling and poignant acknowledgement of otherness, of the paradoxical recognition that the other entails one-self—that what I know is not altogether separate from what I am. Likewise, the past, while it is something alterable, something which changes as the present changes, is also that which we know—and in a sense are—and this leads to the conviction that the writer's most individual accomplishments are, in fact, "those in which the dead poets, his ancestors, assert their immortality."[42] It also leads to the conviction that origin exists as something antecedent to, and mediated by, the past. We do not so much create fresh, brand new gestures so much as we imitate those already made, much in the way that Luke's disciple imitates the master: "The disciple is not above his master: but every one that is perfect shall be as his master."

For Eliot a respect for origin entailed an indebtedness to his literary forbearers, but for Hemingway the matter was, as we see, rather different. He tended to conceive of his profession as a competitive, masculine one, in which authors battled over who could most approximate reality's truth. That there might be more than one truth, one reality, left him unmoved. Rather, he took toward the world an opportunistic stance, believing like Stein before him, that he could "write about the whole damned world if I get to know it" (SL, 764). Here, "it" was a singular, determinate reality, which if one had "an absolute conscience as unchanging as the standard meter in Paris, to prevent faking,"[43] one could "show it as it really is" (SL, 354). The key thing was to be honest and disinterested, to keep one's eye on the object. Meanwhile, Hemingway felt that his own worth as an artist should be located in his extraordinary accuracy. As he told Berenson, "I cannot write beautifully but I can write with great accuracy . . . and the accuracy makes a sort of beauty. . . . I know how to make country so that you, when you wish, can walk into it and I understand tactile values, I hope" (SL, 808). That writing might cease to be writing (and give way, in this instance, to the country that one might walk in) makes for a wonderful trope, one which, in explanation of his work, Hemingway came back to several times, as he did in a memorable passage in *A Moveable Feast*:

> Some days it went so well that you could make the country so that you could walk into it through the timber to come out into the clearing and work up on the high ground and see the hills beyond the arm of the

lake. A pencil-lead might break off into the conical nose of the pencil sharpener and you would use the small blade of the pen knife to clear it or else sharpen the pencil carefully with the sharp blade and then slip your arm through the sweat-salted leather of your pack strap to lift the pack again, get the other arm through and feel the weight settle on your back and feel the pine needles under your moccasins as you started down for the lake. (MF, 91)

Yet even when the writing went well, it never ceased to be writing—a trope for "Country so [real] that you could walk into it." Hemingway, I think, knew this; but he seemed to think that he could also escape it and practice an innocent eye aesthetic. Thus Pound, knowing that Hemingway would understand, could say to him, "I wish you wd. keep your eye on the objek MORE, and be less licherary," and, in the same letter, "ANYTHING put on top of the subject is BAD. Lichersure is mostly blanketing up a subject. Too much MAKINGS. The subject is always interesting enough without blankets."[44] He understood because this was, or had become, Hemingway's own language, that which he used when he spoke of his ambition to "[p]ut down what I see and what I feel in the best and simplest way I can tell it,"[45] or when he spoke of "[t]he indispensable characteristic of a good writer" as being "lucidity."[46] Thus it became Hemingway's own project "to write as truly, as straightly, as objectively and as humbly as possible,"[47] to write not literature but the thing itself. However, like Pound, Hemingway did not fully appreciate the paradox before him. On the one hand, he wished to be master of a literary technique, while, on the other, he believed that he could transcend technique and present something wholly other. When in this latter mood, Hemingway reserved literary "tricks"—technique, in effect—for journalism, and tricklessness for fiction. Recalling the effort he had to make as a young writer changing over from journalism to fiction, Hemingway wrote: "In writing for a newspaper you told what happened and, with one trick and another, you communicated the emotion to any account of something that has happened on that day; but *the real thing,* the sequence of motion and fact which made the emotion and which would be as valid in a year or in ten years or, with luck and if you stated it purely enough, always was beyond me and I was working very hard to get it" (DIA, 2; emphasis added).

That the "real thing"—so far as it was represented in fiction—might also be inextricably intertwined with tricks, with learned techniques, did and did not impress Hemingway. Annoyed by the often heard accusation that he wrote journalism, not fiction, he repeatedly said that a writer does not describe, he makes, that "[i]nvention is the finest thing" (SL, 407), and that a writer, at his best, "make[s] it up so truly that later it will happen that way" (SL, 407). Again, to Berenson, he wrote:

> You know that fiction, prose rather, is possibly the roughest trade of all in writing. You do not have the reference, the old important reference. You have the sheet of blank paper, the pencil, and the obligation to invent truer than things can be true. You have to take what is not palpable and make it completely palpable and also have it seem normal and so that it can become a part of the experience of the person who reads it. (SL, 837)

At the same time, Hemingway believed that the "real thing" was something that stood "outside" language—that the referent possessed its own distinct integrity. And if one were honest enough, if one exercised "terrific concentration," then that which "always was beyond" one might be written. It could be done by "[b]oiling it down always, rather than spreading it thin" (SL, 397), by breaking experience down into its parts, its discrete sensations. To start with what William James called the "first part of reality," "the flux of sensations" and, in Hemingway's words, "to treat of things where simple actions occurred—the simplest—and which I had seen" (SL, 264), seemed the best approach, the best technique. Hemingway wanted to begin at that point before which sensation became conscious thought, before "what really happened in action" became intermixed with that which one "thought" happened. The sense was that one could reach back underneath thought, as if sensations were not themselves a manner of thought. Explaining himself in *Death in the Afternoon*, Hemingway wrote:

> I tried to remember what it was that seemed just out of my remembering and that was *the thing that I had really seen* and, finally, remembering all around it, I got it. When he stood up, his face white and dirty and the silk of his breeches opened from the waist to knee, it was the dirtiness of the rented breeches, the dirtiness of his slit underwear and the clean, clean, unbearably clean whiteness of the thigh bone *that I had seen,* and it was that which was important. (DIA, 20; emphasis added)

Yet even "this first part of reality" is a fiction. And while Hemingway suggests, without really saying how, that an unmediated knowledge of "reality" might be had, what he offers his readers is not the real thing, whatever this might be, but a technique simulating the same, a technique of originality.

To speak this way about Hemingway is not to question his significance as a writer. Literary reputations are all, more or less, relative, yet Hemingway ranks as an important writer. I say this not because I think he offers the "real thing" or "the truth." (Hemingway: "A writer's job is to tell the truth."[48]) No writer does this, exactly. Yet some writers make their fictions persuasive in a way that others do not. They embody in their fictions the "truths" of their time and place, that intersection which Bakhtin calls the chronotope. They offer less an ideal truth, the kind that Hemingway sought to realize, than a concrete one, a truth that seems to be more than it is because it embodies so many of the community's values. They offer a truth for their time, just as they offer a prose for their time. Hemingway, who once wrote a friend, "We need a new prose to handle our own time or that part of it I've seen,"[49] did this splendidly, even as now, in the 1990s, that truth and that prose begin to fray around the edges.

THINKING ABOUT THE SELF

Wallace Stevens once spoke of Hemingway as a poet of extraordinary actuality: "Most people don't think of Hemingway as a poet, but obviously he is a poet and I should say, offhand, the most significant of living poets, so far as the subject of EXTRAORDINARY ACTUALITY is concerned."[50] This is generous praise, but also reflective of the way Hemingway was read by his contemporaries. By this, I mean the sense was that, one, Hemingway not only worked in a "realist" mode, but, two, he somehow inverted the word/object equation, seducing the object to obtrude itself into the place ordinarily reserved for the symbol. And if Stevens's praise accorded itself with the way Hemingway was read, it also accorded itself with the way that he asked to be read:

> You see I'm trying in all my stories to get the feeling of *the actual life* across—not just to depict life—or criticize it—but to actually make it alive. So that when you read something by me you *actually make it alive.* So that when you have read something by me you *actually experience the thing.* (SL, 153; emphasis added)

The two acts are, of course, related, and we should not so much read—or resist the desire to read—Hemingway's prose this way (i.e., as a kind of "presencing" the world) were we not clued in by the author himself that this corresponded with his intention. Still, while acknowledging the powerful suggestiveness of Hemingway's fiction for a prior generation, we should be reluctant to assent, say, to the Stevens proposition as applied to our actuality. Hemingway's fiction is very much of a particular time and place. If we direct our attention to *In Our Time,* the time is circa World War I. The place is Europe and the American Midwest. And the episteme, to borrow from Foucault, is largely a "classical" one that celebrates both "man" and language, and which imagines the latter as "that translucent necessity through which representation and being must pass—as beings are represented to the mind's eye, and as representation renders beings visible in their truth."[51] In this view, how one thinks of oneself and how one uses language are inextricably connected. That is, the belief that language is a field of representations has a way of bestowing special status upon the the receiver of images just as it isolates, distorts, and makes significant the object represented. And while those things which exist out there—elusively just beyond language's periphery—might find their existence questioned, the one thing which generally escapes such questioning is the self which identifies itself with language's point of origin. Developing this idea further, Foucault writes:

> As long as that [Classical] language was spoken in Western culture it was not possible for human existence to be called in question on its own account, since it contained the nexus of representation and being. The discourse that, in the seventeenth century, provided the link between the "I think" and the "I am" of the being undertaking it—that very discourse remained, in a visible form, the very essence of Classical language, for what was being linked together in it was representation and being. The transition from the "I think" to the "I am" was accomplished in the light of evidence, within a discourse whose whole domain and functioning consisted in articulating one upon the other what one represents to oneself and what is.[52]

Foucault's formulation, as I suggested in the first chapter, makes a "discourse" seem a too determinate thing; and while I think he is right to make the connection between the way an epoch conceives language and the way that it imagines both the self and the practice of representation, invariably there will be an element of the "I am" in any linguistic practice, following from the fact that this "I" shall never find itself absolutely determined, nor never wholly without some agency. Still, it seems warrantable to read Hemingway's poetics of the self in the context of Foucault's discourse of the classical, wherein the thinking self naming his or her world finds its greatest articulation. Certainly, Hemingway conceived the individual artist as endowed with an impressive degree of agency. In *Death in the Afternoon* he wrote, "All art is only done by the individual. The individual is all you ever have and all schools only serve to classify their members as failure" (99–100).

Hemingway's work, then, appears aptly described by the epistemic phase "man thinking his world," even as, with time, this phase seems to require more scrutiny. For one, the terms—i.e., "man," "thinking," "world"—are simply not as philosophically secure as they once were. We have not actually thrown them away, of course; they are still part and parcel of everyday usage. Still we are more likely to conceive, with de Man, the self as "a mere metaphor by means of which man protects himself from his insignificance by forcing his own interpretation of the world upon the universe";[53] and, with Nietzsche, to conceive of thinking as "a quite arbitrary fiction, arrived at by singling out one element from the process and eliminating all the rest, an artificial arrangement for the purpose of intelligibility."[54] Granted, these critiques possess their own limitations; nevertheless, they force us to note the difference in assumptions. And here we note the way that Hemingway's world, placing the human at the center of things, admits of tragedy ("I believed that life was a tragedy and knew it could have only one end")[55] and values thinking not only as something real and important, but also as something almost volatile, liable to kindle a tragedy if not properly watched.

What is interesting here is not that Hemingway extols the human—this is something that we all do, almost by necessity—but the way in which he conceives, or constructs, the same. If it is true, for instance, that "[t]here is no such thing as *The* human, where the definite article stands for the universal,"[56] then the question must be what "human" is being spoken of? How does Hemingway understand the term? The answer, at least for *In Our Time,* is that the term overwhelming bespeaks the situation of male Caucasians. That is, Hemingway—whose next collection of stories would be entitled *Men Without Women* for the reason that the author felt that "[i]n all of these [stories], almost, the softening, feminine influence through training, discipline, death or other causes, [is] absent" (SL, 245)— particularly tends to make his heroes reticent, Anglo-Saxon men of action. Nick Adams, the most frequently appearing protagonist, is of this type, as are George, Bill, Krebs, Mr. Adams, and Lieutenant Eric Edward Dorman-Smith, the inspired narrator in Chapters III and IV. Others (women, Indians, blacks, Italians, etc.) fill decidedly subordinate roles and, at times, seem not to matter, like the Hungarian thieves in "Chapter VIII," whom the Irish cop mistakes for Italians ("They're wops, ain't they? Who the hell is going to make any trouble?" [79]) or like the refugee women on the Turkish pier: "You didn't mind the women who were having babies. . . . You just covered them over with something and let them go to it" (12). In fact, women, given their abundance here, are a particularly trod upon group. Though generous interpretations might make protagonists of, say, Marjorie in "The End of Something" or the American wife in "Cat in the Rain," the other women are lucky if they simply go along unnoticed, or relatively unnoticed, like the unwed, pregnant waitress in "Cross-Country Snow" whose lack of cordiality is noticed by George and explained by Nick: "[S]he's touchy about being here and then she's got that baby coming without being married and she's touchy" (110). To which Nick adds, "Hell, no girls get married around here till they're knocked up" (110).

Like Eve in the Garden, women are held responsible for the other sex's unhappiness. Thus they cause men unhappiness by leaving them, like Ad Francis's sister/wife in "The Battler" ("'[O]ne day she just went away and never come back'" [61]) and the American soldier's Luz in "A Very Short Story": "Living in the muddy, rainy town in the winter, the major of the battalion made love to Luz, and she had never known Italians before, and finally wrote to the States that theirs had been only a boy and girl affair" (66). They cause men unhappiness by being difficult, like the American gentleman's Tiny in "Out of Season" ("The wife stayed behind, following rather sullenly" [97]) and George's wife in "Cat in the Rain": "And I want to eat at a table with my own silver and I want candles. And I want it to be spring and I want to brush my hair out in front of a mirror and I want a kitty and I want some new clothes" (94). They cause men unhappiness by being overbearing, like Doctor Adams's wife in "The Doctor and the Doctor's Wife" ("'Remember that he who ruleth his spirit is greater than he that taketh a city,' said his wife" [25]) and Krebs's mother in "Soldier's Home": "'Don't you love your mother, dear boy?'" (75) And finally, they cause men unhappiness in their sexual lives, like Mr. Elliot's wife in "Mr. and Mrs. Elliot" ("He did not like to waken her and soon everything was quite all right and he slept peacefully" [87]) and the American soldier's date in "A Very Short Story": "A short time after he contracted gonorrhea from a sales girl in a loop department store while riding in a taxicab through Lincoln Park" (66).

In a way, Bill's conclusion, in "The Three-Day Blow," that "[o]nce a man's married he's absolutely bitched" (46) is less dire than Hemingway's own ("We are all bitched from the start" [SL, 408]), though it is less comforting to women, who find themselves the origin of so much unhappiness, than to men, who at least can defer unhappiness through bachelorhood. Women, however, do not get off scot-free; they are made to suffer for the unhappiness they cause men. They are abandoned when pregnant, like the waitress in "Cross-Country Snow." They are dismissed when the boy or man finds, as in "The End of Something," that "It isn't fun anymore" (34) or when they simply become, like in "Out of Season," a bother: "'Why don't you go back? Go on back, Tiny'" (100). They are put in their place when they, as in "The End of Something," show intelligence ("'You do. You know everything. That's the trouble. You know you do'" [34].) or, as in "Cat in the Rain," resistance: "'Oh, shut up and get something to read,' George said" (94). And if they happen to be both female and Indian, like the woman trying to have a baby in "Indian Camp," they are treated as if they simply do not exist ("'No, I haven't any anaesthetic,' his father said. 'But her screams are not important. I don't hear them because they are not important'" [16].), that is except as a guinea pig for a grotesque twist in medical practice: "'That's one for the medical journal, George,' he said. 'Doing a Caesarian with a jack-knife and sewing it up with nine-foot, tapered gut leaders'" (18).

Women hardly exist in this world. They might fill a physical space but that is about all. Certainly, it is worth noting that in a book that is filled with conversation (i.e., Nick and Bill in "The Three-Day Blow," Nick and George in "Cross-Country Snow," Joe and his father in "My Old Man," etc.), there is not a single conversation between a man and a woman in which the conversants interact as equals, in which one is not trying to pull away from the other, like Doctor Adams in "The Doctor and the Doctor's Wife," who when pressed by his wife to talk, to say what is on his mind, replies, "'I think I'll go for a walk'" (26). Instead, the ruling gesture seems, unfortunately, more typified by the slightly shell-shocked Krebs, in "Soldier's Home," who, while liking to look at the opposite sex, believes their actual acquaintance something not worth the effort:

He liked the girls that were walking along the other side of the street. He liked the look of them much better than the French girls or the German girls. But the world they were in was not the world he was in. He would like to have one of them. But it was not worth it. They were such a nice pattern. He liked the pattern. It was exciting. But he would not go through all the talking. (72)

Thus the attractiveness, for Krebs, of foreign girls: "That was the thing about French and German girls. There was not all this talking. You couldn't talk much and you did not need to talk. It was simple and you were friends" (72).

The desire to avoid talk expresses itself as a value throughout *In Our Time*. The reason relates to the Hemingway hero's so-called "code" (Hemingway: "It sounds pompous to say so but we who have gone through bad things and times have a certain code.")[57] requiring a general taciturnity whenever the subject turns personal. Again and again here, protagonists turn reticent when the subject touches too close to home. Nick, for example, in "The Three-Day Blow," says about his broken friendship with Marjorie, "'I oughtn't to talk about it'" (48); George, in "Cross-Country Snow," says about the thrill of skiing, "'It's too swell to talk about'" (109); and the American soldier, in "A Very Short Story," goes "under the anaesthetic holding tight on to himself so he would not blab about anything during the silly, talky time" (65).

Here the ethic predicates itself upon the conviction that language fails us when applied to what we hold most sacred. This is, perhaps, ironic given Hemingway's ambition vis-à-vis language. Still, the sense is that in language the true object of one's feelings is readily lost, and that, in this context, there always exists about it a quality of being besides the point, of deceit. This sense of things leads, not surprisingly, to withdrawal or silence as a way to skirt this deception. Thus we have another reason—i.e., a distrust respecting language—for Krebs's taciturnity, which he adopts after feeling betrayed by his effort to say just what it was he experienced during the war:

> At first Krebs . . . did not want to talk about the war at all. Later he felt the need to talk but no one wanted to hear about it. His town had heard too many atrocity stories to be thrilled by actualities. Krebs found that to be listened to at all he had to lie, and after he had done this twice he, too, had a reaction against the war and against talking about it. (69)

There are realms of experience which manage to escape encapsulation by language, and there are times when silence, as a form of metaspeech, constitutes the most proper response to a mystery which appears irreducible. At the same time, silence may be—and often is—misappropriated. This happens when the necessity of negotiating the space between silence and speech is not acknowledged, when silence is granted an excessive value. This is easy enough to do, particularly for those of a religious or an ascetic temper. Here, silence can seem preferable to speech—or a preferable form of speech, for silence always speaks—due to the fact that it acknowledges, as speech often does not, that the "What Is" remains extralinguistic. And yet, this said, speech remains something of a requirement, a necessity, leading us to wonder whether there might not be a single object of desire at all, to wonder whether things might be laid out so that desire and object are inseparable, each implicated in and caught up in the invention of the other. Needless to say, the problem does not omit of ready solution.

Whatever the case might be, silence, in the day to day sense, can be said to function either as a metaspeech or as the refusal of speech. With regard to the majority of male characters in *In Our Time,* their adherence to the "code" causes them to skirt the edge of refusal too often. And so while I would wish to accent the way that speech, or conversation, acts to open up other realities, which, in turn, implicate us in these new realities, the male characters here seem mostly to resist this possibility. Undoubtedly, they know how intertwined the concrete many and the abstract one are, yet they still seem fastened to the belief that reality remains something out there, something apart from one's own interpretation of it. Not surprisingly, then, they tend to conceive of talk as too likely to blur, or to sully, *the* reality, much in the way that an economist might speak of false currency as driving out the good. When all words (or dollars) are not genuine, then all become suspect. Symbolic exactitude is wanted, but barring this, silence seems preferable. For unlike words used loosely, silence respects *the* reality. Silence also creates the condition where one can be receptive, through the five senses, to that reality.[58]

Hemingway, in fact, places great value upon his senses, for they are the means, in paradigmatic fashion, by which he can best experience the world. Sensations (so the claim has it) offer, as intellection does not, an unmediated apprehension of reality, one that the artist can best approximate through the simple report of his sensations. Thus one finds passages, in *In Our Time,* which seem to move in the direction of "pure" description, wherein there is more of an attempt to simply present, or to catalogue, sensations than there is to analyze them. For instance, in "Chapter X," Hemingway largely wishes to objectify the presentation of the picador's dying horse, even as the juxtaposition of images, plus the handful of modifiers (e.g., "jerkily," "wobbly"), makes this an impossible task. In the end, Hemingway is happy to let the juxtaposed images create a meaning—i.e., respecting the cruelty of the men toward the horse, made more evident by the reticence of the bull to inflict further pain upon it. But what he would insist upon is that meaning follows from the sensations rather than vice versa.

Thus while the distinction between felt and abstracted sensation might appear a fiction, it is one that Hemingway regularly employs, accentuating the importance of the former over the latter. In "Big Two-Hearted River," for example, Nick Adams repeatedly makes an effort to leave thinking behind him ("He felt he had left everything behind him, the need for thinking, the need to write, other needs" [134]); to suppress it ("His mind was starting to work. He knew he could choke it because he was tired enough" [142]); and to substitute in its stead sensations in which he could immerse himself: "He did not want to rush his sensations any" (151). Yet Nick never does escape thought; he only changes its color.

As noted earlier, Hemingway extols thinking "man" naming "his" world. Neither Nick nor any of Hemingway's other protagonists truly gives up thinking. That preference is given to sensations over thought makes a nice trope, yet it remains a trope all the same. What is at issue here, then, is not whether the standard Hemingway hero is actively engaged in thinking about his world—he most decidedly is—but rather what form his thinking takes. We have, in a sense, already moved into this discussion with our attention to the gendered bias of Hemingway's code of reticence. Yet I would like to pursue further what Hemingway's own emphasis of sensations over thought means within the order of his own thought and, more concretely, his own stylistics.

The Technique of Originality

Hemingway's fiction offers us not a prose that brings us closer to reality (as if there were such a single entity), but a prose that simulates it. It is a Newtonian reality, a materially hard, atomistic world subject to being divided in both spatial and temporal ways. Hemingway simulates this world, in fiction such as *In Our Time,* through the invention of a technique of originality. He assumes that there is one reality and that this reality, being "outside" both his perception of it and his statements (in language) about it, remains basically inviolate, an autonomous thing-in-itself unaltered by the various ways in which it is framed.

Wishing to know the world as it is, Hemingway assumes a pose of detachment. I say "a pose" for the obvious reason that one can never truly divest oneself of self, of interest. Disinterestness is simply another form of interest. Still, in feigning disinterest, Hemingway adopts a style designed to suggest his objective distance from the events he narrates. Most particularly, he narrates all the stories but one ("My Old Man") in the third person. Beyond this, he does a fine job of pruning modifiers—or any word that evinces too interpretative a color—from his prose. Hemingway shows his greatest self-discipline this way in those interstitial chapters wherein he reduces his narratives to the skeletal reporting of "facts." We've already briefly attended to one of these chapters ("Chapter X"), but I would like to look a little more closely at "Chapter II," the description of the Greek evacuation of Eastern Thrace (Autumn 1922). For example:

> Minarets stuck up in the rain out of Adrianople across the mud flats. The carts were jammed for thirty miles along the Karagatch road. Water buffalo and cattle were hauling carts through the mud. No end and no beginning. Just carts loaded with everything they owned. The old men and women, soaked through, walked along keeping the cattle moving. The Maritza was running yellow almost up to the bridge. Carts were jammed solid on the bridge with camels bobbing along through them. Greek cavalry herded along the procession. Women and kids were in the carts crouched with mattresses, mirrors, sewing machines, bundles. There was a woman having a kid with a young girl holding a blanket over her and crying. Scared sick looking at it. It rained all through the evacuation. (21)

Here, as elsewhere in this text, one is reminded of Foucault's statement that the classical sensibility uses "its ingenuity, if not to see as little as possible, at least to restrict deliberately the area of its experience" (132). Thus Hemingway attempts to reduce experience to definite, discrete "facts," facts which are solid, visible, and determinate. This is a prose which would imitate the photograph, the author suppressing his own personality as much as he might, hoping to delineate, freeze, and make emphatic events that would otherwise go unrecognized. Hemingway himself, in the thinly disguised voice of David Bourne (*The Garden of Eden*), once said about his prose that "he could close it like the diaphragm of a camera and intensify it so it could be concentrated to the point where the heat shone bright and the smoke began to rise."[59] This explains well what Hemingway wishes to accomplish with these interstitial chapters—to offer concentrated, violent images of "our time" which serve as introduction to the stories. In a letter to Edmund Wilson shortly after finishing the volume, Hemingway claimed as much: "Finished the book of 14 stories with a chapter on [of] *In Our Time* between each story—that is the way they were meant to go—to give the picture of the whole between examining it in detail. Like looking with your eyes at something, say a passing coast line, and then looking at it with 15% binoculars" (SL, 128).

To this point of magnified vision, Foucault (without Hemingway in mind, of course) writes: "To attempt to improve one's power of observation by looking through a lens, one must renounce the attempts to achieve knowledge by means of other senses or from hearsay."[60] Hemingway himself does not renounce the other senses, yet as the binoculars metaphor attests, he does seem to celebrate sight—"I know only what I have seen."[61] And he does seem to construct his fiction so as to reflect "all the dimensions of the visible world" (SL, 738). Meanwhile, there is a pertinent passage in "Big Two-Hearted River" wherein Nick, standing on the railway bridge, looks down at the swirling river beneath and through "the clear, brown water, colored from the pebbly bottom" at the steadily holding trout. Nick, writes Hemingway, "watched them a long time":

> He watched them holding themselves with their noses into the current, many trout in deep, fast moving water, slightly distorted as he watched far down through the glassy convex surface of the pool, its surface pushing and swelling smooth against the resistance of the log-driven piles of the bridge. At the bottom of the pool were the big trout. Nick did not see them at first. Then he saw them at the bottom of the pool, big trout looking to hold themselves on the gravel bottom in a varying mist of gravel and sand, raised in spurts by the current. (133)

The passage presents itself as a metaphor both for seeing and for artistic vision. For Hemingway, art might be said to be equivalent to an intensification of vision, to the narrowing down of the field of vision to a few things seen, despite obstacles, with the utmost concentration. Here Hemingway's aesthetic is predicated upon the assumption that the world has an atomistic hardness to it, that it stands out there, and that the best place to start if one wished to be true to it was with the rendering of one's simplest and most individualized sensations. "[W]rite one true sentence. Write the truest sentence that you know" (MF, 12) is the way the young Hemingway goaded himself to write, believing that correspondence, truth-telling, is fiction's most fundamental tenet.

Hemingway's epistemological assumptions colored his own stylistics. I have, in noting the influence of Stein upon the young Hemingway, already named some of the features (i.e., repetition, "-ing" verbals, prose rhythms) most typifying Hemingway's own stylistics of presence. Now, I should like to speak of his prose rhythms, that is, their paratactic form. The explanation for this form, which esteems coordinating above subordinating syntactical relations, is to be found not only in Hemingway's indebtedness to Stein but also in his epistemology. To retreat a bit, William James, in his 1907 volume *Pragmatism,* wrote "that some parts of the world are connected so loosely with some others as to be strung along by nothing but the copula *and*. They might even come and go without those parts suffering any internal change."[62] The construction is not unrelated to our understanding of Hemingway's aesthetic, particularly his prose rhythms, for it is the very same construction upon which Hemingway's artistry is predicated. James's formulation is a modernist representation of "the world," one that was being undermined by relativistic physics even as it was being penned, yet one whose basic currency would keep its value among both the general public and intellectual community for several decades to come. Hemingway's fiction itself is a full-fledged testimony to that value.

What seems most notable about Hemingway's fiction this way is its analytical color: he deliberately attempts to see "reality" in terms of its parts rather than its wholes. Again, like James, who sought to "lay[. . .] the explanatory stress upon the part, the element, the individual, and treat[. . .] the whole as a collection and the universal as an abstraction,"[63] Hemingway sought to break down his perceptions into what were understood to be their singular, atomistic components, an ambition which emphatically shaped the nature and the rhythms of his prose. Hemingway tells one thing at a time, celebrating the uniqueness and the significance of each sensation. Short, simple sentences and coordinated sentences, particularly those making use of the conjunction *and*, are most common. For example, the first two sentences of "Chapter IX" make use of no less than eleven coordinating conjunctions. Also to be noted here (as elsewhere) is the weight Hemingway, anxious to convey a sense of reality's thingness, places upon his nouns, a fact reinforced not only by their omnipresence but also by their combination with the definite article:

> *The first matador* got *the horn* through his *sword hand and the crowd* hooted him. *The second matador* slipped *and the bull* caught *him* through *the belly and he* hung on to *the horn* with one *hand and* held *the other* tight against *the place, and the bull* rammed *him* wham against *the wall and the horn* came out, *and he* lay in *the sand, and* then got up like crazy drunk *and* tried to slug *the men* carrying *him* away *and* yelled for his *sword but he* fainted. (83; emphasis added)

At the same time that Hemingway works, in Tony Tanner's words, "to disentangle each precious single sense impression,"[64] he also narrates events point by point, separate moment by separate moment, emphasizing his understanding that experience is successive and linear. James had stated that "experience as a whole is a process in time, whereby innumerable particular terms lapse and are superseded by others that follow upon them by transitions which, whether disjunctive or conjunctive in content, are themselves experiences, and must in general be accounted as real as the terms they relate."[65] Hemingway follows with a prose that reinforces this sense of ongoing time not only by the repeated use of the adverb "then" but also by the inordinate use of gerunds and participles, as in the following passage from "Big Two-Hearted River":

> He sat on the logs, *smoking, drying* in the sun, the sun warm on his back, the river shallow ahead *entering* the woods, *curving* into the woods, shallows, light *glittering,* big watersmooth rocks, cedars along the bank and white birches, the logs warm in the sun, smooth to sit on, without bark, gray to the touch; slowly the *feeling* of disappointment that came sharply after the thrill that made his shoulders ache. It was all right now. His rod *lying* out on the logs, Nick tied a new hook on the leader, *pulling* the gut out tight until it grimped into itself in a hard knot. (151; emphasis added)

This linear time has an implicit, if unacknowledged, teleology about it. The suggestion is that events move from point A to point B, that time is unproblematic. There is no intuition of repetition or Nietzschean return. Instead, everything happens once, and once only. Events, accordingly, are transitory and ephemeral. They are also tinged with the pain of loss, for an event no sooner transpires than it locates itself in the territory of the unrecoverable. The classical artist tries to circumvent this loss by capturing the event in his or her gelatinous art. Yet the recovery is never complete, never without pathos. And herein, as Milan Kundera writes, "lies the whole of man's plight. Human time does not turn in a circle; it runs ahead in a straight line. That is why man cannot be happy; happiness is the longing for repetition."[66]

Yet if for this reason Hemingway's art appears infected by melancholy, there is also the other side of the teleological equation. That is, if all events recede into an unrecoverable past, they also give way to subsequent events, and these later events point toward an End. History reaches forward toward entelechy, the culminating point which reorders everything that came before, just as (in a less final sense) each successive moment reorders all those that came prior. The End both redeems and forgives history, just as the artist, Hemingway, both redeems and forgives the captured, remembered, and metamophosed moments which make up *In Our Time.* Things may not necessarily be this way, for it is impossible to say; but that the artist makes it *seem* that things are this way is nearly as significant, for the best thing an artist can offer us is "not the assertion that something is true," but rather "its possibilty for being lived" or valued.[67] That in *In Our Time,* Hemingway gives his energies toward making us believe that things and moments are, in truth, valuable, even redeemable, is, in turn, reason enough for us, with respect to his work, to return the favor.

5

William Carlos Williams and *Spring and All*

TRADITION, MODERNISM, AND THE INNOCENT EYE

In the 1923 prose and verse volume *Spring and All*, William Carlos Williams begins by referring to the "moment" that ideally grounds art but to which, in the tradition of the innocent eye, most people remain blind: "If anything of moment results—so much the better. And so much the more likely will it be that no one will want *to see it*."[1] Sight here should expose one's pieties as moth-eaten and untenable, for the "moment" carries disruption within it; it demands that all past practices and future expectations be reordered to correspond to present fact. And yet, even if one should wish "to see it," one's vision will be deflected by all that is not it, including, says Williams, "nearly all writing":

> [M]y theme for the time [is that] nearly all writing, up to the present, if not all art, has been especially designed to keep up the barrier between sense and the vaporous fringe which distracts the attention from its agonized approaches to the *moment*. It has been always a search for the "beautiful illusion." Very well. I am not in search of the "beautiful illusion." (177)

Like Stein and Hemingway, however, Williams intends not to be put off the trail of the real thing, of the "moment": "this moment is the only thing in which I am at all interested" (178). Partly, this follows from the conviction that the moment—i.e., present reality—stands before one as something awaiting discovery. Reality itself constitutes a composite of moments, of discrete facts. Such moments are reality's bedrock, are "the truth" (186), and the less we know about them, the less we know about ourselves. Directing his scorn at the reader, Williams accuses him or her of living too much in either the past or the future, too much in fiction: "The reader knows himself as he was twenty years ago and he has also in mind a vision of what he would be, some day. Oh, some day! But the thing he never dares to know is *what he is at the exact moment that he is*" (177–78; emphasis added).

Meanwhile, that "the moment" itself might also constitute a fiction, a mask for an ever multiplying supply of encapsulated "moments"—i.e., of "moments" within "moments" within "moments"—as well as a never unhinged nexus for an infinitely spun out series of relations, seems less considered. The reason for this has, I believe, something to do with the time, with the assumptions— aesthetic, epistemological, and representational—which Williams shared with writers such as Stein and Hemingway. These assumptions are both spoken and unspoken, yet in the present instance, Williams never questions the reality of the moment. And in this respect he seems much like Stein and Hemingway, both of whom he praises for their own faithfulness to the moment, or, in the case of Stein, to the substance which is antecedent to technique:

> If you like Gertrude Stein, study her for her substance; she has it, no matter what the idle may say. . . . It is substance that makes [her] work important. Technique is part of it—new technique; technique is itself substance, as all artists must know; but *it is the substance under that,* forming that, giving it its reason for existence which must be the final answer and source of reliance.[2]

And, in the case of Hemingway, to the "truth of the object":

> [I]n almost all verse you read, mine or anybody's else, the figures used and the general impression of the things spoken of is vague "you could say it better in prose" especially good prose, say the prose of Hemingway. The truth of the object is somehow hazed over, dulled.[3]

Like Stein and Hemingway, Williams seems to possess a physical sense of things that is noteworthily Newtonian and (after our definition) modern. By this, I mean that his work appears predicated upon the assumption that "reality" presents itself as something separate and slightly beyond one's reach; it is something that one wants to reach out to, even as it remains demonstrably detached and indifferent to one's desires. "[R]eality," says Williams, "needs no personal support but exists free from human action, as proven by science in the indestructibility of matter and of force" (235–36).

Perhaps it is because the "world [is] detached from the necessity of recording it," because it is "sufficient to itself" (207) that it becomes all that much more of a challenge and an imperative to record it. Williams himself makes it his purpose "[t]o refine, to clarify, to intensify that eternal moment in which we alone live" (178), to say, in effect, what this world is. And yet he knows that things shall not be so easy. This is not because he thinks the project essentially unworkable; he does not. Still, Williams is conscious of all the obstacles that might get in one's path, including all of our habitual ways of perceiving the world. We set out to say what the present moment is, and we end up saying something about the past, the future, about who we are, and where we have come from, rather than about what simply is. Thus the person who would read *the world as it is* finds that "[t]here is a constant barrier between the reader and his consciousness of immediate contact with the world. If there is an ocean it is here. Or rather, the whole world is between: Yesterday, tomorrow, Europe, Asia, Africa,—all things removed and impossible, the tower of the church at Seville, the Parthenon" (177).

Like Hulme, Williams claims the biggest obstacle to a fresh appropriation of the world is tradition: scientific, philosophical, and even artistic. And also like Hulme, Williams claims that one can somehow escape not only the frame which is tradition (i.e., Occidental history and thought) but frames themselves: that, if one is faithfully attentive to objects, framing does not take place. For Williams, there are, in short, two potential stances toward the world: either to know it through the lens of institutional forces or to know it directly, as one's senses permit. One can know it either as a Catholic or as a Protestant, and Williams, were he religiously inclined, would like to know it as a Protestant. The result, then, is that the present aesthetic/political conflict breaks down between "[t]hose who led yesterday [and who] wish to hold their sway a while longer" (185) and those who, swearing allegiance to "the truth," would break "through layers of demoded words and shapes" (188):

> [T]hey ask us to return to the proven truths of tradition, even to the twice proven, the substantiality which is known. Demuth and a few others do their best to point out the error, telling us that design is a function of the IMAGINATION, describing its movements, its colors—but it is a hard battle. I myself seek to enter the lists with these few notes jotted down in the midst of the action, under distracting circumstances— to remind myself . . . of *the truth*. (186; emphasis added)

For Williams, tradition is plagiaristic and coercive, yet he also thinks that he can escape its dominion, that he can orient himself toward "the truth." The way involves embracing a method—the imagination—which pretends not to be a method at all. Williams himself should like to think of it as an avenue, which released from the dictates of tradition, shows the way to things as they truly are: "The imagination, freed from the handcuffs of 'art,' takes the lead!"

(185) That one should be so ready to follow the imagination's lead follows from the preformed opinion regarding its specialness. It is spoken of as something electrical, energetic, and magical. "Sometimes," says Williams, "I speak of imagination as a force, an electricity, or a medium, a place. It is immaterial which: for whether it is the condition of a place or a dynamization its effect is the same: to free the world of fact from the impositions of 'art'" (235).

Perhaps the imagination is what Williams says it is; yet one has a right to remain suspicious. The difficulty is that Williams uses the term in such energetic fashion ("The imagination . . . attacks, stirs, animates, is radioactive in all that can be touched by action" [234]) that one may be excused for wondering whether or not the method does not itself mask its own failing. Specifically, one might wonder whether the imagination—in its demarcation of value—works all that differently than the tradition to which it is opposed. Williams himself rejected tradition as an axiological method for the reason that it seemed to adjudicate by fiat. Yet imagination, as proposed here, does much the same. Thus all things felt to be good, fresh, and vital are identified with the imagination just as all things felt to be otherwise are identified with its lumpish antithesis: "there is a sharp division—the energizing force of imagination on one side—and the acquisitive-PROGRESSIVE force of the lump on the other" (220). But how or why such should be the case remains an unanswered question.

This is not to deny the effectiveness of Williams's advocacy. His enthusiasm and passion are impressive, even infectious. And yet we should probably hesitate to follow Williams in his reification of the imagination. It may be that the imagination is no less "real" than the other human faculties (e.g., sight, smell, thinking, etc.), yet its rhetorical dimension does seem to manifest itself a little more readily once we attempt to say exactly what it is or where it is located. The imagination is a trope, and one is tempted to say it is so first and foremost. Whether or not that be true, it is difficult not to be struck by how often, in *Spring and All,* Williams refers to the imagination as if it were an actual—i.e., physical—human faculty:

> Only through the imagination is the advance of intelligence possible, to keep beside growing understanding. (193)

> The imagination is . . . not a plaything but a power that has been used from the first to raise the understanding. (207)

> The reason people marvel at works of art and say: How in Christ's name did he do it?—is that they know nothing of the physiology of the nerv-

ous system and have never in their experience witnessed the larger processes of the imagination. (209–10)

Meanwhile if the imagination is a promoter of the understanding
or an extension of the nervous system, the question remains: In what
way is it so? And if an answer is wanting, then we might question
whether the substitution of imagination for tradition leaves us in a
truly better place, or whether it simply replaces one mythology
with another.

Of course, in 1923, Williams would have felt on the defensive,
for not only was he still, more or less, without reputation, but also
those whose project (i.e., tradition) he castigated—i.e., Eliot and
Pound—were quite well established.[4] This could help to explain the
stridency in *Spring and All,* which might be understood as the consequence of a poet who is less well established trying to route some
attention to the project of the imagination. Whatever the reason,
Williams does present himself here as enormously insistent; time and
again, he tells us that he himself is a man of imagination, that he is a
poet composing modern day classics: "The work the two-thousand-
year-old poet [Homer] did and that *we* do are one piece. That is the
vitality of the classics" (189; emphasis added). Thus throughout
Spring and All one witnesses something of a power play in which
the author, seeing himself in the role of David threatened by the
Goliathan traditionalist, plays to the reader's sympathies, seizes the
moment, and rushes forward to act as his own first fan and critic:
"Who am I but my own critic? Surely in isolation one becomes a
god—At least one becomes something of everything, which is not
wholly godlike, yet a little so—in many things" (198).

Williams recognizes the absurdity of the claims; he is neither a
classic nor a god, yet he does wish to be taken seriously. Self-
promotion does not guarantee that people will rally around one's
work, but it does help, as Williams discovered, to get it an audience.
Meanwhile, at the time of *Spring and All,* Williams found it difficult
not to equate the reception of his work with a personal slight. He
felt excluded and, understandably, wished things were otherwise.
To this end, in *Spring and All,* he appears, through the multiplicity
of his references, almost to create his own community. Included
herein are artists from the past—e.g., Homer, Shakespeare, El
Greco, Poe, Whitman, Cézanne—as well as from the present:
Charles Demuth, Juan Gris, Alfred Kreymborg, Claude Monet,
Marianne Moore. The gesture is not that different from, say, Stein's
linking of her work to Flaubert, William James, Cézanne, Picasso,
and Matisse, or from Hemingway's similar linking, via comparison,

of his work to Shakespeare, Cervantes, Tolstoy, Henry James, and Anonymous. While the gesture appears self-certifying, it still only works with the permission of the larger literary community.

Meanwhile, self-definition proceeds by other means as well. In *Spring and All,* Williams particularly defines himself, as we have partly witnessed, through the imagining of an antithesis between the forces of tradition and those of modernism. Here the modernist is the misunderstood explorer, the one who reaches out to map the terrain of the real, only to find his or her best efforts misrepresented: "You moderns! it is the death of poetry that you are accomplishing. No. I cannot understand this work. You have not suffered a cruel blow from life. When you have suffered you will write differently" (177). And if the modernist is the brave and honest explorer, the traditionalist is the spoiler of these efforts. Here respect for tradition masks a reactionary stance toward the real, and when it finds itself embodied in poetry, it makes due with "demoded words," "[c]rude symbolism" and a mawkish decorousness. The result is that "meanings have been lost through laziness or changes in the form of existence which have let words empty" (188), and even as these poets create "apt similes and pretty thoughts and images" (206), they refuse to acknowledge the fact of the twentieth century.

The traditionalist fares no better when he or she attempts to render the "conscious recording of the day's experiences 'freshly and with the appearance of reality'" (203). The problem results from the artist's failure to distinguish the difference between copying nature and imitating it. Too prepared to accept as true "Shakespeare's familiar aphorism about holding the mirror up to nature" (208), the traditionalist does not realize that "the mistake in it (though we forget that it is not S. speaking but an imaginative character of his) is to have believed that the reflection of nature is nature. It is not. It is only a sham nature, a 'lie'" (208). Here, thinks Williams, echoing Plato, the copy of the thing can never rival the thing-itself. Yet the traditionalist's program has been just this, the furtherance of a mimetic technique, be it Holbein's perspectivism or some other artist's, designed to keep things "continually under cover of the 'beautiful illusion'" (199). The illusion itself might replicate the world quite perfectly, so that "'the birds pecking at the grapes'" in the picture might almost, or even, be mistaken for those outside the frame, yet the fundamental error of the program persists: it "makes nature an accessory to the particular theory he [the artist] is following, it blinds him to his world" (207). Meanwhile the actual problem should be thought of as how to get past the redundant activity of copying nature to the more worthwhile activity of imitating it. The answer should not be merely one of technique, for as Williams understood the matter, the traditionalists—unnamed as they are—were masters of technique. In fact, this was very much their problem. With them all was technique, *trompe l'oeil* tricks which drew one's attention away from the truth of the object itself. Yet for Williams this circumstance bespoke a failure, for the attention wished to go elsewhere, to the object itself or that which existed in a space or a moment prior to technique: "All this being anterior to technique, that can have only a sequent value" (193).

But if technique, say a new realistic technique, was not the answer, what was? Might it not be imagination itself—the "power" which was understood as nothing less than "an actual force comparable to electricity or steam" (207). It seems so, for with it, Williams argued, the artist might "ESCAPE ILLUSION" (199) and move "from the simulations of present experience to the facts of the imagination" (219). That is, by enlarging the artist's sympathies, by elevating him "to some approximate co-extension with the universe" (192), the imagination might facilitate the artist's own unification with his world: "He himself become [sic] 'nature'—continuing 'its' marvels—if you will" (208). The artist becomes, to use Emerson's phrase, a "seeing eye," whereby, to return to *Spring and All,* he "does exactly what every eye must do with life, fix the particular with the universality of his own personality" (193). Success becomes dependent upon the quality of his detachment, for "[w]hen in the condition of imaginative suspense only will the writing have reality" (206). Assuming the proper detachment, it then becomes necessary only "to write down that which happens at that time" (206). Hence, for Williams, the artist aspires "[t]o perfect the ability to record at the moment when the consciousness is enlarged by the sympathies and the unity of understanding which the imagination gives, to practice skill in recording the force moving, then to know it, in the largeness of its proportions" (206).

The difference between copying and imitating the world is that in the former, the artist holds back too much and demonstrates not enough faith in the "unification of experience" (207). Here the artist tries to make the art "like life" rather than life (or reality) itself (215). Yet Williams should prefer that the artist, possessed of imagination, attempt "NOT TO COPY them [the world's facts], not to holding the mirror up to them but to equal, to surpass them as a creator of knowledge, as a vigorous, living force above their heads" (209). The artist creates things which have the quality of separate existence: "'works of art' cannot be left in this category of [Anatole] France's 'lie,'" that is as imitative and hence false things; rather "they must be real, not 'realism' but reality itself" (204).

THE POET AND HIS WORLD

In *Spring and All,* Williams's aesthetic project imagines a situation where the traditional separation between subject and object is overcome. To begin with, there is no material difference between subject and object, the subject (or imagination) being "not 'like' anything but transfused with the same forces which transfuse the earth" (207). Likewise, the object (nature) is "not opposed to art but apposed to it" (208), it (the object) possessing that "quality of independent existence, of reality which we feel in ourselves" (207–8). The long-standing metaphysical differentiation of subject and object being one not only of function but also of substance (spirit versus matter) gives way then in Williams to a state where functional difference alone seems to matter. Yet if Williams, like James, imagines subjects and objects as being composed of more or less the same substance, he still maintains a firm sense of the subject's autonomy, and still imagines the "space" between the subject and the object as at the heart of the poetic problem. In this sense, he is more a modernist than a postmodernist, if these terms satisfy. Thus Williams speaks of how, through the imagination, he came to reconfigure his own "I" in relation to experience: "*I* let the imagination have its own way to see if it could save itself. Something very definite came of it. *I* found myself alleviated but most important *I* began there and then to revalue experience, to understand what *I* was at" (203; emphasis added). And this, in turn, further confirms his sense of a "world" standing independent of this "I": "A world detached from the necessity of recording it, sufficient to itself, removed from him (as it most certainly is) with which he has better and delicious relations and from which he is independent—moving at will from one thing to another—as he pleases, unbound—complete" (207).

For Williams, then, "subject" and "world" are not understood as tropes, concepts inescapably entangled in language, but as "real" entities, things-in-themselves which are understood to be bridgeable by another real entity: the imagination. The imagination, meanwhile, is understood (Williams's modernist presuppositions showing here) very much in optical terms—vision, clarity, intensification, magnification. Understood this way, there follows the desire to break one's visual field down, to detach and to abstract the individual "thing" from the scene's welter, and, mindful of the camera, to celebrate this thing's uniqueness. Thus Williams, referring to Juan Gris's exercise of imagination, takes note of those

> things with which he is familiar, simple things—at the same time to detach them from ordinary experience to the imagination. Thus they are still "real" they are the same things they would be if photographed or painted by Monet, they are recognizable as the things touched by the hands during the day, but in this painting they are seen to be in some peculiar way—detached. (197)

In Williams's view, things-in-themselves are important. Things might appear to be in flux and values might appear to be contingent; still, the important things, the universal things, are fixed: "The fixed categories into which life is divided must always hold" (224). The world of things bespeaks a hidden presence—call it God, spirit, or whatever, Williams, himself a materialist, does not name it—which gives value to all things, a confirmation which the poetics imitates. The poet, however, acts as if he were giving value for the first time, forgetting just how much his own poetics is predicated upon the presumption of inherent value: "My whole life has been spent (so far) in seeking to place a value upon experience and the objects of experience that would satisfy my sense of inclusiveness without redundancy—completeness" (202).

Much of what Williams does in *Spring and All* involves the simple presentation of people, places, and things with the understanding that they have inherent value. As a poet, Williams conceives his obligation as not to transform or subvert value but to affirm and celebrate it: "poetry does not tamper with the world but moves it— It affirms reality most powerfully" (234). Thus the greatest tribute the poet can bestow upon a found experience, upon this "wordless/ world" (228), is to offer it up without a word, silence being the most exquisite form of acknowledgment, of recognizing value independent of one's will. In a way, this is the theme of the collection's eleventh poem, which starts with the poet/narrator telling of an ostensibly ordinary Sunday-like drive in his car, nothing at all on his mind: "In passing with my mind / on nothing in the world // but the right of way / I enjoy on the road by // virtue of the law—" (205). With his mind a blank tape, ready for recording, he soon begins to take note of certain sensations, particularly people. First, "I saw // an elderly man who / smiled and looked away // to the north past a house—". Then his attention moves to "a woman in blue / who was laughing and / leaning forward to look up // into the man's half / averted face[,]" followed by "a boy of eight who

was looking at the middle of / the man's belly / at a watchchain—".
The poet then comments:

> The supreme importance
> of this nameless spectacle
> sped me by them
> without a word—
>
> (206)

In a sense, Williams as poet is caught in a bind. On the one hand, he wishes to acknowledge that silence is the most perfect response to that which, in its uniqueness, fills us with awe and respect; on the other hand, he is a poet, forced to speak this silence, or at least to speak of it. Maybe a more genuine awe should refrain from utterance, but as Williams says, "the form of poetry is related to the movements of the imagination revealed in words" (219), not in silences. And so if words do not, in the words of a rival poet, quite "reach / Into the silence," they do, nevertheless, speak of a respect for silence, a respect for the mystery which refuses dissection. Meanwhile, for Williams beauty is to be found everywhere. The ordinary is replete with the extraordinary, and to meet it, all one has to do is, in effect, set one's wheels rolling:

> Why bother where I went?
> for I went spinning on the
>
> four wheels of my car
> along the wet road until
>
> I saw a girl with one leg
> over the rail of a balcony
>
> (206)

"[I]t is the common thing," then, "which is anonymously about us" (189) that Williams makes his theme, believing that it is this which is "of a piece with the 'nature' which Shakespeare mentions and which Hartley speaks of so completely in his 'Adventures'" (189). Perhaps Williams shows his innocence when he equates this italicized or literary nature with that other, "realer" Nature, though that too works as a trope. In any case, nature as found in Homer and Shakespeare is conflated with nature as such, and "[t]heir compositions [are said] to have as their excellence an identity with life since they are as actual, as sappy as the leaf of the tree which never moves from one spot" (189).

Williams seems confident that he knows what nature is. He is somewhat like Hemingway or Stein in this respect, for the confidence seems premature. Yet as he stresses the necessity of a "residual contact between life and the imagination" and as he sets out to make the "common thing" which is all about us his theme, this confidence might prove an advantage. In any event, Williams seems somewhat certain that in populating his poems with "old ladies / that darn socks" (210), "young slatterns, bathed in filth" (212), "Drivers for grocers or taxidrivers / white and colored—" (221), and retarded servant girls with "ungainly hips and flopping breasts" (218), he is populating them with essential human types, telling not only of human nature but of "nature" itself. The result is a sort of proletarian equation made between drivers, farmers, fishermen, housekeepers, nurses, and "Nature." They are nature; nature is they.

This is probably a little unfair to Williams, for certainly his value as a poet connects with the fact that he, like Whitman before him, made a concerted effort to de-prettify and to de-gentrify the realm of poetry. Still, in *Spring and All,* Williams, even as he deconstructs the prevailing formulas, does appear to resort too readily to formulas of his own. Thus individuals are reduced to types, and farmers and fishermen are romanticized for the reason that they are farmers and fishermen. Accordingly, "[t]he farmer and fisherman who read their own lives there (in the sky)" are said to "have a practical corrective for . . . demoded meanings" (187). And the farmer himself (in the volume's third poem) is likened to the artist—singular, silent, strong, thoughtful, and a little detached from the world even as he does battle with it, creating its shape:

> The farmer in deep thought
>
> is pacing through the rain
> among his blank fields, with
> hands in pockets,
> in his head
> the harvest already planted.
> A cold wind ruffles the water
> among the browned weeds.
> On all sides
> the world rolls coldly away:
> black orchards
>
> darkened by the March clouds—
> leaving room for thought.
> Down past the brushwood

bristling by
the rainsluiced wagonroad
looms the artist figure of
the farmer—composing
—antagonist

(186)

    Williams's sympathies are in the right place, but the praise he offers farmers, fishermen and the elderly seems remarkably generous. One appreciates the sentiment but struggles to believe it. Meanwhile, apart from this, there is something surprisingly Arnoldian here, by which I mean the world is conceived as a rather lost place so long as it does not heed the message of its artists: "A terrific confusion has taken place. No man knows whither to turn. There is nothing! Emptiness stares us once more in the face" (184). Once men and women possessed a unified understanding of knowledge and culture. But no longer. Somewhere alone the way a kind of Eliotian "dissociation of sensibility" occurred and now all is either fragmented or lost: "In other times—men counted it a tragedy to be dislocated from sense—Today boys are sent with dullest faith to technical schools of all sorts—broken, bruised" (225). The farmer and fisherman might thus exemplify some "residual contact between life and the imagination" (187), yet on the whole humankind is not very well spoken of. In poem twenty-six, for instance, Williams, attending to a crowd of sports fans, accents both its vacuity—

The crowd at the ball game
is moved uniformly

by the spirit of uselessness
which delights them—

—and also its bestiality—"It is alive, venomous // it smiles grimly / its words cut—"—prepared to lash out at any easy prey:

The flashy female with her
mother, gets it—
The Jew gets it straight.

Oddly, Williams finds this spectacle somehow beautiful:

It is beauty itself
that lives

day by day in them
idly—

(233–34)

Still, it seems an abstract beauty at best, and makes one wonder whether Williams's detachment does not have its less attractive side. Williams, it is true, makes a point of saying how much he loves people:

> I love my fellow creature. Jesus, how I love him: endways, sideways, frontways and all the other ways—but he doesn't exist! Neither does she. I do, in a bastardly sort of way. (178)

But the affection comes close to annihilating what it professes to embrace, and should this happen, we should be left only with the vatic I. While Williams, on the whole, seems generous and concerned, he does, clearly, have his boastful moments, moments when he too readily assumes it his place to be a legislator of the world. In such moments, his criticisms seem less pointed than indiscriminate. For instance, in the same poem twenty-six, the ballgame crowd is represented as an undifferentiated mass, condemned, it would seem, for lacking what no mass has ever evidenced: individuality and intellection:

> It is summer, it is the solstic
> the crowd is
>
> cheering, the crowd is laughing
> in detail
>
> permanently, seriously
> without thought
>
> (234)

Williams's critique predicates itself upon the assumption that what we have in the present century "is not a civilization but stupidity" (225), with "few escap[ing] whole" (225) the widespread slaughter of knowledge. Given later historical events, the conviction seems not so wild. Still, Williams's penchant for categorical judgments ultimately weakens his appeal. Here it is not just a matter of statements that seem overwrought, as when Williams labels Anatole France "a fool" for celebrating art's artifice, but it is also a matter that such judgments enhance his detachment. Williams is simply too much the observer, the distanced judge who makes proximity appear a risk. Occasionally, this detachment can turn cruel, as it does in poem nine, wherein a love relationship is described with a nurse named Miss Margaret Jarvis. What goes wrong, what turns lovemaking into heartbreak, is not actually stated. What does seem clear, however, is that the poet/lover has said something not so much deliberately unkind as unconsidered or thoughtless:

> All I said was:
> there, you see, it is broken
>
> stockings, shoes, hairpins
> your bed, I wrapped myself round you—
> I watched.
>
> You sobbed, you beat your pillow
> you tore your hair
> you dug your nails into your sides
>
> I was your nightgown
> I watched!

(201)

In a perceptive essay on Williams's friendship with Marianne Moore ("Something Inescapably Typical . . ."), John Slatin argues that the relationship cooled due to Moore's disenchantment with attitudes typified by, for instance, Williams's "deeply seated and unconscious contempt for the predicament of a woman [Marcia Nadia, fictionalized as 'C' in *Paterson*] trying desperately to make poetry."[5] I agree with Slatin, and think that these lines from *Spring and All* foreshadow Williams's use or misuse (for he was not granted permission to use them) of the Nadia letters in *Paterson*. There, according to Slatin, "Nardi's private, impassioned analysis of the forces that combine to thwart and stifle her creative energies becomes 'literature,' that is, public property" (97), and here, too, a situation which seems essentially private (i.e., Williams's affair with a nurse, Miss Margaret Blake Purvis, with whom he worked while an intern at a New York hospital) is offered up as something irrefragably public. Meanwhile, whether one wishes, or not, to identify Williams with the doctor/poet here, one finds a narration wherein the author appears as a shallow and unmoved lover ("I merely / caress you curiously"), who seems unaware of the import of his own story. Granted, there is some self-conscious irony in the repeated line "I watched," offered the second time with a spatial pause between the first and second word and a final exclamation point: "I watched!" Nevertheless, the overall mood appears voyeuristic, with the speaker demonstrating little empathy with the woman's pain. I find it too cool and, at the risk of being unkind, would suggest that the poem's motivation includes Williams's unrepressed longing to boast about a sexual "conquest" that took place fifteen years earlier. In any event, the nurse's sobs go unheard except by the furniture, the same furniture that the doctor/poet/lover makes the receptacle of what emotion he has:

> In my life the furniture eats me
> the chair, the floor
> the walls
> which heard your sobs
> drank up my emotion—

                                                                        (200)

POLEMICIZING THE IMAGINATION

If in *Spring and All* Williams handles his theme—"the common thing which is anonymously about us"—with detachment, it might also be noted that his theme remains a little too much the object of poetry rather than poetry itself. Thus while Williams hopes, keeping Shakespeare in mind, to dramatize his theme—to offer not a discussed reality, but an actualized reality—he often veers off in the direction of literary talk—less offering us poetry than telling us what it should be. (For example, "poetry has to do with the dynamization of emotion into a separate form" [219].) This might seem unfair, for *Spring and All* includes both poetry and prose. Yet Williams, both here and elsewhere, presents himself as a polemicist, arguing for a "modernist" poetics which is self-consciously differentiated from previous poetic practice by means of its clean, sharp images, faithful attention to the object, and governance by the imagination.

Often Williams chooses to play the polemicist in the poetry itself. At his best, he carries this off subtly and beautifully as when, in poem eighteen, he, following the story of the servant girl Elsie and her cheap jewelry, so attractive to "rich young men with fine eyes," apotheosizes the imagination and its nameless, unaccountable object:

> as if the earth under our feet
> were
> an excrement of some sky
>
> and we degraded prisoners
> destined
> to hunger until we eat filth

while the imagination strains
after deer
going by fields of goldenrod in

the stifling heat of September
Somehow
it seems to destroy us

It is only in isolate flecks that
something
is given off

No one
to witness
and adjust, no one to drive the car

(218–19)

Another beautiful example occurs in poem seven when Williams, attending to the distinct lines which radiate out from the rose petal's edge, celebrates the geometrically sharp quality of modern poetry itself:

The rose is obsolete
but each petal ends in
an edge, the double facet
cementing the grooved

columns of air—The edge
cuts without cutting
meets—nothing—renews
itself in metal or porcelain—
whither? It ends—

But if it ends
the start is begun so that to engage roses
becomes a geometry—

Sharper, neater, more cutting
figured in majolica—

(193)

Yet there are probably more instances, in *Spring and All,* when the polemic does not work well, or when it is simply too enigmatic for the general reader to grasp the meaning. For instance, I suspect few contemporary readers, not to mention later reader unsupplied with notes, would have recognized the following lines' allusion:

>That is why boxing matches and
>Chinese poems are the same—That is why
>Hartley praises Miss Wirth
>
>(190)

The allusion, in fact, is to the the painter Marsden Hartley's *Adventures in Art* (1921) wherein the author praises circus rider Mary Wirth. Her art, says Hartley, "gives the body a chance to show its exquisite rhythmic beauty . . . the beautiful plastic of the body, harmonically arranged for personal delight" (502). A minor bother, perhaps, but one which is compounded by Williams's overall stridency. For instance, in the following lines, Williams, seemingly a populist, can still be arrogantly dismissive of people in general:

>Time does not move. Only ignorance and stupidity move.
>   Intelligence (force, power) stands still with time and forces change about itself—sifting the world for permanence, in the drift of nonentity.
>
>(220)

And, on other occasions, his voice can turn almost manic, as in the volume's first dadaist pages wherein Williams devotes his attention to the recreation of the world from scratch by the Imagination:

>If I could say what is in mind in Sanscrit or even Latin I would do so. But I cannot. I speak for the integrity of the soul and the greatness of life's inanity; the formality of its boredom; the orthodoxy of its stupidity. Kill! Kill! let there be fresh meat. (179)[6]

In addition to the polemic, one hears numerous literary echoes in *Spring and All.* That is, despite the pride Williams takes in his attention to his immediate contacts, there is a surprising literariness to the volume, allusions and mimicry abounding. Beyond the references to Baroja, Cézanne, El Greco, France, Gris, Hartley, Holbein, Homer, Kreymborg, Marlowe, Monet, Moore, Poe, Sandburg, Shakespeare, and Whitman among others, one hears any number of familiar voices, such as the Pound of *Cathay:*

>The grief of the bowmen of Shu
>moves nearer—There is
>an approach with difficulty from
>the dead—the winter casing of grief
>
>(181)

the Eliot of "Prufrock,"

> No that is not it
> nothing that I have done
> nothing
> I have done
>
> (191)

or the Whitman of "Crossing Brooklyn Ferry": "We are one. Whenever I say 'I' I mean also 'you.' And so, together, as one, we shall begin" (178).

As Williams himself might say, the smell of literature hangs over *Spring and All,* which is surprising as it is the work of one who admonishes others that "the greatest characteristic of the present age is that it is stale—stale as literature" (219). Still, Williams is an innovator, and if his innovation is self-conscious in a literary manner, this is not to be regretted. What might be regretted is the suggestion that things are otherwise. But even here perhaps the fairest thing to say is that the suggestion connects less with fact than with desire. Certainly, Williams wants to suggest that he is discovering or rediscovering an origin—a world that lies ever before us, free of us— that has been so blackened and marked over by literary artists that it is no longer recognizable:

> The man of imagination who turns to art for release and fulfillment of his baby promises contends with the sky through layers of demoded words and shapes. Demoded, not because the essential vitality which begot them is laid waste—this cannot be so, a young man feels, since he feels it in himself—but because meanings have been lost through laziness or changes in the form of existence which have let words empty. (188)

The desire for origin is, then, important for Williams. He would, if he could, present the world as it is, free of art, free of intellection. He thinks he can do this, that his own art is not art, "not a matter of 'representation'" but of presentation, or "of separate existence" (204). It is a mistake, of course, and while the more pertinent matter might be to address the question of *whose* representation shall hold sway (a question which Williams, in one sense, never stopped asking), we should do well to remember that technique and substance are never, in fact, dissociable. Hence, I would argue that Williams, like Stein and Hemingway, offers us not origin itself, but a technique of originality, a technique which celebrates the thing-in-itself as a value and which offers a simulacrum of the same. In *Spring and All* the technique is characterized by, among other things, a polemical celebration of the world as it is; a valuing of the trope of the common life, that is "the common thing which is anonymously about us"; a belief that subject-object dualisms can be overcome and thereafter replaced by a subject/object monism; a privileging of sight over the other senses; a paratactical accent in the syntax; a celebration of cubistic technique for the reason that it reinforces the atomistic, detached nature of things-in-themselves; a renewed attention to poetic measure, here again in conjunction with the understanding that the world is, at bottom, arithmetical in nature; and, lastly, an atheistic affirmation of the world as an all in all solid and material thing.

Some of these concerns I have already spoken to, and will not repeat; others, however, need to be addressed. First, respecting Williams's polemical celebration of the world as it is, one is aware of the large role Williams played in shaping the critical understanding of his work. We read his work as fresh, innovative, and attuned to a "realer," less poeticized world partly in response to his own urging. Things of course are not this simple. Still, readers are grateful to be partly led by Williams or by any other writer who demands to be read with his or her newness in mind. Thus it is not unusual that we so often read Williams as he reads himself, that is, as one who, like his generous description of Marianne Moore, "is most constantly a poet in her work because the purpose of her work is invariably from the source from which poetry starts—that it is constantly from the purposes of poetry. And that it actually possesses this characteristic, as of that *origin,* to a more distinguishable degree when it eschews rhythms than when it does not. It has the purpose of poetry written into it and therefore it is poetry" (230; emphasis added).

In *Spring and All* Williams makes a concerted effort to say what poetry is. The definition, however, remains somewhat obscure. For instance, while the values of "imagination," "newness," "cleavage," and "actual existence" are extolled, their critical value seems uneven. They do not translate easily into a practical poetics, and they appear subject to manipulation. Williams is surely sincere when he says "that there is work to be done in the creation of new forms, new names for experience" (203) and also when he speaks of his wish "to give created forms reality, actual existence" by means of the "unique power" which is the "imagination" (207). Nevertheless, such a standard seems too plastic—too malleable to Williams's own needs and moods. One admires flexibility, but a poetic standard needs to be predicated upon more than a sincerely felt "something": "I search for 'something' in the writing which moves me in a certain way—It offers a suggestion as to why some work of Whitman's is bad poetry and some, in the same meter is prose" (230). For all his mention of a standard, discriminations do seem to boil down to a matter of Williams's taste.

Williams's taste and, perhaps, Williams's need. To write free verse in the 1920s was, after all, to raise questions respecting legitimacy. Williams felt the need to defend his efforts, to offer a reason for doing things differently. He argued that traditional poetry, organized along the principles of rhyme and meter, was too artificial, too removed from "reality," its source of power. Along with symbol and metaphor, rhyme and meter might be sacrificed if it meant greater attention to this source:

> What I put down of value will have this value: an escape from crude symbolism, the annihilation of strained associations, complicated ritualistic forms designed to separate the work from "reality"—such as rhyme, meter as meter and not as the essential of the work, one of its words. (189)

Here Williams might have demonstrated greater knowingness about the way "reality" finds itself constructed, and shown less readiness to think of it as something out there. In any event, he felt the world was something approachable, and what one said about it—that is, how one poetically presented it—could either be near the mark or not. Thus by eschewing rhyme and meter, Williams conceived of himself as bringing poetry closer to the mark, closer, that is, than more recent poets. Up to this point, one always had, with certain notable exceptions (Homer, Shakespeare), "the illusion relying on composition to give likeness to 'nature'" (204), so that what one had was not the thing itself but its copy. But Williams thought he could offer the real thing by simply naming it:

> Understood in a practical way, without calling upon mystic agencies, of this or that order, it is that life becomes actual only when it is identified with ourselves. When we name it, life exists. To repeat physical experiences has no— (202)

Williams assumed that as mind and world were substantively alike, there should exist no insurmountable barrier between them. Differences there might be, but the integers at play could always be recoordinated to the point where mind and world could be brought more or less into line. The poet had only to get some kind of fix on the world, to attend to its elements with unfailing concentration, and then to lock it, or them, with the imagination, securing such as a permanent thing and value: "All that appears to the senses on a work of art does so through . . . fixation by the imagination of the external as well as internal means of expression the essential nature of technique or transcription" (193). Here technique, conceived as self-effacing and invisible, becomes synonymous with transcription, and as such is readily identified with the object itself. "Nature is the hint to composition" (207); and composition only has value when it aligns itself with nature or life. "Composition is in no essential an escape from life. In fact if it is so it is negligible to the point of insignificance" (189).

Williams's readiness to say what nature is appears premature. And while he exhibited an enviable confidence this way, the suspicion is that Williams's poetry approaches no nearer the mark of "reality" than that of previous poets. The error can be found in Williams's understanding of the problem, particularly in the sense that reality is separate and determinate. But "reality," as much as anything else, appears a linguistic concept. And while there are undoubtedly things which exist beyond the boundaries of both our bodies and minds, these things, like ourselves, do not possess the quality of independent existence but are enmeshed in a web of relations. One relation from which they cannot be easily freed is that with language. This is not the same thing as saying that their existence is dependent upon language. The key phrase here is "for us." Thus, for us, language gives these "things" both reality and shape. Meanwhile, there are, in fact, no individual "things," and the word "thing" or "things" constitutes a convenient trope, giving us a way to deal with the matter even as it falsifies it. The word suggests that "things" are autonomous entities possessing distinct edges, even as they are not the first and have not the latter. In short, "reality" is less an autonomous thing existing in three-dimensional space than it is an event, a cluster of relations which, while standing in relation to other events, cannot be said to be either qualitatively inferior or superior.

Without a discussion of the contingencies, for instance, Williams's "reality" possesses no more truth than, say, Longfellow's or Tennyson's. And yet, when interests are declared, it might. That is, though the poet cannot secure the truth of his or her representation by reference to some absolute (e.g., nature or reality), he or she can speak of certain realities as being more congenial to one's temper or values. Depending upon the time and place, one can anticipate measures of agreement or disagreement, to the point where one representation—say Williams's—starts to appear more true than another. In fact, Williams's present canonical status offers evidence that his representation of things remains attractive to a large group of readers.

Why does Williams's reputation remain secure? Though we understand that Williams presents us not with origin, with things as they really are, but with a technique of origin, many of us continue to find intellectual, emotional, and aesthetic satisfaction in the world that his poetry makes available. Despite Williams's detachment and Heraclitean pronouncements, a stable world remains, grounded in the individual's understood humanity. This world may not really be "true" but many of us should like to believe it so. Williams's celebration of the imagination is a testimony to the fact that he, in any event, believes it to be true—believes that the poet bestows value upon the world: "The only means he has to give value to life is to recognize it with the imagination and name it: this is so" (202). The world might be infinite in its parts, its number, yet the only aspect of it to which real value attaches is that which has been lighted upon by our imagination: "It is not necessary to count every flake of the truth that falls: it is necessary to dwell in the imagination if the truth is to be numbered. It is necessary to speak from the imagination" (199).

THE TECHNIQUE OF ORIGINALITY

Williams places the imaginative person at the center of things, and thereby also places value upon the means by which this individual's imagination is fed—his or her senses: "A work of the imagination which fails to release the senses in accordance with this major requisite—the sympathies, the intelligence in its selective world, fails at the elucidation" (192) of this world. Here again, sight is more privileged than the other senses. The reason may have to do with the fact that the world is conceived as something out there, distinct from the imagination. Whereas touch, smell, taste, and (to a lesser extent) hearing depend upon a certain proximity to the sensed object, sight is capable of operating at a distance from the apprehended object and, when magnified, at an extraordinary distance. It is not surprising, then, that a modernist such as Williams should conceive of the artist as, in his words, a kind of "seeing eye" (192). This eye both opens up the world and delimits it, fending off the infinity of sensations which equals the universe. This, however, does not mean that the "seeing eye" is a mostly passive instrument; it is not. All the while, says Williams, it is guided in what it should attend to by the imagination; for as the imagination is the value-bestowing faculty, it is also the composing faculty, shaping the particular objects of its vision through recourse to its own universal blueprint, the same blueprint which it shares with nature itself: "In the composition, *the artist does exactly what every eye must do with life,* fix the particular with the universality of his own personality—Taught by the largeness of his imagination to feel every form which he sees moving within himself, he must prove the truth of this by expression" (193; emphasis added).

Williams's meaning here seems somewhat unclear (e.g., "The universality of his own personality"), and his aesthetic theory sometimes begs the question. Williams presses a little too hard upon his theoretic terms, asking them to explain more than is their wont. And yet, when one turns to the poetry, the aesthetic values are apparent. For one we find in *Spring and All* a poetics that is particularly pictorial, presenting a scene the way a painter might.[7] For example, in the first paragraphs of the first poem, the arrangement is noticeably spatial and, with participles standing in for verbs, also remarkably quiescent:

> By the road to the contagious hospital
> under the surge of the blue
> mottled clouds driven from the
>
> northeast—a cold wind. Beyond, the
> waste of broad, muddy fields
> brown with dried weeds, standing and fallen
> patches of standing water.
> the scattering of tall trees
>
> All along the road the reddish
> purplish, forked, upstanding, twiggy
> stuff of bushes and small trees
> with dead, brown leaves under them
> leafless vines—
>
> (183)

Things are presented as isolated, disparate, with few observable relationships other than the spatial. These include the road that leads to the hospital but which is more spatially defined as being beneath "the surge of the blue / mottled clouds," and things which themselves are defined in terms of their distinct attributes: "surge," "blue," "mottled." The clouds, meanwhile, are spatially defined as moving from the direction of the northeast, pushed by "a cold wind" which again seems presented, particularly given the syntax (here the dash both connects and isolates), as a self-contained entity. All this (the road under the clouds) then becomes a spatial point by which to locate "the / waste of broad, muddy fields," said to be "[b]eyond" the road just as "the reddish / purplish, forked, upstanding, twiggy / stuff of bushed and small trees" is said to be "along" it. At the same time, things continue to be sharply delineated—"One by one objects are defined— / It quickens: clarity, outline of leaf" (183)—reminding one of William James's suggestion that the world might amount to no more than the mutiplicity of its parts.

In *Spring and All,* Williams acknowleges both the unity and the disparateness of experience, and one might (keeping with the James reference) label the text radically empirical. Certainly the imagination is understood as a unifying, universal force, offering coherence and meaning to all that it touches. Yet what it touches, "the world's" particulars, are themselves recognized as standing opposed to this unity—that is, as being arithmetic, disparate, and individually autonomous. Williams would, if he might, lift these separate objects up to the point of the imagination without transforming them, without having them give up their quality of separateness. Yet it is not possible, for poetry's grammar, even when it is as syntactically paratactic as Williams's, is always in some way coercive. Still, Williams believed it could be done, that if one simply pressed the matter, making use of a cubist technique that detached things from their ordinary environment and placed them in a new situation, celebrating their separateness, one might present things as they actually are, unaltered by "[c]rude symbolism" (188). The cubist painters, particularly Juan Gris, were proof that it could be done: "But such a picture as that of Juan Gris . . . is important as marking . . . what the modern trend is: the attempt is being made to separate things of the imagination from life" (194).[8] Hence, looking at a Gris painting, one saw that individual things did not lose their separate identity and were not coerced by the larger composition: "Here is a shutter, a bunch of grapes, a sheet of music, a picture of sea and mountains (particularly fine) which the onlooker is not for a moment permitted to witness as an 'illusion'" (197).

Yet the cubist painters were not the only proof that the separateness of things could be carried over into art. There were also literary artists, notably Gertrude Stein and Marianne Moore, who, adopting techniques similar to those of the painters, also gave evidence that such could be done. Williams, to his credit, generously praises both for their invention. First Stein:

But if one remain in a place and reject satire, what then? To be democratic, local (in the sense of being attached with integrity to actual experience) Stein, or any other artist, must for subtlety ascend to a plane of almost abstract design to keep alive. To writing, then, as an art in itself. *Yet what actually impinges on the sense must be rendered as it appears, by use of which, only, and under which, untouched, the significance has to be disclosed.* It is one of the major problems of the artist.[9]

And then Moore:

> There is almost no overlaying [in Moore's poetry] at all. The effect is of every object sufficiently uncovered to be easily recognizable. This simplicity, with the light coming through from between the perfectly plain masses, is however extremely bewildering to one who has been accustomed to look upon the usual "poem," the commonplace opaque board covered with vain curlicues. They forget, those who would read Miss Moore aright, that white circular discs grouped closely edge to edge upon a dark table make black six-pointed stars.[10]

The point here is not that Williams did not recognize that to write poetry was to engage in an inherently self-reflexive endeavor. He did recognize this, and much of his commentary points to this fact. As he says, words represent poetry's ultimate substance: "Of course it must be understood that writing deals with words and words only and that all discussion of it deals with single words and their association in groups" (231). Yet it is another aspect that most interests me, partly perhaps for the reason that it goes so much against the grain of his first assumption, now our assumption, that writing is inescapably rhetorical and self-reflexive. And from this side, one hears something quite different: writing is a form of revelation, a revelation of a world that stands opposed to the poet, even as it is conceded that the world includes the poet. Here the poet's position as subject and creator appears magnified, enhanced as well by the sense that the poet's role is to reach out and lift the world's objects to the level of the imagination: "THE OBJECTIVE in writing is, to reveal. It is not to teach, not to advertise, not to sell, not even to communicate (for that needs two) but to reveal, which needs no other than the man himself."[11]

This revelation has two dimensions: one, the object is seen for what it is; but, two, the poet also finds himself or herself revealed: "Reveal what? That which is inside the man."[12] The suggestion is that the artist endowed with imagination feels no division between his or her apprehension of things and things-in-themselves. Such a poet might be likened to Shakespeare, who "[f]eeling the force of life, in his peculiar intelligence, the great dome of his head, he had no need of anything but writing material to relieve himself of his thought" (208). Hence whatever this poet writes will possess that quality of actuality which things themselves possess. And should we find the fusion difficult to grasp, it is probably, says Williams, because we have (as was earlier noted) given too little study to physiology: "The reason people marvel at works of art and say: How in Christ's name did he do it?—is that they know nothing of the physiology of the nervous system and have never in their experience witnessed the larger processes of the imagination" (209–10).

Meanwhile if "the larger processes of the imagination" require the lifting of the world's particulars above their plane ("To discover separate things from the amorphous, the conglomerate normality with which they are surrounded and of which before the act of 'creation' each is a part"),[13] there will need to be a third plane in which to locate the art-object. This art-object (painting, poem, etc.), while spatially distinct from both the subject and object, is nevertheless one with them. It is the place where subject and object meet, constituting a kind of secular trinity: three entities (subject, object, and art object) in one (art-object). Understood this way, the poem not only presents nature as it is but also becomes part of that nature, an addition to it: "Poetry has to do with the crystallization of the imagination—the perfection of new forms as addition to nature" (226). These forms are not so much "like" their counterparts in nature as they are them—in the sense that they constitute their celebration by the imagination—and are not them, in the sense that they are themselves material (paint, words, etc.). Two truths then, less contradictory than paradoxical, for even as Williams acknowledges, for instance, that "the mountain and sea" in the Gris painting "are obviously not 'the mountain and sea', but a picture of the mountain and the sea" (198), he presses the point that the imaginative artist creates something which "gives the feeling of completion by revealing the oneness of experience" (194), which "lives as pictures only can live: by their power TO ESCAPE ILLUSION and stand between man and the sky" (199). Pictures and poems of this kind are, then, not a form of realism but something else entirely: "experience dynamized into reality" (220). They compete with things-in-themselves even as they present the same and are themselves things-in-themselves. "The exaltation men feel before a work of art is the feeling of reality they draw from it" (215), for as Williams writes, "[t]he same things exist, but in a different condition when energized by the imagination" (224).

Williams's claims are brash and confident. The brashness seems part of an armored ego, the confidence of a strong aesthetic faith. As for the latter, it is mostly a faith in technique: the cubist technique so identified with modernism. As observed, what Williams most valued in this technique was its quality of cleavage, the practice of lifting ordinary objects from their ordinary surroundings in order to call attention to their specialness. "[B]y simply rotating the object // cleaving away the root of / disaster which it / seemed to foster" (214), Williams hoped to forge "new forms to embody this reality of art" (198), "to replace not the forms but the reality of experience with its [the art-object's] own" (204). The poem or painting would then have a quality of "independent existence" about it, cleaving itself free from all its surroundings.

If Williams's ambition appears adventurous and new, there also is, as with cubism itself, something quite conservative about it. For even as such a poetics results in somewhat surrealistic effects and finds otherwise able readers uncomprehending—e.g., "The incomprehensibility of her [Moore's] poems is witness to at what cost [she cleaves herself away] as it is also to the distance which the most are from a comprehension of the purpose of composition" (188)—the attempt to isolate, elevate, and preserve the otherwise anonymous sensations of experience is a gesture which would, in effect, stay time's passing and raise a measured monument to the moment that never was. Measured, for the reason that, again, Williams works from the assumption that all is divided up into three-dimensional space within which each autonomous "thing" finds its separate location, edge to edge beside other equally autonomous things. Yet not measured in the sense of formal meter. "[M]eter has nothing to do with the question, whatever" (229), for the reason that spatial "difference is felt" not dictated (230). Not an *a priori* science, not something fixed, measure for Williams is a supple response to bodies, objects, and things and the space that separates them. As both measure and syntax, it is paratactical, keeping distinct those things which press themselves upon the poet's attention differently, as do, for example, in the first verse paragraphs of poem sixteen, the "tongue," "sore," "netherlip," "toppled belly," "passionate cotton," "matted hair," "elysian slobber," and "folded handkerchief."

> O tongue
> licking
> the sore on
> her netherlip
>
> O toppled belly
> O passionate cotton
> stuck with
> matted hair

    elysian slobber
    upon
    the folded handkerchief

                                    (215)

As Williams later wrote, "The first thing you learn when you begin to learn anything about this earth is that you are eternally barred save for the report of your senses from knowing anything about it. Measure serves for us as the key: we can measure between objects."[14] And as objects themselves were discrete, it followed that words—conceived as bridges between objects and language—should also possess this quality of separation. For Williams, the word turns to the fact which gives it occasion and reality—the fact needing the word less than the word the fact—and in turn finds itself liberated from the coercive influences of usage and language: "The word is not liberated, therefore able to communicate release from the fixities which destroy it until it is accurately tuned to the fact which giving it reality, by its own reality establishes its own freedom from the necessity of a word, thus freeing it and dynamizing it at the same time" (235). Faithful to the facts of a pluralistic universe, words acquire license: they not only "remain separate, each unwilling to group with the others except as they move in one direction" (231), they are also capable of comporting themselves in surreal fashion, as for example in poem four, after the poet has challenged himself to find the essential verbal equivalent—

        Burst it asunder
        break through to the fifty words
        necessary—

—to present the relation between the Easter sky, the city skyline and a young girl:

              a crown for her head with
        castles upon it, skyscapers
        filled with nut-chocolates—

              dovetame winds—
        star of tinsel
        from the great end of a cornucopia
        of glass

                                  (187)

Williams puts the matter differently. He speaks not of surrealistic effects but of words approaching the condition of music, as when they are linked with "natural objects" and liberated by the imagination: "According to my present theme the writer of the imagination would attain closest to the conditions of music not when his words are dissociated from natural objects and specified meanings but when they are liberated from the usual quality of that meaning by transposition into another medium, the imagination" (235). For Williams, the work of the imagination frees us by, paradoxically, more fully attaching us to "reality." The freedom follows from the creative act, the cleaving of the object away from the unnamed flux. Once, says Williams, such an act would have been thought unnecessary, for then "the subject of art was not 'reality' but related to the 'gods'— by force or otherwise." Here "[t]here was no need of the 'illusion' in such a case since there was none possible where a picture or a work represented simply the imaginative reality which existed in the mind of the onlooker. No special effort was necessary to cleave where the cleavage already existed" (198). But now, with the world understood as a wholly material place, cleavage is necessary if we are to escape "illusion"—the warping influences of art, philosophy, religion, science, tradition, etc.

Finally, Williams's claim to know what "reality" is appears premature; just as his dismissal of everything that is not it seems rash. Doubtless, there is more than a modicum of truth about the statement, "Religion is continued as a form, art as a convention" (221), yet Williams errs if he thinks that this situation can be altogether transcended. New forms push out old but form and convention persist, for it is they (including the form of the classical *trivium*) which transcend, more or less, our contingencies. This holds true as much with a poetics of "reality," of origin, as it does with anything else. One can speak of the absolute otherness of things, but one cannot offer them up, for, as far as we are concerned, they exist only within the forms of our thinking about them; otherwise, they are a fiction; they do not exist.

One suspects that, at bottom, Williams himself knew all this; knew, that is, that what he really offered his readers was not origin itself but a simulacrum of the same. What was new was not what Williams said it was—the world presented as it is—but the technique for doing or, better, suggesting this, what I have hitherto called the technique of originality. That Williams was able to carry things off as well as he did—that he was so successful in promoting a critical response to his work that marched in step with his own self-projections—has much to do with the fact that he, like Stein and Hemingway, was, in the language of Harold Bloom, a strong poet, one who by force of will was able to accomplish much that was denied others. That this work and the manner in which it is presented should nevertheless bear such resemblances to the contemporaneous work of other "strong" writers is, meanwhile, the problem which this study seeks to investigate.

6

Marianne Moore and *Observations*

What constitutes the aesthetic changes from place to place, and from historical moment to moment? For American literary artists working in the first decades of this century, an interest in aesthetics often went hand in hand with an interest in epistemology. Certainly this was true for Stein, Hemingway, and Williams, and I would argue that it was also true for Marianne Moore. Yet, if so, why was this the case? I believe it had much to do with the historical moment in which they worked. We usually accent the aesthetic differences which distinguish one artist from another, and there are good arguments supporting the importance of differences over whatever continuities there are that bind. And yet, with the artists under discussion, there are shared assumptions that are so elemental that they have not been recognized. Here, I have in mind particular assumptions about space, time, subject, object, representation, and the aesthetic function, assumptions which should have been almost invisible to the authors.

Why did they not see what we ourselves do? It is not because we are, overall, more seeing. Rather, it is because we see different things. And if we understand their aesthetic assumptions differently than they themselves did, it is because their assumptions are no longer ours, and we note the difference. What we particularly note, to borrow from Foucault, is the way in which their sense of space is conceived "as a *common place* for representation and for things, for empirical visibility and for the essential rules, which unite the regularities of nature and the resemblances of imagination in the grid of identities and differences."[1] Here space is conceived as three-dimensional and time, a separate measure, as chronological and progressive. The world might appear to be infinite, yet the more pressing sense was that it was atomistic, or countable and finite.

If the world was, at bottom, arithmetic in nature, this, in turn, meant that every object possessed its own distinct edges and boundaries. Objects became identical with the spatial volume which they occupied. And the world in sum equalled its parts, a concept which fostered the notion that each thing possessed a unique value, for it constituted an essential part of the larger whole. In this way, things had, more or less, inherent value, if not because they found corresponding ideas in the mind of God, then because they were a part of that field which stood before the Artist, the present bestower of value; and because this field could not be understood in its totality— the ultimate ambition—without them. They had their parts to play in the unfolding drama, the main plot of which was the precise, scientific rendering of the world as it is. All (scientists, philosophers, artists) were implicated in this epistemological ambition even as all were not scientists.

Science had become the premier intellectual discipline and there were few intellectuals who did not take a passing interest in, or possess a passing understanding of, general science. Stein, Hemingway, Williams, and Moore were not exceptions. It is interesting to note that each, at one point, evinced an interest in the science of medicine, illustrating, in effect, Moore's belief that "[p]hysicians are not so often poets as poets are physicians."[2] Thus we find that Gertrude Stein all but completed the medical program at Johns Hopkins; Ernest Hemingway's father was a doctor and Hemingway himself, an ambulance driver in the First World War, always showed a keen interest in human physiology; William Carlos Williams was a general practitioner; and Marianne Moore at one time aspired to study medicine. Moore told the poet Donald Hall that in college she "found the biology courses—minor, major, and histology—exhilarating" and "thought, in fact, of studying medicine."[3] She did not actually study medicine, but throughout her career Moore called attention to the similarities which united poetry and science. Here the most fundamental similarity was that of methodology itself: both the poet and the scientist were interested in discovering connections among dissimilar things, in the patient, disciplined pursuit of a truth that could be found in no other way. "Do the poet and the scientist not work analogously?" asked Moore.

Both are willing to waste effort. To be hard on himself is one of the main strengths of each. Each is attentive to clues, each must narrow the choice, must strive for precision. As George Grosz says, "In Art there is no place for gossip and but a small place for the satirist." The objective is fertile procedure. Is it not? Jacob Bronowski says . . . that science is not a mere process of discovering. In any case it's not established once and for all; it's evolving.[4]

In one of her later poems, "The Student," Moore, paraphrasing Albert Einstein, again tells us that "science," or learning, "is never finished."[5] Yet in both that and the present instance, it is understood that knowledge (which includes both science and poetry) is in the process of moving or "evolving" toward *something*—some kind of immutable reality or truth. The "oppositions of science are not oppositions to poetry but oppositions to falseness" (CP, 157), something which Moore believes poetry should also be opposed to. For science and poetry, then, the enemy is the same, just as the object— truth—is the same. Or as Moore puts the matter in "Picking and Choosing,"

> Words are constructive
> when they are true; the opaque allusion—the simulated
> flight
>
> upward—accomplishes nothing.

(55)

Thus it should not surprise anyone that Moore, who wrote that "[t]oo much cannot be said for the necessity in the artist, of exact science" (CP, 53), felt her early scientific training fed into her work as a poet and played a part in her understanding of the imagination: "[D]id laboratory studies affect my poetry? I am sure they did. . . . Precision, economy of statement, logic employed to ends that are disinterested, drawing and identifying, liberate—at least have some bearing on—the imagination, it seems to me."[6]

Like the scientist classically defined, Moore wished to be a good observer, to be one who suppressed her ego before the world's bounty, wishing not to take possession of what lay before her but rather to present it, to master, as the artisan masters, the techniques of his or her trade in order to be a better craftsperson, a better presenter of the case. Moore writes, "One's work would not be the potent and accomplished thing it is, if it were done for any reason but to fulfill the instinct for technical mastery. What scientist thinks of being thanked for what he does? It is a pleasure to be so gifted that one's work is important as science is important. There is no pleasure subtler than the sensation of being a good workman" (CP, 284).

The good artisan has not the romantic artist's vaunted sense of self, of one's originality: he or she is more like the Flemish master, the guild member, who knows that one must learn from those greater than oneself, that one must master the trade and so too become a master. Good students require good teachers; otherwise all is for naught. Moore, in any event, felt this to be the case: "No mannerisms; you are not selecting notoriety or a fortune; you are a student of art" (CP, 657). Hence she sought out those master word-smiths who might teach her about her chosen trade, who might provide her with examples of "the honest unaffected natural force of plain declarative statements."[7] As she often noted, "the first aid to good writing . . . is the reading of such masterworks as one enjoys and would read for one's independent pleasure," among which, she was "inclined to put first, scientific works such as Darwin's and technical books of instruction such as Xenophon's on horsemanship, reports of research in a special subject such as Albert Reese The Alligator and Its Allies." "[D]esigned primarily for use-fulness," these works also served as models in which "sincerity pro-vides strength, humility provides grace, professional honor conscience and moderation a conscious tentativeness," which, in ef-fect, "demand the precise effect that hyperbole is striving for."[8]

Not all her models were scientists, of course. There were also artists (e.g., Gordon Craig, Henry James, Gustave Flaubert), among whom Ezra Pound was one of the most influential: "Our debt to Ezra Pound is prodigious for the effort he has made to share what he knows about writing and, in particular, about rhythm and mel-ody; most of all, for his insistence on liveness as opposed to dead-ness" (CP, 447). Moore particularly took to heart Pound's famous strictures in "A Few Don'ts by an Imagiste," slightly conflating them in the formula described as "[d]irect treatment, economy of words; compose in the sequence of the musical phrase rather than that of the metronome" (CP, 504). When Hugh Kenner questioned whether Pound had ever made clear what he meant by exact definition, Moore replied: "What is it? a neatening or cleancutness to begin with, as caesura is cutting at the end (*caedo*, cut off). For Dante, it was making you see the things that he sees, Mr. Pound says; and speaking of Rimbaud, says there is 'such firmness of coloring and such certitude'" (CP, 447).

Perhaps the definition still remains in doubt, yet what does not is Moore's allegiance to "vigilant exactness" (CP, 165), to Flaubert's admonition to "describe a tree so no other could be mistaken for it."[9] Whether or not it is possible (and the thrust of this study is to say that it is not) to detach things from their surroundings, present-ing them as things-in-themselves, separate, free, inherently valuable, Moore often wishes to do just this, "seized," like Valéry, whom she quotes, "with the sickness of precision[,] . . . tend[ing] to an extreme of an insane desire to understand."[10] What she would understand,

Moore writes in "Poetry," are those things which seldom find their home in poetry but which, nevertheless, "are important":

> The bat, upside down; the elephant pushing,
> a tireless wolf under a tree,
> the base-ball fan, the statistician—
> "business documents and schoolbooks"—[11]

The way she would understand them is principally twofold: first, "to acknowledge the spiritual forces which made" them ("When I Buy Pictures," 59); and second, to see them as the innocent eye might see them, as in the days of prismatic color. The former articulates Moore's belief that all things bespeak significance, the source of which is found in Divinity. (Here, Moore's Christianity sets her apart from both Stein and Williams, and less so from Hemingway, though all four writers start, whether they acknowledge it or not, with metaphysical predispositions.) And the latter, sight, or the "held eye," bespeaks Moore's principal means of understanding her objects. Intensity of vision—of concentration upon the object—is everything. Again quoting Valéry, it makes, Moore says, "the object inescapable."[12] Poetry, in this sense, is conceived not only as a form of "heightened consciousness" ("The Past is the Present," 32), but also as a form of superior seeing, a kind of unmediated apprehension of things. To this effect, Moore quotes both Ruskin ("Thousands of people can see for one who can think; but thousands can think for one who can see. To see clearly is poetry, prophecy, and religion all in one" [CP, 184]) and Conrad ("It [the object of art] is above all, in the first place, to make you see" [CP, 590]).

THE VALUE OF OBSERVATION

Moore thought of herself as an observer—"I seem to myself an observer" (CP, 648)—and named her volume (*Observations*) accordingly.[13] She felt herself a describer ("I like to describe things" [CP, 505]), not a doer ("I seem to myself . . . an interested hack rather than an author" [CP, 648]). Yet even though she put both herself and her method forward in a self-deprecating fashion, she did nevertheless put them forward. Observation—detached attentiveness to, and interest in, those things about one—did remain very much a value with her, something that she looked for not only in her own work but in that of others. Hence Ms. Adele Greeff is said to be "an observer who 'ties outer to inner act'" (CP, 633); Charlie Chaplin, in a volume of travel writing, is said to be "entirely the artist" for the reason of "detachment attained in descriptions of places and of himself, in the penetrating, unembellished force of the observer;"[14] and Stanley Kunitz, "value[d] for his 'poetic eye,'" is said to write with "[i]mpassioned feeling [and] accurate observation" (CP, 635). Like George Moore, then, whose "expertness as an observer made one feel as if sensation might at any time wander all the way to the heart" (CP, 64), Moore, overtaken by the "rapture of observation" (CP, 321), wished to contribute to "a new vocabulary of seeing,"[15] wished to be like H. D., who "[o]f what she saw, her eyes made poems, stated with a lyrical conciseness" (CP, 558).

Given, then, Moore's valuation of self-effacement, craftsmanship, and the plentitude of the visible world, it does not surprise that one of her favorite forms is the still life. Hers are not poems in which much happens, in the conventional sense of large-scale historical events, or even small-scale narratives. Except for the action of intellection, of the human mind seizing upon an object to its liking, there is little in the way of action in *Observations*. As Eliot famously wrote in the preface to *Selected Poems,* Moore's poetry is essentially "'descriptive' rather than 'lyrical' or 'dramatic.'"[16] Things, rather, are seen, or observed, the way that in "When I Buy Pictures," she tells us "I fix upon what would give me pleasure in my average mo-/ ments," which in that poem include "the old thing, the medieval decorated / hat-box, / in which there are hounds with waists diminishing like the waist of the hourglass / and deer and birds and seated people" (59), or which in "New York" include "the ground dotted with deer-skins—white with white spots / 'satin needlework in a single color may carry a varied / pattern,' and wilting eagles' down compacted by the wind; and picardels of beaver skin; white ones alert with snow" (65). "[T]hese things," as Moore argues in the longer version of "Poetry," "are important not because a // high-sounding interpretation can be put them upon but because / they are / useful."[17]

What Moore intends by this adjudicating term "useful" has always left me a little puzzled. The term, of course, is familiar; one sees it in James's *Pragmatism;* one sees it in Stein's *Tender Buttons.* Yet in Moore's poem "Poetry" the word appears to beg a question. I do not quite believe that Moore thinks that these things are important because they can be put to use; rather, it seems these things are deemed important simply because they are, because they exist. Or perhaps they are important not because they make "use" of, or in, time, but because they "redeem the time," because they point to a purpose or an end which is not completely at one with them, but of which they are nevertheless a part. In any case, the conviction is that "glory shall spring from in-glory" (24), not only in the case of persons, which is how she puts the matter in "'The Bricks are Fallen Down, . . . We will Build with Hewn Stones. The Sycamores Are Cut Down, we will Change to Cedars,'" but also in the case of things themselves.

And because for Moore things are, more or less, important in themselves, the still life presents itself as a most appropriate genre. Again and again, we find Moore deferring to the things themselves, bringing them forward, letting them announce themselves. Things are allowed to be. Yet this said, I wish to demur from Norman Bryson's embracing understanding of the still life, which is that "we never see the human form at all," that the "[s]till life negates the whole process of constructing and asserting human beings as the primary focus of depiction."[18] The argument is interesting, yet a little too strict; and I think for this reason we should be wary of applying it either to still lifes in general or to Moore's still lifes in particular. Granted, in *Observations,* Moore is most self-effacing, and the "I" more often tries to function as an "eye," an instrument for seeing rather than saying. Still, *there is an "I" here,* albeit one which appears to manifest itself less in the enunciation than in the effects of its intention:

> The pulse of intention does not move so that one
> can see it, and moral machinery is not labelled, but
> the future of time is determined by the power of volition.
> ("Reinforcements," 42)

That there is an I, an intention, has consequences. For one, it has been argued, again by Bryson, that it is the nature of the still life to deconstruct the single perspective:

> The enemy is a mode of seeing which thinks it knows in advance what is worth looking at and what is not: against that, the image presents the constant surprise of things seen for the first time. Sight is taken back to a vernal stage before it learned how to scotomize the visual field, how to screen out the unimportant and not to *see,* but scan.[19]

This seems true, yet true not only of still lifes, but of texts in general. No text exists without its inherent complexities or contradictions, properties which invariably undermine the attempt to say what it is. Thus, in one way, the text also demands to be seen, or read, anew. This does not mean, however, that sight is ever truly "vernal," or innocent. Screening always takes place. That is, as long as the viewer

THE VALUE OF OBSERVATION   189

remains part of the visual equation. For instance, Moore herself might think that she is forging a significant separation when she speaks of a thing as "[i]t belongs first to the eye; then [the] eye of the mind,"[20] but the separation collapses as quickly as it is spoken. There is no seeing divorced from intellection, and intellection always entails its own counter demands upon the text.

Hence despite the acknowledgment of complexities which reside in the text and which make the text immune to final definition—"'complexities which still will be complexities / as long as the world lasts'" ("An Octopus," 83)—one still meets with the counter purpose which is to press past complexity in order to arrive at "the initial great truths":

> complexity is not a crime but carry
>   it to the point of murki-
>   ness and nothing is plain. Complexity
> moreover, that has been committed to darkness, instead of
>   granting it—
>
> self to be the pestilence that it is, moves all a-
>   bout as if to bewilder us with the dismal
> fallacy that insistence
>   is the measure of achievement and that all
> truth must be dark. Principally throat, sophistication is as
>   it al-
>
> ways has been—at the antipodes from the init-
>   ial great truths.
>   ("In the Days of Prismatic Color," 49)

Faithfulness to "the initial great truths" requires an intention; and if in one sense, this means an openness to the valency of what is, in another sense it means a narrowing down of perspective. For Moore, as for Stein, Hemingway, and Williams, perspective, in many ways, involves a veridical ambition. It involves less the seeing of things from different angles than the marshalling of one's faculties to see "with piercing glances into the life of things" ("When I Buy Pictures," 59). One's "admiration now con-/ verges upon this" and that, and "one is compelled to look" at that "which from the earliest times, importance / has attached" ("Snakes, Mongooses . . . Charmers and The Like," 69). Perspective here entails not so much an arc as a line, drawn between the optic and the object.

Meanwhile, Moore's optical agenda also frequently assumes a panoramic aspect, as it does in "People's Surroundings." Here, in

the last stanza, Moore begins with a meditation on the "poetic eye,"
the scotomizing eye which knows what to attend to and what not,
which knows the difference between appearance and the real thing,
and which all along sees things with intensity:

> in these noncommittal, personal-impersonal expressions of
> appearance,
> the eye knows what to skip;
> the physiognomy of conduct must not reveal the skeleton;
> "a setting must not have the air of being one"
> yet with x-ray like inquisitive intensity upon it, the
> surfaces
> go back;
> the interfering fringes of expression but a stain on what
> stands out,
> there is nothing up nor down to it;
>
> (68)

This is followed by the fulsome presentation of what is seen:

> we see the exterior and the fundamental structure—
> captains of armies, cooks, carpenters,
> culters, gamesters, surgeons and armourers,
> lapidaries, silkmen, glovers, fiddlers and ballad-singers,
> sextons of churches, dyers of black cloth, hostlers and
> chimmey-sweeps,
> queens, countesses, ladies, emperors, travellers and
> mariners,
> dukes, princes and gentlemen
> in their respective places—
> camps, forges and battlefields,
> conventions, oratories and wardrobes,
> dens, deserts, railway stations, asylums and places where
> engines are made,
> shops, prisons, brickyards and altars of churches
> in magnificent places clean and decent,
> castles, palaces, dining-halls, theatres and imperial
> audience—
> chambers.
>
> (68)

Moore here would like to think that there is "no trace of sentimen-
tality" in her observations; that she is "a faithful friend of the objects
[she] portrays" (CP, 35); and that curiosity is enough—enough in
the sense that no strong privileging occurs, that all is seen with a
poetic and democratic eye. As she says, reversing the intellectual's

ordering of things, "People ask me, 'How do you think of things
to write about?' I don't. *They think me.* They become *irresistible*"
(CP, 663). Perhaps they do. Yet even while one is prepared to allow
for the metaleptic reversal—with cause changing places with effect—
one also suspects that despite the panoramic gaze and the Whit-
manesque catalogs, Moore's visual field reflects an interest, an
axiology. And here things become particularly irresistible if they
identify themselves with that which is "natural" and unconscious,
as for instance the child and her pet in "Critics and Connoisseurs":

> There is a great amount of poetry in unconscious
>   fastidiousness. Certain Ming
>   products, imperial floor coverings of coach
> wheel yellow, are well enough in their way but I have
>   seen something
>   that I like better—a
>   mere childish attempt to make an imperfectly
>   ballasted animal stand up,
>   similar determination to make a pup
>   eat his meat on the plate.

(35)

They also become irresistible (perhaps not without some contradiction) if they be exotic. Moore takes a particular delight in "'the
eccentric as the 'base of design.'"[21] Reviewing Stevens's *Harmonium*
in 1924, Moore wrote, "One is excited by the sense of proximity to
Java peacocks, golden pheasants, South American macaw feather
caps, Chilcat blankets, hair seal needlework, Singhalese masks, and
Rousseau's paintings of banana leaves and alligators" (CP, 92), excited, in part, for the reason that these are much akin to the exotica
which is so much a feature of her own poetry. Thus in *Observations,*
one is excited by the sense of proximity to crow-blue mussel shells,
parakeets from Brazil, Chinese cherries, emeralds from Persia, Flor-
entine gold work, teepees of ermine, Sevres china, bronze dromios,
old Persian velvets, Chinese lacquer carvings, black obsidian Dianas,
Britannia's sea unicorns, Egyptian vultures, Foo dogs, pine-lemurs,
etc. Whether these are, at the same time, all examples of what Moore
would understand as "natural," and value for their being so, is a
question worth pursuing.

THE VALUE OF NATURALNESS

"Naturalness" is a paramount value for Moore. Again and again
she judges art, artists, and other things and people by this one crite-

rion. Pound is accordingly praised for having "raised naturalness to an art" (CP, 587); and Shakespeare himself, characterized by an "elate and fearsome rightness" is only saved "from the offense of being 'poetic' by his well-nested effects of helpless naturalness" (CP, 398). To be natural is a good, to be poetic the opposite. As Moore writes in the first line of her famous poem "Poetry," "I, too, dislike it" (31), the antecedent of "it" being poetry itself.

What Moore dislikes about poetry—which is to say bad poetry or poetry lacking in naturalness—is its artificialness: "When we think we don't like art it is because it is artificial art" (CP, 398). It is elliptic, ostentatious, and self-conscious. It shows itself forgetful, says Moore (by way of Voltaire), that "[p]rincipally throat, sophistication is as / it al-// ways has been—at the antipodes from the initial great truths" ("In the Days of Prismatic Color," 49). Finally, Moore refuses the name of poetry to that which is deliberately pretentious, deliberately dark:

> It may be said of us all
> that we do not admire what we cannot understand
> enigmas are not poetry.
>
> ("Poetry," 31)

Naturalness, then, has much to do with honesty, with, in the case of Moore's cat, Peter, the matter of being one's self:

> What is the good of hypocrisy? It
> is permissible to choose one's employment, to abandon
> the wire nail, the
> roly-poly, when it shows signs of being no longer
> a pleas—
>
> ure, to score the adjacent magazine with a double line of
> strokes. He can
> talk, but insolently says nothing. What of it? When one
> is frank, one's very
> presence is a compliment. It is clear that he can see
> the virtue of naturalness . . .
>
> ("Peter," 52)

Criticism of Moore on the point of "naturalness" might appear unwarranted. After all, unlike Williams, she is never overly insistent with the trope of the imagination; she never puts forward her own concerns in all or nothing terms. She is, instead, attractively deferential and circumspect, and her concept of naturalness never offends.

Quite the contrary, for in its simplicity it has an extraordinary appeal and one has to force oneself back from it to see what a trope it is. Yet seeing this, one also begins to see just how much Moore's relation to the concept predicates itself upon trust, of just how much reliance she places upon her ability to discriminate between what is natural and what is not. The problem, for us, mostly follows from Moore's turning a personal value into something more universal. Moore too readily overlooks the concept's artifice and uses it to arbitrate worth in more instances than are warrantable. Thus when she says that she does not "like verse that is self-conscious and haughty" for the reason that she "think[s] we ought to be natural" (CP, 664), the reader is reminded of Kenner's questioning Pound's concept of exact definition, and wonders whether Moore does not too much beg the question with this discrimination, does not assume a too complete agreement as to what does and what does not constitute the "natural."

Perhaps Moore's most forced use of this value is found in her understanding of poetic voice. Here she adopts the rather uncritical stance that free verse is somehow inherently more natural than rhymed verse. In the 1916 essay "The Accented Syllable," Moore claims that "a distinctive tone of voice is dependent on naturalistic effects, and naturalistic effects are so rare in rhyme as almost not to exist" (CP, 34). Yet when one reads further, with the hope of learning what exactly makes for "naturalistic effects," one is disappointed, for what Moore offers is less a definition than an illustration: "By naturalistic effect I mean the sort of thing we have in Hamilton Sorley's 'Barrabas,' D. F. Dalston's 'Blown,' and Wallace Stevens' 'As Before'" (CP, 34). Needless to say, none of these poems seems to escape its time and place; each is as artificial as it is natural; and together they do not so much evidence Moore's remark as they call it into question.

And yet Moore critics continue to extoll the naturalness of her verse. For example, Margaret Holley, one of Moore's best readers, writes about "A Grave" and the effect of the poet's revisions:

> The effect of letting the phrasing have its way with the line is to remove a certain visceral evidence and to increase the sense of naturalness in the poem's appearance as written on the page. The fact that Moore changed such an insignificant fraction of her wording throughout these transformations (two or three phrases in an average of thirty lines) attests to the already natural flow of her poem as speech and to the visceral or written nature of her free verse form. "A Grave" looks quite different but sounds much the same as in its two incarnations, for with the help of the light

or inaudible rhyme, Moore had already achieved the "naturalistic effects" which she admired in 1916 in "The Accented Syllable."[22]

The irony here is that while the desire to be more "natural" propels Moore to write a kind of free verse, this verse is only verified as verse via reference to the printed page. This is, perhaps, even more true when the verse is less free than syllabic (wherein the syllabic pattern, or count, of the first stanza is mimicked in subsequent stanzas), and one can only acknowledge the pattern through *reading* the poem. Moore herself seemed, at least at first, to believe that the accents conveyed by this method would be so strong that they would resist any sort of verbal realignment, intended or not. She spoke of "that intonation in which the accents which are responsible for it are so unequivocal as to persist, no matter under what circumstances the syllables are read or by whom they are read . . . ; if an author's written tone of voice is distinctive, a reader's speaking tone of voice will not obliterate it" (CP, 32). But this is not true; if a reader does not obliterate the voice, he or she most definitely transforms it. In what fashion depends upon the reader, but no matter who this reader's listener may be, it seems clear that this person will need to return to the written page to appreciate the more formal aspects of Moore's poetry. And with this return to the page, what will most obtrude itself is less the "natural" than the artificial aspect of Moore's poetry.

THE VALUE OF IMAGINATION

The same reservations which I have expressed with regard to to Moore's celebration of the natural might also be extended to her extolling of the imagination, for here too she seems to embrace a debatable concept. Once more, the problem is that in Moore's hands, imagination, a working concept, begins to serve as a universal principle. Certainly, the concept is very important to Moore. Often she announces its value, praising Williams for his "acknowledgement of our debt to the imagination" (CP, 56), quoting Wallace Stevens when he says that "the imagination always makes use of the familiar to produce the unfamiliar" (CP, 443–44), and deferring to Kenneth Burke when he "speaks of the imagination as the most intensive province of pleasure and pain and defines it as a creative power of the mind, representing at pleasure the images of things in the order and manner in which they were received by the senses or in combining them in a new manner and according to a different order" (CP, 56). As Moore herself writes:

> In making works of art, the only legitimate warfare is the inevitable warfare between imagination and medium and one finds it impossible to convince oneself that the part of the artist's nature which is "rash and combustible" has not been tamed by the imagination, in those instances in which the result achieved is especially harmonious. (CP, 177)

Moore of course was not alone in celebrating the imagination. As her references make clear, many of her contemporaries, including Stevens and Williams, also thought it a given principle. Still, it is important for us to recognize the said principle of the imagination for what it is, a trope, a culturally and historically contingent concept, a successor to a line of figures (muse, spirit, afflatus, fancy) articulative of artistic invention, which finds its moment during an epoch in which the classical conceptions of time and space are accepted. This is evident, for instance, in Moore's last quoted statement, when she forcefully sets up an opposition between imagination and medium—mind and matter—the distance between the two being understood as a spatial distance—that is, as a spatial distance *alone*. (Time, a transcendent entity, is understood as equal for both.) Reality, here, is a stable thing, composed of an unchanging number of facts, all of which were capable of being ordered or conceived of from one point of view, that of the transcendent imagination. Imagination is not itself divinity; rather, for the modern individual living in an age of science, it stands in for divinity; it relieves one, proudly no longer superstitious, of having to think about Clockmakers even while it perpetuates the fiction that if all things are not seen by the eye of God, they are, nevertheless, seen by the eye of the Artist, the god manqué. Occasionally the space and time equation is reconceived—

> Time present and time past
> Are both perhaps present in time future,
> And time future contained in time past.
> (Eliot, "Burnt Norton")

—but for the most part, the classical schema holds up, and the artist is conceived of as the all-important recognizer of value in, and conferrer of value upon, things which are spatially distanced. Thus Moore can write: "the artist—the mind which creates what it needs for its own subsistences and propitiates nothing, willing—indeed wishing to seem to find its only counterpart in the elements" (CP, 80).

The world in all its disparateness stands before one. It is, from the modernist point of view, the ultimate fact, and when the artist, the metaphor-making animal, is not comparing the elements of one genus with that of another, he or she is, as Moore says, deferentially reserved, a stance often laden with strong emotion: "reserve is a concomitant of intense feeling, not the cause of it" (CP, 80). The deference itself follows from the assumption that What Is—the world—is identical with What Is True. Here, however, Truth presses itself forward less as an absolute—"Truth is no Apollo / Belverdere, no formal thing" ("In the Days of Prismatic Color," 50)—than as an equation of correspondence, as one thing being equal to another, as A is equal to B. Things appear to stand, more or less, in place, and art, accordingly, "'must praise all it can for being as for happening,'" for being itself is the point from which one starts. From this perspective, there are material things which have the quality or aspect of being first facts, and this leads to a situation in which the assertion "'every poem is'" might be said to be "'rooted in imaginative awe'" (CP, 506).

Awe itself is something that best expresses itself less in words than in silence. Words themselves always seem, no matter how well intended, to mask over or obscure the inspiring object. And yet silence, while perhaps the most fitting response, cannot be the poet's formal response, except as it locates itself in the work's interstices. In a sense, silence does this in Moore's work. For instance, one might take Moore's epigraph to her 1967 *Complete Poems*—"Omissions are not accidents"—not only as a statement having reference to that particular collection but also as a more general statement about her poetic practice. For Moore, omissions function as a sort of absent presence. Like the nightingale "with its silence—not its silence but its silences" ("Marriage," 76), omissions seem to determine meaning, the way for instance the tabled longer version of "Poetry" seems to determine our understanding of its shorter versions (including the version in *Observations*). There, we find a situation which prompted Hugh Kenner to wonder "[h]as a text ever before become a footnote to an excerpt from itself?"[23] Yet whether we prefer one version or the other, neither version can now be read without calling forth its other (or others, for there are more than two). Similarly, throughout Moore's work there exists the sense that the visible is always suggestive of the invisible, that, in Bonnie Costello's words, "[h]er indirection becomes an alternative form of intensification, the restraint that shows deep feeling, rather than a repression or sublimation of feeling."[24] In *Observations,* in addition to one's impression that this is so, one also finds Moore's testimony that she thinks it so. Thus in "Silence," Moore writes, "The deepest feeling always shows itself in silence; / not in silence, but restraint" (82). And in "England," praise is bestowed upon "The sublimated wisdom / of China, Egyptian discernment, the cataclysmic torrent of / emotion compressed / in the verbs of the Hebrew language," with the additional advice that "should one not have stumbled upon it in America, / must one imagine / that it is not there? It has never been confined to one locality" (58).

"Feeling at its deepest . . . tends," says Moore, "to be inarticulate" (CP, 396). It tends toward silence, or if not this, restraint. And here restraint often expresses itself as a faithfulness to the object. And as we saw with Stein, Hemingway, and Williams, a fidelity to the object often went hand in hand with the belief that representation could be pushed to the point of presentation and that the art object could aspire to the place of the given object, something that Moore is convinced takes place in Williams's poem "Struggle of Wings": "Likenesses here are not reminders of the object, they are it" (CP, 326). At the same time, there was a general recognition, predicated on the assumption of truth as correspondence, that while one thing (A) might be like or similar to another (B), or roughly $A = B$, it could never actually be that $(A \neq B)$, that the otherness of the object B was essentially inviolable. One might play with the idea that the word was, in fact, the thing (Eliot: "Language in its healthy state presents the object, is so close to the object that the two are identified.")[25] but all along one knew that the two were separate, distinct. Which is not to say, to refer back to the argument made in Wittgenstein's *Tractatus,* that many did not believe that there existed an invisible logic joining word with thing. Most did believe this, and the consequence of this belief is that quite a number of modernists tried to use language as if it were the focusing lens of a camera, the ambition being to line up a language along the sight line of the invisible connective which was logic in order to offer up something possessed of "an unbearable accuracy" (CP, 396). As Susan Sontag put the matter in *On Photography,* "A modernist would have to rewrite Pater's dictum that all art aspires to the condition of music. Now all art aspires to the condition of photography."[26] For Moore, meanwhile, this meant that while the "'ultimate poem'" might be "'beyond the rhetorician's touch,'" one did not stop trying to realize it.

The modernist approached the object via language. He or she demanded a stricter exactitude, the measure of account being the degree of correspondence felt to be extant between the planes of language and thing. Here, one might wish that the medium was something other than language (Moore: "[F]or anyone with 'a passion for actuality' there are times when the camera seems preferable to any other medium" [CP, 543]), the conversion of that which is composed of color, sound and structure into language not being the most easy thing. Still, language was flexible; it could be endlessly shaped and molded until that point when "'justice to the meaning'" (CP, 435), to the object, is done. As Moore said, this "implies restraint, that discipline is essential" (CP, 435). It also implies an intense concentration, "an impassioned perceptiveness" that sees the "governance of the emotions" (CP, 582) as a virtue claiming the way for "exact portrayal" (CP, 330). "At the *Dial*," Moore writes, "we talked about 'intensity' as a test for what purported to be art. What is the individual thing that lasts, that can not be counterfeited" (CP, 563). What is it but "an intensity which finds a way of surpassing intensity" (CP, 649), a precision which, faithful to the object, expresses it "so well that it could not be expressed better" (CP, 657). Or as Moore says in "An Egyptian Pulled Glass Bottle in the Shape of a Fish,"

> And art, as in a wave held up for us to see
> In its essential perpendicularity;
>
> Not brittle but
> Intense—

(20)

THE TECHNIQUE OF ORIGINALITY

To put things the way Moore does—that is, to speak in terms of precision, concentration, intensity, and a single best way of representing something—is to reveal just how predicated one's poetics are upon a belief in origins, a belief in disparate and autonomous things which, falling under the heading of "objects," exist at something like arm's length from that which thinks of itself as "subject." Like Stein, Hemingway, and Williams, what Moore offers us in her poetry are not natural objects which have somehow managed to free themselves of the dress of the poet's rhetoricity, not things-in-themselves, but their poetic constructs. They are not things which are original but a technique of originality, replete with rhetorical strategies designed to simulate the presence of things. Among these strategies are, first, handsomely delineated descriptions, often displaying scientific-like discriminations, as in the following lines from "Peter":

> Strong and slippery, built for the midnight grass-party con-
>   fronted by four cats,
> he sleeps his time away—the detached first claw on his
>   foreleg which corresponds
> to the thumb, retracted to its tip; the small tuft of fronds
>   or katydid legs above each eye, still numbering the
>   units in each group;
>   the shadbone regularly set about his mouth, to
>   droop or rise
>
> in unison like the porcupine's quills—motionless.
>
> (51)

Second, we encounter an emphatically paratactical syntax which celebrates the uniqueness of objects, either by arranging things in, so to speak, democratic and unhierarchical catalogues (as we have already had examples of in the lines quoted from "People's Surroundings") or by introducing things (linguistically symbolized by the *nomen substantivum*) by the definite article. Both are normative features of standard discourse, yet are used to the point of mannerism in Moore's poetry, as they are, together, in the following lines from "Dock Rats":

> On what a *river;* wide-twinkling like a
>   chopped *sea* under some
>   of *the* finest *shipping* in *the*
>
> *world: the* square-rigged *Flemish four master, the liner,*
>   *the battleship* like *the* two-
>   thirds submerged *section* of an *iceberg; the*
>   dipping and pushing, *the bell* striking as *it* comes;
>   *the*
>   *steam yacht,* lying
>   like a new made *arrow* on *the*
>
> *stream:* the *ferry-boat* a *head* assigned, one to each *com-*
>   *partment,* making
>   a *row* of *chessmen* set for play.
>
> (53; emphasis added)

Third, we find an ordering principle given over to "a classifying, a botanizing, a voracity of contemplation" (CP, 329). Moore, who likes the poetic imagination to the scientific, emphasizing that they both celebrate "the ability to see resemblances in things which are dissimilar" (CP, 65), is herself devoted to the discovery of a thing's differentiae, of those attributes which distinguish it from all other things, including members of its own classificatory family. As Moore writes, "in the ability to see . . . differences, a special kind of imagination is required" (CP, 56), most typified by her own poetry, wherein, as in "The Monkey Puzzler," a coniferous tree native to the Southern hemisphere is most amusingly and expertly classified:

> A kind of monkey or pine-lemur
>> not of interest to the monkey,
>> but to the animal higher up which resembles it,
>> in a kind of Flaubert's Carthage, it defies one—
>> this "Paduan cat with lizard," this "tiger in a bamboo
>
>> thicket."
>> "An interwoven somewhat," it will not come out,
>> Ignore the Foo dog and it is forthwith more than a dog,
>> its tail superimposed upon itself in a complacent half
> spiral,
>> incidentally so witty;
>> but this pine-tree—this pine-tiger, is a tiger, not a
> dog.

(30)

And finally, she makes a rich use of quotation which paradoxically celebrates origin even as it suggests that all things are "part of a series, a series of the original, a series that never existed."[27] In sum, what Moore's poetry most fabulously illustrates is Stanley Cavell's claim that "[t]here is a locale in which quotation becomes more original than its original,"[28] an observation (or shall we say a quotation) which recalls Wittgenstein's two levels of quotation: imitation and repetition. "In one we imitatively declare our uniqueness (the scheme of skepticism); in the other, we originally declare our commonness (the theme of acknowledgement)."[29] The question then is whether quotation speaks origin or origin speaks quotation, or both. Respecting the first formulation, Moore decidedly thinks this way, and said so several times:

"Why the many quotation marks?" I am asked. Pardon my saying more than once, When a thing has been said so well that it could not be said better, why paraphrase it? Hence my writing is, if not a cabinet of fossils, a kind of collection of flies in amber. (CP, 551)

Few have ventured to acknowledge their commonness to the degree that Moore does; few have been so original. Certainly, in *Observations*, "The deepest feeling always shows itself in silence; / not in silence, but" in quotation (82). Repeatedly, Moore borrows from her wide ranging readings, offerings quotations from both well knowns—e.g., Democritus, Duns Scotus, Isaiah, Hegel, Leigh Hunt, William Hazlitt, Anatole France, Anthony Trollope, Henry James, Pliny, Edmund Burke, Daniel Webster—and unknowns: Rev. J. W. Darr, Frank Alvah Parsons, Arthur Hayden, P. T. Forsyth, M. C. Carey. Likewise, source texts are both familiar—the *Bible, The Tempest, The Rape of the Lock, Philosophy of History*—and unfamiliar: *The Rockies of Canada*, "The Mystery of an Adjective and of Evening Clothes" (in the *London Graphic*), *Adventures in Bolivia, History of the Goths and Swedes*. Still, whether the quotations' antecedents be proud or not, Moore uses them to much the same purpose: to tell a truth; to return to etymon, to origin, much in the way she would purchase a certain kind of dictionary as a means of returning to "headquarters":

> Renouncing a policy of boorish indifference
> to everything that has been said since the days of Matilda,
> I shall purchase an Etymological Dictionary of Modern
>   English
> that I may understand what is written
> and like the ant and the spider
> returning from time to time to headquarters,
> shall answer the question
> as to "why I like winter better than I like summer"
>
> ("Bowls," 70)

Yet if Moore uses her quotations to tell a truth, she also seems to use them to deflect a truth. That is, if "poetry is not a thing of tunes, but of heightened consciousness" (CP, 590), there nevertheless remains a certain desire to pull up short, to settle for re-cognition as opposed to cognition. The reason follows from fear that the world, looked at directly, threatens us with its beauty; its exquisiteness is, at the same time, both immensely pleasurable and painful:

> Below the incandescent stars,
> below the incandescent fruit,
> the strange experience of beauty;

its existence is too much;
it tears one to pieces
and each fresh wave of consciousness
is poison.

("Marriage," 74)

Like Moore's conception of humility, quotation is, in effect, an "an armor, for it realizes that it is impossible to be original, in the sense of doing something that has never been thought of before" (CP, 420–21). As she notes elsewhere, "we adopt a thought from a group of notes in the song of a bird, from a foreigner's way of pronouncing English, from the weave in a suit of clothes. Our best and newest thoughts about color have been known to past ages" (CP, 328). And yet this said, origin still seems to find a way to speak through these things, to speak itself through quotation. "Originality," says Moore, "always comes in disguise,"[30] the sense being that "an indebted thing does not interest us unless there is originality underneath it" (CP, 328).

That there be such a thing as "origin" seems likely; that it is locateable "underneath" that which is "not-origin" seems less so. Co-presence seems a more fitting metaphor here, as the quest for origin is always something that throws us back into quotation or language. Moore seems both to act—and not act—as if this were the case. That is, she knows that origin *qua* origin always eludes us; yet she acts as if it were less something extant than as if it were something lost and perhaps even recoverable. So seems the case in the beautifully elegiac "In the Days of Prismatic Color," which begins

> Not in the days of Adam and Eve but when Adam
>   was alone; when there was no smoke and color was
> fine, not with the fineness of
> early civilization art but by virtue
> of its originality; with nothing to modify it but the
>
> mist that went up, obliqueness was a varia-
>   tion of the perpendicular, plain to see and
> to account for: it is no
>   longer that;

(49)

The consequence of all this is that when one takes the just mentioned four features—i.e., description, parataxis, classification, and quotation—and combines them with the somewhat coordinate interests in clarity, precision, "straight writing" ("this is my mania—the natural order of words, the subject, the predicate, and the object" [CP, 433]), and the trope of the natural, they together comprise Moore's technique of originality, her technique of presentation. She wishes to reveal things as they are, refusing to be diverted "from / what was originally one's / object—substance at the core" ("England," 57). And while she knows of the difficulties which adhere to such a project, she is nevertheless taken with the "love of doing hard things" ("An Octopus," 89), with "the transparent equation" ("Novices," 72). Poetry might never escape its rhetoricity, yet there are still "things that are important beyond all this fiddle" ("Poetry," 31), things which, so to speak, exist out there. And about them, Moore remains curious.

CURIOSITY AND A SACRED WORLD

Curiosity, then, is, for Moore, a value in itself. She esteems those who have it, like Edmund Burke—"Burke is a / psychologist—of acute, raccoon- / like curiosity" ("Picking and Choosing," 55)—and Henry David Thoreau: "Thoreau, you may recall, demurred when commended for originality and said that it was curiosity: 'I am curious from top to bottom'" (CP, 516). She associates it with the recognition of value: "Curiosity seems to me connected with this sense of significance" (CP, 516). Tied into this sense, of course, is the understanding that things have inherent value, that the poet does not so much make as discover value. The world is a rather stable place, and every object has a part to play in its story. Only inertia prevents one—the poet, in this instance—from recognizing the value of each disparate thing. The need, accordingly, is to reawaken ourselves to what is about us, to demonstrate an interest in things. Reviewing Williams's first *Collected Poems,* Moore, partly quoting Williams, writes: "The 'ability to be drunk with a sudden realization of value in things others never notice' can metamorphose our detestable reasonableness and offset a whole planetary system of deadness" (CP, 327). It causes "ordinariness to be clothed with extraordinariness" (CP, 194) and reminds us, once again, that like the work of Stein and Williams, Moore's art is one that would handle the world's things with a kind of religious reverence, an attitude attributable to their one-of-a-kindness and hence rarity, though in Moore, also attributable to religious belief itself. About the latter, Moore writes, "[t]he realm of the spirit is the only realm in which experience is able to corroborate the fact that the real can also be the actual" (CP, 74).

The religious attitude, shared by the four artists vis-à-vis objects, whether self-conscious or not, also shows up in their redemptive ambitions. Each speaks of a desire to rescue things from the fate of oblivion, as if this were possible or as if this were the only way to frame the problem of a thing's beingness. Things are considered sacred, though why they should be thought this way remains unclear. Their attitude, however, seems to have been also shared by the late English Victorians, something which the critic Valentine Cunningham takes note of:

> For a world stripped bare of transcendence seemed to demand from them a scrupulously mean writing, realistically attentive to things simply as they are. At the same time, their realistic fictions seemed to be smuggling the mythic back in by various side entrances, even granting a kind of post-transcendent otherness, a fetishistic or magical luminosity, to things as such. This kind of result became for some . . . a kind of programme, a post-sacramental sacramentalism.[31]

Meanwhile, Moore, who, given her more pronounced religious belief, probably has a better reason for thinking things sacred than say, a Stein or a Williams, whose sense of such (as the Valentine Cunningham quotation suggests) would be more vestigial, conceives of things almost requiring her attention. As I have quoted her as saying, Moore claims she does not think things so much as things think her—things demand to be rescued from the nameless flux. On her part, Moore never knows how long her engagements this way will last, never knows how long she will continue to find herself interested enough in things so as to make the effort needed to preserve them in art. Yet the interest and the responsibility appear not to stop: "When I have finished a thing it is, so far as I know, the last thing I shall write; but if taken unaware by what charms or stirs me up, I may write again" (CP, 648).

If then "'Ecstasy / affords / the occasion and expediency determines the form'" ("The Past is the Present," 32), one might say, "What a thing is the interested mind with the disinterested motive" (CP, 406)—that is, if one could believe any motive disinterested. Still, I like the idea, the celebration, in writing, of the "disinterested focused zeal" (CP, 632) aspiring to achieve a "quiet objectiveness" (CP, 420) wherein "something [is] so well expressed that it could not be better expressed" (CP, 657). And if any artist might move one, once again, to believing "that the writer's object is 'to render the highest kind of justice to the visible world'" (CP, 590), Moore, with her "impassioned interest in life" (CP, 516) and her "burning desire to objectify what it is indispensable to one's happiness to express" (CP, 507), is my candidate. I would, finally, pay Moore the compliment which she herself paid to Williams: "The poem often is about nothing that we wish to give our attention to, but if it is something [s]he wishes our attention for, what is urgent for [her] becomes urgent for us" (CP, 327).

Conclusion

In *Ferocious Alphabets,* his critique of contemporary literary theory, Denis Donoghue criticizes Hugh Kenner for grouping together, with the intention of reifying a single modernist poetics, writers such as Pound, Eliot, Joyce, Lewis, Williams, and Moore: "These writers are so different, one from another, their linguistic principles so diverse and divergent, that the attempt to make a single Modernism out of them is doomed."[1] Meanwhile, in *The Dance of the Intellect,* her critique of the Pound tradition, Marjorie Perloff, wishing perhaps to avoid a like accusation, broadens the concept of literary modernism to include two schools: The School of Stevens and The School of Pound. In the first, modernism means "MAKE IT OLD," which is to say that its antecedents are firmly rooted in Anglo-American Romanticism, "with a slight influx of French Symbolisms to add piquancy."[2] Such a poetics, writes Perloff, "takes the lyric paradigm for granted; it answers to the demand for organic unity and symbolic structure, avoiding all contact with the language of ordinary prose and therefore with the discourses of the novel and of historical writing" (21). In the second, modernism means "MAKE IT NEW." It represents not a continuation of the past into the present, but a distinct break from the past. "*Modernism,* in this context, means rupture—not, of course, with the distant past which must be reassimilated, but with all that has become established and conventional in the art of one's own time" (14). Stylistically, it sets itself in opposition to Romantic self-consciousness and the lyric, choosing instead to celebrate the objective properties of things-in-themselves, poetically rendered through the structural techniques of "collage, fragmentation, [and] parataxis" (22).

Perloff is not against choosing sides here; she clearly prefers Pound's poetics, thinking it more authentically modern (modernism here being defined as much by what was happening in the other arts as in literature itself). Thus, "[r]ead synchronically, against the backdrop of the avant-garde arts of Europe in the period *entre deux guerres,* Pound's strictures seem quintessentially modern. Read diachronically, against the paradigm of the Anglo-American lyric from Blake to Emerson to Emily Dickinson, Pound will seem, as he did

to Stevens, 'an eccentric person'" (23). Meanwhile, that only one of
the two schools should be conceived as "quintessentially modern"
appears equivalent to saying that what we have here is both a true
(Pound's) and false model (Stevens's) for modernism. The falseness
of Stevens's model is, perhaps, ameliorated by the acknowledgment
that it is actually Stevens's critics who make a bad situation worse:
"What matters, to Harold Bloom and Hillis Miller as to Frank Kermode and Helen Vendler, is Stevens's restatement, in chastened,
qualified, and ironic form, of the Romantic position, his Emersonian
(for Bloom) or Coleridgean (for Kermode) or Keatsian (for Vendler)
ethos" (14). And it is conceivable that the poet might be brought
back into the true modernist fold did we not have to deal with
his critics:

> A concordance of Stevens criticism, if there were such a thing, would
> probably show that the following words had a very high incidence: *being,
> consciousness, fiction, reality, self, truth.* These are, of course, Stevens's own
> words, and the poet's advocates have adopted them quite naturally. But
> it does not follow that they have some sort of absolute value as nodes
> of critical discourse. Certainly they are not the words we meet in discus-
> sion of the *Cantos.* (9)

Esteeming Pound's over Stevens's school, Perloff might be accused of simply inverting Bloom's judgment that "Modernism in
literature has not passed; rather, it has been exposed as never having
been there."[3] In either case—that is, whether one chooses to see
American poetics in this century as largely a continuation of the
Romantic (Bloom) or as the rupture of the Modern (Perloff)—one
practices a criticism of exclusion. Such exclusion, in the first instance, denies authentic canonical status to Pound's *Cantos* for the
reason that, in Perloff's words, they "violate . . . the norms of the
lyric, specifically the Romantic lyric," (17) and, in the second instance, consigns Eliot to limbo for the reason that his poetics seem
not easily categorizable: "Eliot's poetry does not fully pose the problem that came to obsess Modernism: whether poetry should be lyric
or collage, meditation or encyclopedia, the still moment or the jag-
ged fragment" (23).
Donoghue and Perloff are both excellent critics, and it is not my
purpose to contradict their understandings. At the same time, I wonder whether beneath the differences that distinguish the writers spoken of by Donoghue and Perloff there is not a structural subtext—
unspoken and perhaps also unconscious—which escapes even their
close scrutiny. For instance, to reach for a comparison, might we
not liken the dispute between Pound's and Stevens's modernism to,

say, the fourth-century debate between Homoiousian and Homoou-sian Christianity? There, too, the issues (whether Christ, as the son of God, was of like but different substance from the Father or whether He was consubstantial with the Father) were thought—and doubtless were—significant, even as what held these polar arguments together (the assumption that Christ was the Son of God) was, in fact, even more significant. It is this assumption, invisible and unaddressed by the opposing Homoiousian and Homoousian factions, which we now, distanced from the fray, register as the thing most important, the Homoiousian/Homoousian debate itself now appearing but an incidental matter.

Similarly, might not future historians find the debate between Stevens's (subjective) and Pound's (objective) poetics less interesting than those shared assumptions which did not get foregrounded, yet acted as determinants for all that did? Might they not come to see Pound's discussion of the distinction of the "subjective" Image and the "objective" Image—

> The Image can be of two sorts. It can arise within the mind. It is then "subjective." External causes play upon the mind, perhaps; if so, they are drawn into the mind, fused, transmitted, and emerge in an Image unlike themselves. Secondly, the Image can be objective. Emotion seizing upon some external scene or action carries it intact in the mind; and that vortex purges it of all save the essential or dominant or dramatic qualities, and it emerges like the external original. [4]

—as exemplifying the rule "[t]hat things change as one thinks them through logically and become their opposite."[5]

Granted, I, too, prefer one pole to the other, for like Perloff I, too, find myself more attentive to the "Objective" school, believing that it presents the problem of cognition in fresher dress and, more times than not, even presents itself as a successor to the "Subjective" school. (Hence Chapter I and the charting of the inversion of an Emersonian or Subjective poetics by a Jamesian or Objective poetics.) Still, for me, what is more interesting here is less the debate itself—i.e., subjective versus objective poetics—than the assumptions which give legitimacy to the debate. These frame the debate and determine what is, and what is not, discussable. And in the case of writers such as Stein, Hemingway, Williams, Moore, Pound, Eliot, Stevens, and the rest, one of the things which seems most discussable is the problem of cognition, the relation of the knower and his or her relation to what there is to be known, what there is out there, which assumes the status of the "object" in relation to the knower's "subject." That modernism might be conceived completely apart from the question of subject and object, I do not deny. That Stevens and Pound are different writers and that all kinds of fruitful discoveries may follow from this investigation of difference, I also do not deny. Still, when the question of cognition is foregrounded, I think we can say that while Stevens and Pound work differently, they also work alike; and what J. Hillis Miller writes about one—"The dialogue between subject and object is Stevens' central subject"[6]—might just as well be written about the other.

This said, it seems that we fool ourselves if we proceed too far with the notion that in a Poundian or imagistic poetics the subject ever truly dissolves itself. Perloff writes not without caution when she argues that "[i]f the 'I' becomes 'another,' the Romantic dualism of subject and object is resolved; the self no longer contemplates nature but becomes part of its operational processes."[7] Still, we want to remember that even as artists such as Pound, Stein, Hemingway, and Williams simulate, by means of a technique of originality, an objective poetics, theirs is nevertheless very much a story of the subject. What, after all, comes through in their poems and stories is just how seriously these people—these "Artists"—take themselves. The "Artist" is Ruler; and when Williams, speaking for them all, writes "that life becomes actual only when it is identified with ourselves. When we name it, life exists,"[8] he means it.

It is with this sense of things—i.e., that, respecting the issue of cognition, the "classical," the "modern," the "romantic," and the "post-romantic" can be read as variations upon a single theme or assumption—that the present essay has been constructed. What I have tried to attend to then has been the tradition of a problem: the problem of the artist attempting to know his or her world; the problem of subjects and objects; of minds and things. The focus, accordingly, is narrow, and the history offered is not a history of American literature but a history of this problem as it surfaces in American literature. It is, of course, but one history or narrative, one that I hope will be judged not by whether it tells the Truth but whether it tells a truth. There is no such thing as a reified narrative: the story of the event is not itself the event; and we make a mistake when, speaking of narratives, we use a term like "definitive." There are no definitive narratives; only good narratives and bad narratives. Good narratives are persuasive; they may, in fact, suggest definitiveness, yet the suggestion will turn upon not an act of substitution, of reification, but upon a host of favorable contingencies acting in conjunction with an inherent logic.

My argument posits that the received notion that the subject is fully present to itself and that there stands an objective world before

it, situated like one parallel plane next to its other, is one that, in
European and American intellectual discourse, holds good from
roughly the seventeenth century onward. Conjoined here is the argument that the writers studied in this essay work from this assumption, not truly questioning it even as, at times, they push the matter
so far that they undermine it. While it has been the aim of many a
literary history to see these writers as the vanguard of something
quite new, it is my aim to demonstrate that there is also a way in
which we can conceive these same writers as the rearguard of something (i.e., a discourse) not so new. In any case, art, for the most
part, seems to be understood here as a veridical ambition, celebrating
not only Truth, Self, Object, and Itself, but also notions like depth,
profundity, transparency, revelation, and silence. Art is performative; it is an act; the self manifesting itself in an intention. If there is
rupture, it is to be found in the rupturing of Silence, the first state.

What is to be understood here is that for this episteme and for
these artists, the world, in Heidegger's formulation, has become a
picture, something that is not the case today, at least not quite. The
decisive change here is predicated upon a prior change, that in the
individual's status. What is significant "is not that man frees himself
to himself from previous obligations, but that the very essence of
man itself changes, in that man becomes subject."[9] This change
("man" becoming subject) leads to the situation in which

> the world becomes picture, [wherein] what is, in its entirety, is juxta-
> posed as that for which man is prepared and which, correspondingly,
> he therefore intends to bring before himself and have before himself, and
> consequently intends in a decisive sense to set in place before himself.
> Hence world picture, when understood essentially, does not mean a
> picture of the world but the world conceived and grasped as a picture.[10]

For Stein, Hemingway, Williams, and Moore, the world is conceived as something at arm's length, out there, framed, waiting to
be known. This is not the same thing as saying that it depends upon
them. As Williams wrote in Spring and All, "reality needs no personal support but exists free from human action, as proven by science in the indestructibility of matter and of force."[11] It is, however,
to say that, through the artist, its factness—its metaphysical presence—is articulated and made known. This conception of things is
again articulated by Heidegger when he writes: "man sets himself
up as the setting in which whatever is must henceforth set itself
forth, must present itself [sich präsentieren], i.e., be picture. Man
becomes the representative [der Repräsentant] of that which is, in the
sense of that which has the character of object."[12]

That things are known is, of course, made manifest in language. Yet here language is not a troubled thing. Rather, language is—or is conceived to be—translucent, if not transparent: it mediates between subject and object; it bridges the gap. Poetically used, language would call attention to itself. Yet whether language was used this way (subjectively) or descriptively (objectively), it would still be implicated in the presencing of things; it would still be caught up in the activity of naming things. Which, in turn, reminds us of Stein's statement about what was learnt in the writing of *Tender Buttons:* "I began to discover the name of things, that is not discover the names but [to] discover the things to see the things to look at and in doing so I had of course to name them not to give them new names but to see that I could find out how to know that they were there by their names or by replacing their names."[13]

Poetics, conceived this way—that is, as bringing into presence, through naming, the anterior object—predicates itself upon the faith that "[e]very representation finds its genuine fulfillment . . . in the fact that what it represents is emphatically there,"[14] and celebrates recognition as a cognition of the truth, wherein "we do not differentiate between the representation and the represented,"[15] between the thing named and the thing. More than most, it is a poetics of adequation, of maximum accord between one thing (the image) and the other (the thing represented), the maximum which "cannot be represented by concepts but only in a singular presentation,"[16] a presentation which, in the case of the authors studied, privileges the present moment, the now which is thought indivisible and unique enough almost to be timeless. "This moment is the only thing in which I am interested,"[17] wrote Williams, believing, it seems, that if one could situate one's poetics between the walls of the individual moment, one could engage the object one to one, free of history, free of intellection, free of distortion. The thing was not to think the object but to see it, "to see the thing itself without forethought or afterthought but with great intensity of attention."[18]

Sight, accordingly, was the privileged sense, it being assumed, in Hegel's words, that "[v]ision finds itself in a purely theoretical relationship with objects,"[19] or, in Hans Jonas's, "seeing requires no perceptible activity either on the part of the object or on that of the subject. Neither invades the sphere of the other: they let each other be what they are and as they are."[20] That sight prioritized might be less than innocuous—that it might, for instance, give too much away to the impulse to distance, to objectify, to master the putative other—did not assume the weight of a concern, so impressed were the majority in the paradigm of representation and the metaphysics of presence. Respecting the latter, the radical materialism of a Stein, a Hemingway, or a Williams did not, denials aside, equate itself with the rejection of metaphysics. Metaphysics does not require deities and angels to be what it is: a giving credence to an absolutized, transcendental other. It evidences itself as much in Stein's conception of "things as they are" as in Hemingway's "the real thing" or in Williams's "world of fact." Or, as Derrida writes,

> It is not only idealism in the narrow sense that falls back upon the transcendental signified. It can always come to reassure a metaphysical materialism. It then becomes an ultimate referent, according to classical logic implied by the value of the referent, or it becomes an "objective reality" absolutely "anterior" to any work of the mark, the semantic content of a form of presence which guarantees the movement of the text in general from the outside.[21]

Meanwhile, if the distance between subject and object is maintained, even as the aesthetic project calls for its abolition, it no doubt has something to do with the celebration of the Imagination. Imagination might be (in Derrida's words) "the faculty of *presentation,*" yet while it is so, it altogether divides and conquers: consigning to one side all that is passive, inert and controllable; and to the other, all that is active, vital and controlling. As W. J. T. Mitchell, speaking to the point of imagery, observes: "Under the aegis of 'imagination' . . . the notion of imagery is split in two, and a distinction is made between the pictorial or graphic image which is a lower form— external, mechanical, dead, and often associated with the empiricist model of perception—and a 'higher' image which is internal, organic, and living."[22] The division between the subject and the object is maintained, as the first assumes its role of bestowing life upon the latter, bringing it forward, announcing its presence. Here presence is particularly established by the image. As used by a Stein or a Williams, "[t]he image," in Mitchell's words, "is the sign that pretends not to be a sign, masquerading as (or, for the believer, actually achieving) natural immediacy and presence."[23] It is "the real thing," achieved by a perspective which is thought to be objective, the product of a "terrific concentration," but which perhaps most gives itself away by "the way" (again I am quoting Mitchell) "it denies its own artificiality and lays claim to being a 'natural' representation of 'the way things look,' 'the way we see,' or 'the way things really are.'"[24] To "see," with Moore, "the virtue of naturalness" might appear an innocuous enough wish; yet it can readily enough become a prescription for difficulty if one presses too hard upon it, if one begins to act as if "naturalness" were a contingentless category, or if one begins to confuse the image with the thing it represents, to think, with Stein, that one can "express things not as one knows them but as they are when one sees them without remembering having looked at them."[25]

The most salient feature of this poetics, I have argued, is the belief that there exists something anterior to language, something original. The poetic project itself proceeds from a follow-up assumption: the belief that it is required of the artist to do justice to this "something." It leads to a poetics of originality, wherein representation is placed in the service of a theory of adequation. Mostly here representation was enough. Yet in the present century, one saw artists—Matisse, Cézanne, Pound, Stein, Hemingway, Williams, Moore, Zukofsky— who pressed the common assumption quite hard, who "experimented," we might say, with the language. Yet if they did experiment, they did so within certain bounds. And these bounds are best conceived as the bounds of representation. Certainly, each of the writers examined presses hard on the assumptions of this representation—each, it might be further stated, wishes to press representation to that ever receding point where it becomes presentation. The ambition is quixotic, and the artists must know this; yet the zeal with which they keep to the quest suggests that they themselves find it difficult to structure the artistic project along other lines or upon another assumption. They are captive to an episteme—an episteme which they do much to overturn or revolutionize yet which nevertheless plays a determinant role in what they produce.

In the case of Stein, Hemingway, Williams, and Moore, what they produce is less "the world" as it is found then the world as it is constructed, abetted by a set of assumptions which helps both to state and answer the questions, What is important? What is real? What is art? The answers revolve around the sense that the world is a distinctly stable and factual place; that it is the artist's responsibility to give voice to this place and to celebrate, more or less, its thereness. That there are limits as to what may be achieved this way—limits as to representation itself—is less admitted than sidestepped. It is particularly sidestepped by the invention of a technique of originality, a technique which simulates the presence of things without actually calling them forth. As exemplified in *Tender Buttons, In Our Time, Spring and All,* and *Observations,* it is a literary technique that circumscribes the area of attention by reducing the size of the canvas or frame. Here it is appropriate to borrow terms (canvas, frame) from painting for the reason that each of these works is, to some extent, modeled on the form of the still life, modeled not only in the sense that visual and tactile values are celebrated, but also in the sense that vision is circumscribed, concentrated, intent simply on letting something be there without trying to do anything more with it. In specifically literary terms, this translates into a technique which is unusually reliant upon the *nomen substantivum*, parataxis, catalogs, the temporal present and the suppression of the poetic "I" (even as it celebrates the "I" as eye). In short, it translates into an attempt to suppress the literary in favor of the object, the belief being that the thing has a value all its own, one which the artist feels duty bound to discover. Metaphysics might be dead (or thought dead) but things remain holy.

Perhaps we still think things are holy. Perhaps the assumptions which Stein, Hemingway, Williams, and Moore bring to their art are not very much different from those which artists today bring to theirs. (A point, with reference to the classical *trivium*, which I made in the first chapter.) Still, there appears to be reason for believing that a discernible shift in our assumptions has taken place, that the belief that art is a vertical, veridical act of discovery has been elbowed aside by one that sees the literary project in more "letteral" terms: not as an experience that seeks to get beyond language but as an experience that locates its pleasure precisely in language; as an exploration of "language itself, . . . a horizontal investigation of the polysemous meanings simultaneously available in the words themselves—in etymologies and puns—and in the things the words name."[26] Or, if this is overstating the case, might we simply say that what has most fundamentally changed is our understanding of language's relation to the "real." That language and the real are implicated in one another we now take as a given, something that we have not always done. Certainly, Stein, Hemingway, Williams, and Moore did not appear to begin with this assumption; and yet the fact that we do is perhaps in no small way due to writers such as they who so persistently pressed forward the possibilities of one description that they cleared the way for another.

Notes

CHAPTER 1. THE PROBLEMS OF REPRESENTING AN AMERICAN LITERARY MODERNISM

1. Paul de Man, *Resistance to Theory* (Minneapolis: University of Minnesota Press, 1986), 13. (All subsequent references to this text will be indicated by the abbreviation RT.)

2. The descriptions of both logic and grammar are found in Christopher Norris, *What's Wrong With Postmodernism: Critical Theory and the Ends of Philosophy* (Baltimore: Johns Hopkins University Press, 1990), 116.

3. De Man writes, "Rhetoric, by its actively negative relationship to grammar and to logic, certainly undoes the claims of the *trivium* (and by extension, of language) to be an epistemologically stable construct" (RT, 17).

4. Quoted in Paul de Man, "The Epistemology of Metaphor," *Critical Inquiry*, 5, no. 1 (Autumn 1978): 15.

5. Ludwig Wittgenstein, *Philosophical Investigations*, trans. G. E. M. Anscombe (1953; reprint, Oxford: Basil Blackwell, 1981), 138.(All subsequent references to this text will be indicated by the abbreviation PI.)

6. Wallace Stevens, *The Necessary Angel: Essays on Reality and the Imagination*. (New York: Vintage, 1951), 20. (All subsequent references to this text will be indicated by the abbreviation NA.)

7. Ludwig Wittgenstein, *Tractatus Logico-Philosophicus*, trans. C. K. Ogden (1922; reprint, London: Routledge, 1990), 22. (All subsequent references to this text will be indicated by the abbreviation T.)

8. Quoted in Brian McGuinness, *Wittgenstein: A Life* (Berkeley: University of California Press, 1988), 100.

9. See Jacques Derrida, "How to Avoid Speaking," in *Language of the Unsayable*, eds. Sandford Budick and Wolfgang Iser (New York: Columbia University Press, 1989). In response to Wittgenstein's command that we be silent respecting that which we cannot clearly articulate, Derrida writes,

> The nature of this "one must" . . . is significant here: it inscribes the injunction to silence into the order or the promise of a "one must speak," "one must—not avoid speaking"; or rather, "it is necessary . . . that there be a trace." No "it is necessary that there have been a trace," a sentence that one must simultaneously turn toward a past *and* a future that are as yet unpresentable. (11)

10. Quoted in McGuinness, 288. The difficulty of delimiting the bounds of semantic meaning are poignantly testified to in the short correspondence which Wittgenstein had with Gottlob Frege, the German logician whom the younger man hoped would serve as a mentor. After reading the *Tractatus*, Frege wrote Wittgenstein, saying, "You see from the very beginning I find myself entangled in doubt as to what you want to say, and so make no proper headway":

Right at the beginning I come across the expression 'is the case' and 'fact' and I suspect that *is the case* and *is a fact* are the same. Is not every fact the case and is not that which is the case a fact? Is it not the same if I say, A is a fact, A is the case? Why then this double expression? Now comes a third expression: "What is the case, a fact, is the existence of *Sachverhalte*." I take this to mean that every fact is the existence of a *Sachverhalt*. Couldn't one delete the words "existence of" and say "every fact is a *Sachverhalt*, every other fact is another *Sachverhalt*." Could one perhaps also say, "Every *Sachverhalt* is the existence of a fact?" (Quoted in Ray Monk, *Ludwig Wittgenstein: The Duty of Genius* [New York: The Free Press, 1990], 163.)

11. Quoted in McGuinness, 245.

12. Paul de Man, "Hegel on the Sublime," in *Displacement: Derrida and After*, ed. Mark Krupnik (Bloomington: Indiana University Press, 1983), 148.

13. Gertrude Stein, *Tender Buttons* (1914; reprint, Los Angeles: Sun & Moon, 1991); Ernest Hemingway, *In Our Time* (1925; reprint, New York: Scribner, 1970); William Carlos Williams, *Spring and All*, in *The Collected Poems of William Carlos Williams, vol. 1 (1909–1939)*, eds. A. Walton Litz and Christopher MacGowan (New York: New Directions, 1986); and Marianne Moore, *Observations* (New York: The Dial Press, 1925).

14. George Steiner, *Real Presences: Is There Anything in What We Say?* (Chicago: University of Chicago Press, 1989).

15. Roland Barthes, "The Death of the Author," in *The Rustle of Language*, trans. Richard Howard (Berkeley: University of California Press, 1989), 53. My discussion of the author here is indebted to Marilyn Edelstein's unpublished essay, "Authors: Implied, Extrafictional, and 'Real.'"

16. Donald Davidson, *Essays on Actions and Events* (Oxford: Clarendon Press, 1980), 255. Terry Eagleton says something similar: "Understanding my intention is grasping my speech and behaviour in relation to a significant context. When we understand the 'intentions' of a piece of language, we interpret it as being in some sense *oriented*, structured to achieve certain effects; and more of these can be grasped apart from the practical conditions in which the language operates." Quoted in Linda Hutcheon, *A Poetics of Postmodernism: History, Theory, Fiction* (London: Routledge, 1988), 81–82.

17. W. K. Wimsatt and Monroe C. Beardsley, *The Verbal Icon* (Lexington: University of Kentucky Press, 1954), 5. Perhaps a more reasonable way to understand this posited quality of the text's objectivity is offered by Anthony Giddens ("Action, Subjectivity, and Meaning," in *The Aims of Representation: Subject/Text/History*, ed. Murray Krieger [New York: Columbia University Press, 1987], 173):

[I]t should be stressed—again as [Paul] Ricouer says—texts become distanciated from their authors. The concept of textual distanciation can be usefully substituted, in most respects, for that of the autonomy of the text. What this means . . . is that texts have a relative autonomy from the context of their production; but that there is a two-way relation of interpretation which needs to be accomplished between the analysis of the conditions of their original production and the meanings which can be glanced from them in other conditions. It is only, of course, in such a manner that we can speak of "distanciation" at all, since this presumes that we have some notion of the "distance" which a text has traveled from the initial conditions of its generation.

18. Michel Foucault, "What Is an Author?," trans. Josué V. Harari, in *The Foucault Reader*, ed. Paul Rabinow (New York: Pantheon, 1984), 102–3.

19. Milan Kundera, *The Art of the Novel*, trans. Linda Asher (New York: Grove Press, 1988), 25.

20. Davidson, *Essays*, 258.

21. Foucault asks the question in "What Is an Author?," 120; Cheryl Walker, "Feminist Literary Criticism and the Author," *Critical Inquiry* (Spring 1990), 557.

22. Paul de Man, *Blindness and Insight* (New York: Oxford University Press, 1971), 25.

23. Quoted in Robert Scholes, *Protocols of Reading* (New Haven: Yale University Press, 1989), 71.

24. Jacques Derrida, "'Eating Well,' or the Calculation of the Subject: An Interview with Jacques Derrida," in *Who Comes After the Subject?*, eds. Eudardo Cadava, Peter Connor, and Jean-Luc Nancy (New York: Routledge, 1991), 111.

25. Michel Foucault, *The Order of Things: An Archaeology of the Human Sciences* (1971; reprint, New York: Vintage, 1973). (All subsequent references to this text will be indicated by the abbreviation O.)

26. Richard Rorty is most identified with the concept of conversation. See his *Philosophy and the Mirror of Nature* (Princeton: Princeton University Press, 1979), 170; The phrase "finished signified" is Jacques Derrida's: "These [Marxist] texts are not to be read according to a hermeneutical or exegetical method which would seek out a finished signified beneath a textual surface." *Positions,* trans. Alan Bass (Chicago: University of Chicago Press, 1982), 63.

27. David Couzens Hoy, "Foucault: Modern or Postmodern?," in *After Foucault,* ed. Jonathan Arac (New Brunswick, N.J.: Rutgers University Press, 1988), 14–15.

28. Michel Foucault, *The Archaeology of Knowledge,* trans. A. M. Sheridan Smith (New York: Pantheon Books, 1972), 47–48.

29. Richard Rorty, "Foucault and Epistemology," in *Foucault: A Critical Reader,* ed. David Couzens Hoy (Oxford: Basil Blackwell, 1986), 43.

30. For example, in "Nietzsche, Genealogy, History," Foucault writes,

[T]he historical sense can invade metaphysics and become a privileged instrument of genealogy if it refuses the certainty of absolutes. Given this, it corresponds to the acuity of a glance that distinguishes, separates, and disperses; that is capable of liberating divergence and marginal elements—the kind of dissociating view that is capable of decomposing itself, capable of shattering the unity of man's being through which it was thought that he could extend his sovereignty to the event of his past. (In *Language, Counter-Memory, Practice: Selected Essays and Interviews,* [Ithaca: Cornell University Press, 1977] 152–53.)

31. Jürgen Habermas, *The Philosophical Discourse of Modernity: Twelve Lectures,* trans. Frederick Lawrence (Cambridge: MIT Press, 1987), 268.

32. Scholes, 71.

33. See Jean-François Lyotard, *The Postmodern Condition: A Report on Knowledge,* trans. Geoff Bennington and Brian Massumi (Minneapolis: University of Minnesota Press, 1984).

34. Jacques Derrida, *Writing and Difference,* trans. Alan Bass (Chicago: University of Chicago Press, 1978), 280.

35. Jean Baudrillard, "The Precession of Simulacra," in *Art After Modernism: Rethinking Representation,* ed. Brian Wallis (New York: New Museum of Contemporary Art, 1984), 254. About this matter of "liquidation," Derrida, wisely I think, says:

I wouldn't agree to enter into a discussion where it was imagined that one knew what the subject is, where it would go without saying that this "character" is the same for Marx, Nietzsche, Freud, Heidegger, Lacan, Foucault, Althusser, and others, who would somehow all be in agreement to "liquidate" it. For me, the discussion would begin to get interesting when, beyond the vested confusion of this *doxa,* one gets to a more serious more essential question. For example, if throughout all these different strategies the "subject," without having been "liquidated," has been re-interpreted, displaced, decentered, re-inscribed, then, first: what becomes of those problematics that seemed to presuppose a classical determination of the subject (objectivity, be it scientific or other—ethical, legal, political, etc.), and second: who or what "answers" to the question "who"? ("'Eating Well,'" 98)

36. Roland Barthes, *Image Music Text*, trans. Stephen Heath (New York: Hill & Wang, 1977), 124.

37. Quoted in Christopher Norris, *Paul de Man: Deconstruction and the Critique of Aesthetic Ideology* (London: Routledge, 1988), 71.

38. De Man, *Blindness and Insight*, 162.

39. J. Hillis Miller, *Versions of Pygmalion* (Cambridge: Harvard University Press, 1990), 75.

40. Rodolphe Gasché, "In-Difference to Philosophy: de Man on Kant, Hegel, and Nietzsche," in *Reading de Man Reading*, eds. Lindsay Waters and Wlad Godzich (Minneapolis: University of Minnesota Press, 1989), 273. Elsewhere, Brook Thomas writes,

> My problem with de Man's argument is not the implication that the attempt to construct a permanent rational foundation for historical investigations is doomed to failure. It is instead the implication that because those investigations are forced to rely on inherently unreliable language they cannot get started until they have answered fundamental questions that by nature are unanswerable. We are being prodded not only continually to reinvent the wheel, but also to invent it knowing that it will be asked to serve the function of a firm and stationary foundation. Meanwhile, numerous other questions of historical importance go unexplored. (*The New Historicism: and Other Old-Fashioned Topics* [Princeton: Princeton University Press, 1991], 74–75.)

41. Barbara Johnson, interviewed in Imre Salusinszky, *Criticism in Society* (New York: Methuen, 1987), 163.

42. Lillian S. Robinson, for instance, writes:

> In marking off 'the Renaissance,' say, as a historical epoch, historians are already making a statement about its existence as a positive era. So if we ask, as [Joan] Kelly herself does in the title of another well-known essay, "Did Women Have a Renaissance?" we are questioning not only whether the centuries usually encompassed by the acrobatically flexible term "Renaissance period" were salutary for women, but also, if they were not, what sense it makes to talk about them as constituting a meaningful period. ("Sometimes, Always, Never: Their Women's History and Ours," *New Literary History*, Vol. 21, No. 2 [Winter 1990], 380.)

43. Frank Kermode, *History and Value* (Oxford: Clarendon Press, 1989), 123. Also, Walter Benjamin, in *Arcades Project*, writes:

> For the materialist historian, every epoch with which he occupies himself is only a fore-history of that which really concerns him. And that is precisely why the appearance of repetition doesn't exist for him in history, because the moments in the course of history which matter most to him become moments of the present through their index as "fore-history," and change their characteristics according to the catastrophic or triumphant determination of that present. (Quoted in Jonathan Crary, *Techniques of the Observer: On Vision and Modernity in the Nineteenth Century* [Cambridge: MIT Press, 1990], xii.)

44. Quoted in Kermode, 123.

45. Frank Kermode writes,

> My contention is that the forces which control our treatment of history in general are the same forces which insist that we think in terms of period, and, especially when the documents are literary, in terms of canon. That the choices made in all these fields are controlled by the desires of the mind and even by the desires of power I cannot contest, though conscience may also have its part. (125)

46. Cecelia Tichi writes that Henry James, along with William Dean Howells and Jack London, "engaged the figure of the new woman; but they portrayed her, like Mr. Dooley's Molly, as an upstart or rebel who would be brought to heel by male authority and by her susceptibility to fashion, frippery, and, above all, social convention." "Women Writers and the New Woman," in *Columbia History of the United States,* ed. Emory Elliott (New York: Columbia University Press, 1988), 593.

Meanwhile, with respect to the way in which our classifications determine our literary histories as much as they are the product of the same, I would refer the reader to David Perkins's fine essay "Literary Classifications: How Have They Been Made?" (in *Theoretical Issues in Literary History,* ed. David Perkins [Cambridge: Harvard University Press, 1991]) and particularly to the following paragraph:

> Wittgenstein's famous remark on "family resemblance" are relevant to these dilemmas [of classification] but do not resolve them. When we align a number of instances under the same concept, the reason is not, Wittgenstein says, because they share an "essence," but because of "a complicated network of similarities of detail." Texts are grouped together when they exhibit a number of features that belong to the set, even if they also have anomalous features. But as Wittgenstein clearly says, before we look for "family resemblance," we assume there is a "family": "Don't look for similarities in order to justify a concept, but also for connections. The father transmits his name to his son even if the latter is quite unlike him." In other words, the taxonomy is prior to our observation and comparison of individuals, and is based on "external facts" of filiation. (260–61)

47. Paul Smith, *Discerning the Subject* (Minneapolis: University of Minnesota Press, 1988), 86.

48. Quoted in Miles Orvell, *The Real Thing: Imitation and Authenticity in American Culture, 1880–1940* (Chapel Hill: University of North Carolina Press, 1989), 220, 219.

49. The terms "megalography" (i.e., "the depiction of those things in the world which are great—the legends of the gods, the battles of heroes, the crises of history") and "rhopography" (i.e., "from *rhopos,* trivial objects, small wares, trifles") are borrowed from Norman Bryson's incisive discussion of still-life painting in *Looking at the Overlooked: Four Essays on Still Life Painting* (Cambridge: Harvard University Press, 1990).

50. Bryson, 65.

51. Charles Altieri, "'Ponderation' in Cézanne and Williams," *Poetics Today,* 10, no. 2 (Summer 1989), 382.

52. Virginia Woolf, *To the Lighthouse* (1927; reprint, New York: Harcourt Brace Jovanovich, 1955), 299–300. Also, Wallace Stevens quotes, in *The Necessary Angel,* a Cézanne letter to Emile Bernard, to similar effect:

> I am able to describe to you again . . . the realization of that part of nature which, coming into our line of vision, gives the picture. Now the theme to develop is that—whatever our temperament or power in the presence of nature may be—we must render the image of what we see. (47)

53. Roland Barthes, *Camera Lucida,* trans. Richard Howard (New York: Hill and Wang, 1981), 87, 88.

54. Barthes, 76–77.

55. Walter Benjamin, *Illuminations,* trans. Harry Zohn (New York: Schocken, 1969), 221.

56. Quoted in Orvell, 278.

57. Quoted in Orvell, 222–23.

58. Quoted in Orvell, 220.
59. Marianne Moore, *The Complete Prose of Marianne Moore,* ed. Patricia C. Willis (New York: Viking, 1986), 543.
60. Quoted in Carlos Baker, *Hemingway: The Writer as Artist,* 4th ed. (Princeton: Princeton University Press, 1972), 64.
61. William Carlos Williams, *Selected Essays* (1954; reprint, New York: New Directions, 1962), 266.
62. Gertrude Stein, *Picasso* (1938; reprint, Boston: Beacon Press, 1959), 35.
63. Matei Calinescu writes,

Modernity in the broadest sense, as it has asserted itself historically, is reflected in the irreconcilable opposition between the sets of values corresponding to (1) the objectified, socially measurable time of capitalist civilization (time as a more or less precious commodity, bought and sold on the market), and (2) the personal, subjective, imaginative durée, the private time created by the unfolding of the "self." The latter identity of time and self constitutes the foundation of modernist culture. (In *Five Faces of Modernity: Modernism, Avant-Garde, Decadence, Kitsch, Postmodernism* [Durham: Duke University Press, 1987], 5.)

64. Quoted in Orvell, 203.
65. Quoted in Orvell, 199.
66. Susan Sontag, *On Photography* (New York: Anchor Books, 1990), 22–23. Sontag also makes the connection between photography and a modern poetics:

The ethos of photography—that of schooling (in Moholy-Nagy's phrase) in "intensive seeing"—seems closer to that of modernist poetics than that of painting. As painting has become more and more conceptual, poetry (since Apollinaire, Eliot, Pound, and William Carlos Williams) has more and more defined itself as concerned with the visual. ("No truth but in things," as Williams declared.) Poetry's commitment to concreteness and to the autonomy of the poem's language parallels photography's commitment to pure seeing. Both imply discontinuity, disarticulated forms and compensatory unity: wrenching things from their context (to see them in a fresh way), bringing things together elliptically, according to the imperious but often arbitrary demands of subjectivity. (95–96)

67. The phrase is Emile Zola's, and is expanded into a working concept designed to illuminate Paul Cézanne's own artistic interest in origins, by Richard Shiff in *Cézanne and the End of Impressionism: A Study of the Theory, Technique, and Critical Evaluation of Modern Art* (Chicago: University of Chicago Press, 1984). The study is an important influence on the present essay.

CHAPTER 2. SHIFTING PARADIGMS: EMERSON, JAMES, AND HULME

1. Ralph Waldo Emerson, "Nature," in *Ralph Waldo Emerson: Essays & Lectures* (New York: Library of America, 1983), 7. (All subsequent references to this text will be indicated by the abbreviation N.)
2. Ralph Waldo Emerson, *The Selected Writings of Ralph Waldo Emerson,* ed. Brooks Atkinson (1940; reprint, New York: Modern Library, 1968), 93.
3. Immanuel Kant, *Critique of Pure Reason,* trans. F. Max Muller (New York: Anchor-Doubleday, 1966), 21–22.
4. Quoted in Charles Feidelson, Jr., *Symbolism and American Literature* (1953; reprint, Chicago: University of Chicago Press, 1983), 120.
5. Kant writes,

The transcendental conception . . . of all phenomena in space, is a critical warning that nothing which is seen in space is a thing by itself, nor space a form of things supposed to belong to them by themselves, but that objects by themselves are not known to us at all, and that what we call external objects are nothing but representations of our senses, the form of which is space, and the true correlation of which, that is the thing by itself, is not known, nor can be known by these representations, nor do we care to know anything about it in our daily experience. (28)

6. Quoted in Leon Chai, *The Romantic Foundations of the American Renaissance* (Ithaca: Cornell University Press, 1987), 64.
7. Ernst Cassirer, *The Philosophy of Symbolic Forms,* vol. 1, trans. Ralph Manheim (1923; reprint, New Haven: Yale University Press, 1977), 161.
8. Ralph Waldo Emerson, "Plato; or, The Philosopher," in *The Selected Writings of Ralph Waldo Emerson,* 492.
9. Kant writes,

The solution of this problem (of pure reason), or a sufficient proof that a possibility which is to be explained does in reality not exist at all, is the question of life or death to metaphysics. David Hume, who among all philosophers approached nearest to that problem, though he was far from conceiving it with sufficient definiteness and universality, confining his attention only to the synthetical proposition of the connection of an effect with its causes *(principium causalitatis),* arrived at the conclusion that such a proposition *a priori* is entirely impossible. According to his conclusions everything which we call metaphysic would turn out to be a mere delusion of reason, fancying that it knows by itself what in reality is only borrowed from experience, and has assumed by mere habit the appearance of necessity. If he had grasped our problem in all its universality, he would never have thought of an assertion which destroys all pure philosophy, because he would have perceived that, according to his argument, no pure mathematical science was possible either, on account of its certainly containing synthetical propositions *a priori;* and from such an assertion his good sense would have saved him. (13)

10. Herman Melville, writing in his journal, described this Kantian argument as it was explained to him by a friend, George J. Adler:

He believes that there are things *out* of God and independent of him—things that would have existed were there no god:—such as that two and two make four, for it is not that God so decrees mathematically but that in the very nature of things, the fact is thus. (Quoted in Leon Howard, *Herman Melville* [Berkeley: University of California Press, 1951], 140.)

11. Kant, p. 76.
12. John Randall, "The Changing Import of Darwin on Philosophy," in *Darwin,* ed. Philip Appleman (New York: Norton, 1970), 420.
13. Charles Darwin, *The Origin of Species,* in *Darwin,* ed. Philip Appleman (New York: Norton, 1970), 152.
14. Stephen Kern, *The Culture of Time and Space, 1808–1918* (Cambridge: Harvard University Press, 1983), 37.
15. Bruce Kuklick, *The Rise of American Philosophy: Cambridge, Massachusetts, 1860–1930* (New Haven: Yale University Press, 1977), 1.
Meanwhile, Richard Rorty writes,

After Darwin, it became increasingly difficult to use the notion of "experience" in the sense Kant had tried to give it. For Darwin, by making Spirit continuous with Nature, completed the historicizing process which Hegel had begun. So those who wanted to preserve the notion of philosophy as a nonempirical science *relativized* the Kantian *a priori.* . . . They tried to keep intact the notion of a distinction between the formal and the material—the domain of philosophy and the domain of natural science. But this relativizing cast doubt on the notion of a "transcendental standpoint," and thus on the notion of "possible experience" as something the conditions of which could be specified. For a plurality of forms of experience or forms of consciousness looks much like a plurality of actualities, each of which may be presumed to have casual, naturalistically explicable conditions. Further, if the *a priori* could change, then it is no longer *a priori* enough, for philosophical arguments can no longer culminate in immutable, apodeictic truths. (*Essays on Heidegger and Others* [Cambridge: Cambridge University Press, 1991], 53.)

16. John Dewey,"The Influence of Darwin on Philosophy," in *Darwin*, ed. Philip Appleman (New York: Norton, 1970), 394.

17. Kuklick, 9.

18. Anonymous quotation in Kuklick, 24.

19. Charles Peirce, *Selected Writings,* ed. Philip P. Wiener (New York: Dover, 1966), 189.

20. Richard Rorty, *Philosophy and the Mirror of Nature* (Princeton: Princeton University Press, 1979), 165.

21. A discussion of this group is provided in Kuklick, chapter 3.

22. Kuklick, 49.

23. Peirce, 182.

24. Peirce, 181.

25. Peirce, 124.

26. Peirce, 107–8.

27. Ralph Waldo Emerson, "Experience," in *The Selected Writings of Ralph Waldo Emerson,* 359.

28. Ralph Waldo Emerson, "Experience," 359.

29. Peirce, 153.

30. Peirce, 197.

31. Peirce, 196. Respecting the tendency to idealize language in twentieth-century thought, Richard Rorty writes,

"Language" was the twentieth-century philosopher's substitute for [Kantian] "experience" for two reasons. First, the two terms had an equally large scope—both delimited the entire domain of human inquiry, of topics available to human study. Second, the notions of "language" and "meaning" seemed, at the beginning of the century, immune to the naturalizing process. . . .
Philosophy of language . . . was supposed to produce conditions of describability. . . . Describability . . . was supposed to be the mark of everything studied or exemplified by all areas of study other than philosophy. Language seemed able to avoid relativization to history, for description was thought to be a single indissoluble activity, whether done by Neanderthals, Greeks, or Germans. If one could give *a priori* conditions of the activity of description, then one would be in a position to offer apodeictic truths. (*Essays on Heidegger and Others* [Cambridge: Cambridge University Press, 1991], 53.)

32. William James, *Pragmatism,* ed. A. J. Ayer (1907; reprint, Cambridge: Harvard University Press, 1978), 31. (All subsequent references to this text will be indicated by the abbreviation P.)

In *Poetry and Pragmatism* (Cambridge: Harvard University Press, 1992), Richard Poirier offers statements from Peirce that suggest the link between him and James was not completely happy. The first is in a 1905 letter to Mrs. Ladd-Franklin: "Although James calls himself a pragmatist, and no doubt derived his ideas on the subject from me, yet there is a most essential difference between his pragmatism and mine." The second occurs in the same year, in an essay in *Monist*: "So then, the writer, finding his bantling 'pragmatism' so promoted, feels that it is time to kiss his child good-by and relinquish it to its higher destiny; while to serve the precise purpose of expressing the original definition, he begs to announce the birth of the word 'pragmaticism,' which is ugly enough to be safe from kidnappers" (5).

33. Quoted in Kuklick, 272.

34. William James, *Essays in Radical Empiricism,* ed. Richard J. Bernstein (1909; reprint, New York: Dutton, 1971), 24. (All subsequent references to this text will be indicated by the abbreviation RE.)

35. Quoted in Kuklick, 323–24.

36. William James, *The Principles of Psychology,* vol. 2. (New York: Henry Holt, 1893) 6. (All subsequent references to this text will be indicated by the abbreviation *Psych.*)

37. Quoted in Denis Donoghue, *Reading America* (New York: Alfred A. Knopf, 1987), 182.

38. José Ortega y Gasset, quoted in Kern, 218. The quotation is bracketed by Kern's own remarks.

39. Wallace Stevens, *The Necessary Angel: Essays on Reality and the Imagination* (New York: Vintage-Random House, 1951), 138. Fredric Jameson argues Stevens's position here somewhat differently, saying first that "the subject–object framework of Stevens' poetic practice . . . [is] rigorously epistemological in all the worst senses of this word. In Stevens we never have anything but an abstract subject contemplating an object world which is thereby constructed as being abstract" (179). But then Jameson qualifies his remarks, suggesting that Stevens's poetics is, in fact, less attentive to objects than to language itself, and hence is postmodern: "[A]s damaging as the restriction to an epistemological framework may be, we must here too immediately add the qualification that somehow, again in ways that remain to be determined, Stevens' poetry manages to transcend the limits of traditional epistemology: here, as in the gradual foregrounding of the theme of language in his work, he may best be read as registering a process analogous to that we will observe in French 'structuralism,' namely a dissolution of the older epistemological subject-object framework, which is bought at the cost of a certain reification of 'Language.'" ("Wallace Stevens," in *Critical Essays on Wallace Stevens,* eds. Steven Gould Axelrod and Helen Deese [Boston: G. K. Hall, 1988], 179–80.)

40. Denis Donoghue, *The Sovereign Ghost* (Berkeley and Los Angeles: University of California Press, 1976), 7.

41. Frank Lentricchia, *Ariel and the Police* (Madison: University of Wisconsin Press, 1988), 167.

42. Title of one of Stevens's poems.

43. T. E. Hulme, "Humanism and the Religious Art," in *Speculations: Essays on Humanism and the Philosophy of Art,* ed. Herbert Read (New York: Harcourt, 1924), 113; emphasis added. (All subsequent references to this and other Hulme essays included in the *Speculations* volume will be indicated by the abbreviation *Spec.*)

44. William Carlos Williams, *Imaginations* (New York: New Directions, 1970), 81.

45. Alfred North Whitehead, *The Concept of Nature* (Cambridge: Cambridge University Press, 1920), 30.

46. William Carlos Williams, *Imaginations,* 8.

47. Gertrude Stein, *Lectures in America* (1935; reprint, New York: Vintage-Random House, 1962), 196.

48. Ezra Pound, *Poetry: A Magazine of Verse* (March 1913), 201.

49. Quoted in Richard Bridgeman, *Gertrude Stein in Pieces* (New York: Oxford University Press, 1970), 270.

50. William Carlos Williams, *Selected Essays* (New York: New Directions, 1969), 127.

51. Louis Zukofsky, *Prepositions: The Collected Critical Essays of Louis Zukofsky* (New York: Horizon Press, 1968), 22.

52. William Carlos Williams, *The Selected Letters of William Carlos Williams,* ed. John C. Thirlwall (New York: New Directions, 1957), 23.

53. Isaac Newton, quoted in Kern, 11; emphasis added.

54. William James, quoted in Kern, 83.

55. James Joyce, *Ulysses* (1922; reprint, New York: Random House, 1961), 186.

56. See Kern, 55.

57. Gertrude Stein, quoted in Tony Tanner, *The Reign of Wonder* (Cambridge: Cambridge University Press, 1965), 196.

58. Cassirer, 160.

59. Edmund Wilson, *Axel's Castle* (New York: Scribner's, 1931), 5.

60. Ezra Pound, "Vorticism," *The Fortnightly Review,* 1 September 1914, 44; emphasis added.

61. Gertrude Stein, *What Are Masterpieces?* (1940; reprint, New York: Vintage-Random House, 1966), 32.

62. Gertrude Stein, quoted in John Malcolm Brinnin, *The Third Rose: Gertrude Stein And Her World* (Boston: Little, Brown, 1959), 288.

63. William Carlos Williams, *Selected Essays,* 116, 28.

64. Ernest Hemingway, quoted in Carlos Baker, *Hemingway: The Writer as Artist,* 4th ed. (Princeton: Princeton University Press, 1972), 58.

65. Louis Zukofsky, *Prepositions,* 22.

66. William Carlos Williams, *Selected Essays,* 197.

67. Marianne Moore, *Collected Poems* (1951; reprint, New York: Macmillan, 1979), 41.

68. Ezra Pound, "A Few Don'ts by an Imagiste," *Poetry: A Magazine of Verse,* I.6 (March 1913), 201.

69. Wallace Stevens, *The Necessary Angel,* 174–75.

70. Marianne Moore, *Collected Poems,* 49.

71. T. S. Eliot, *Knowledge and Experience in the Philosophy of F. H. Bradley* (London: Faber & Faber, 1964), 51 & 48.

72. Jacques Derrida, *Dissemination,* trans. Barbara Johnson (Chicago: University of Chicago Press, 1981), 139.

73. Hans-Georg Gadamer, *Truth and Method* (New York: Crossroad, 1985), 134.

74. Gadamer, 135.

75. Stanley Cavell, in a discussion of Heidegger, argues, "The redemption of the things of the world is the redemption of human nature, and chiefly from its destructiveness of its own conditions of existence." In *Quest of the Ordinary* (Chicago: University of Chicago Press, 1988), 66.

76. George Steiner, *Real Presences: Is There Anything in What We Say?* (London: Faber and Faber, 1989), 216.

Chapter 3. Gertrude Stein and *Tender Buttons*

1. Roger Shattuck, *The Innocent Eye* (New York: Farrar, Straus & Giroux, 1984), 237.

2. Shattuck, 238.

3. Shattuck, 23.

4. Steven Knapp and William Benn Michaels, "Against Theory," *Critical Inquiry*, 8 (Summer 1982), 724.

5. William C. Dowling, "Intentionless Meaning," *Critical Inquiry*, 9 (June 1983), 784. Meanwhile, Christopher Norris, in his book *Derrida* (Cambridge: Harvard University Press, 1987), attempts to clarify the post-structuralist conception of intentionality. Referring to and quoting Derrida, he writes, "He is not denying that language possesses an 'intentional' aspect that allows us—again, for all practical purposes—to interpret various kinds of performative utterance in keeping with the relevant conventions. But he *is*, most emphatically, denying the idea that philosophy can lay down the rules of this procedure by explaining how language *should or must* work if its workings are to make good sense. 'What is limited by iterability is not intentionality but its character of being conscious or present to itself'" (179).

6. Shattuck, 238. Meanwhile, John Frow, offering a summary of Jean-François Lyotard's distinction between the aesthetic practice of modernism and postmodernism, writes,

> The modernist artist (Duchamp, Mies and Corbusier, Schoenberg and Webern, Mallarmé, Joyce, Kafka, Stein) is the one who explores the given material with absolute commitment and to the point of silence or madness. But this narrative continues, not with a simple succession but with a dialectical reversal: having reached the point of absolute aporia, having taken the exploration of the material to its end, the modernist project becomes both complete and irrelevant. The intervention of postmodernism at this point would involve not a linear succession but a change of ground. Losing faith in both the purity and the futility of modernist practice, postmodernism takes up the discarded or marginalized materials of modernism (figure and representation, for example, or humor and directness of enuciation), and exploits them with a quite different kind of rigor. In particular, it ceases to structure its project on the opposition between high and low culture. ("Postmodernism and Literary History," in *Theoretical Issues in Literary History*, ed. David Perkins [Cambridge: Harvard University Press, 1991], 133.)

Frow himself does not accept this representation of modernism and postmodernism. He critiques Lyotard's promotion of a "closed epochal unity" (133) and the rupture between unities which attends this formulation: "Were it to be qualitatively different, postmodernism would have to be grounded in a quite different temporality, and would thus have to be the paradoxical reversal of its own act of rupture" (134).

Frow's criticism is well taken. There is no need to promote a radical differentiation between one epoch and another. Continuities will always exist side by side with discontinuities; and the historian's task will always require a negotiation between them. And yet the description offered here of the modernist project—though undermined by Frow's own one-sidedness (e.g., "absolute commitment," "absolute aporia," "complete and irrelevant," "purity," etc.)—is interesting and suggestive. And I should think of myself as structuring my own history of Stein, Hemingway, Williams, and Moore within the frame of American literary modernism somewhat along these lines. I hope my description is more modulated than the one Frow disapproves of. At the same time, I am willing, with Dilthey, to concede that periods themselves are "fixed representations of something in progress, giving fixity in thought to that which in itself is process or movement in a direction" (quoted in David Perkins, "Literary Classifications," in *Theoretical Issues in Literary History*, ed. David Perkins [Cambridge: Harvard University Press, 1991], 251).

7. Gertrude Stein, *The Autobiography of Alice B. Toklas* (1933; reprint, New York: Vintage, 1961), 211. (Subsequent references to the text will be indicated by the abbreviation ABT.)

8. In *The Autobiography of Alice B. Toklas,* Stein tells us that she once informed an editor "that everything that is written in the manuscript [of *Three Lives*] is written with the *intention* of its being so written and all he has to do is to print it and I will take the responsibility" (68; emphasis added).

9. See E. H. Gombrich, *Art and Illusion* (1960; reprint, Princeton: Princeton University Press, 1972).

10. Quoted in Gombrich, 296.

11. William James, *Principles of Psychology* (1893), vol. 2, 243.

12. Quoted in Allegra Stewart, *Gertrude Stein and the Present* (Cambridge: Harvard University Press, 1967); also in Gertrude Stein, *Everybody's Autobiography* (New York: Random House, 1937), 242.

13. In her "Radcliffe Themes," Stein writes (25 April 1895):

Is life worth living? Yes, a thousand times yes when the world still holds such spirits as Prof. William James. He is truly a man among men; a scientist of force and originality embodying all that is strongest and worthiest in the scientific spirit; a metaphysician skilled in abstract thought, clear and vigorous and yet too great to worship logic as his God, and narrow himself to a belief merely in the reason of man.

A man he is who has lived sympathetically not alone all thought but all life. He stands firmly, nobly for the dignity of man. His faith is not that of a cringing coward before an all-powerful master, but of a strong man willing to fight, to suffer and endure. He has not accepted faith because it is easy and pleasing. He has thought and lived many years and at last says with a voice of authority, if life does not mean this, I don't know what it means.

What can one say more? He is a strong sane noble personality reacting truly on all experience that life has given him. He is a man take him for all in all. (*A Primer for the Gradual Understanding of Gertrude Stein,* ed. Robert Bartlett Haas [Los Angeles: Black Sparrow Press, 1971], 41.)

Meanwhile, in *Poetry and Pragmatism* (Cambridge: Harvard University Press, 1992), Richard Poirier reports that Stein told Richard Wright, "William James taught me all that I know" (92).

14. Gertrude Stein, *Lectures in America* (1935; reprint, New York: Vintage, 1975), 156–57. (Subsequent references to the text will be indicated by the abbreviation LIA.)

15. Gertrude Stein, "Cultivated Motor Automatism," *Psychological Review,* 5 (1898), 295.

16. Stein, "Cultivated Motor Automatism," 297.

17. Stein, "Cultivated Motor Automatism," 299.

18. Leon Katz, introduction to *Fernhurst, Q.E.D., and Other Early Writings* (New York: Liveright, 1971).

19. Gertrude Stein, *Three Lives* (1909; reprint, New York: Random House, 1936), 85.

20. Gertrude Stein, *How Writing is Written* (Los Angeles: Black Sparrow Press, 1974), 156. (Subsequent references to the text will be indicated by the abbreviation HWW.)

21. Gertrude Stein, *The Making of Americans* (1925; reprint, New York: Something Else Press,1966), 275. (The several page references following are to this text.)

22. Lisa Ruddick's reading of this "bottom nature" matter demands quoting:

Stein's characterological scheme, which slowly takes over the novel, is directed at uncovering the "bottom nature"—or, as she sometimes rephrases it, the "bottom"—in each person. The notable feature of each character is thus not membership in the class male or female . . . but instead the sort of "bottom" the person has, as if Stein were unconsciously marginalizing genital sexual difference in favor of a weird and indistinct notion of anal identity. (83)

Ruddick's further attention to "Stein's fantasy of anal omnipotence" (85) leads her to say that in *The Making of Americans* Stein "developed a mode of writing that is the stylistic analogue to what Shengold calls 'making stool and making lists'" (118). In effect, a "poetics of the tush." (*Reading Gertrude Stein: Body, Text, Gnosis* [Ithaca: Cornell University Press, 1990].)

23. Gertrude Stein, "Composition as Explanation" (London, 1926), reprinted in *Selected Writings of Gertrude Stein*, ed. Carl Van Vechten (New York: Vintage, 1972), 517.

24. Quoted in Wendy Steiner, *Exact Resemblance to Exact Resemblance: The Literary Portraiture of Gertrude Stein* (New Haven: Yale University Press, 1978), 51.

25. Quoted in Steiner, 46.

26. Stein, *The Making of Americans*, 34.

27. Stein, *The Making of Americans*, 540–41.

28. Hayden White, *Tropics of Discourse* (Baltimore: Johns Hopkins University Press, 1985), 253.

29. Gertrude Stein, *Geographical History of America* (1936; reprint, New York: Vintage, 1973), 76. (Subsequent references to the text will be indicated by the abbreviation GHA.)

30. Quoted in Richard Bridgman, *Gertrude Stein in Pieces* (New York: Oxford University Press, 1970), 262; Stein, *Geographical History of America*, 44.

31. Gertrude Stein, *Portraits and Prayers* (New York: Random House, 1934), 12.

32. Pamela Hadas refers to Leo Stein's biographical fragment, wherein he "notes that geniuses always seem to have excellent memories of their childhood, as he of course does, and reveals that ' . . . Gertrude remembers almost nothing. Was it because her childhood was happy and mine was not? I don't know the answer, but the difference is enormous.'" "Spreading the Difference: One Way to Read Gertrude Stein's *Tender Buttons*," *Twentieth Century Literature* (Spring 1978), 68.

33. Michel Foucault, *The Order of Things* (New York: Vintage, 1973), 133.

34. Gertrude Stein, *Tender Buttons* (1914; reprint, Los Angeles: Sun & Moon Classics, 1991), 12. (Subsequent page references will be in the text.)

35. Martin Heidegger, *Being and Time*, trans. John Macquarrie and Edward Robinson (New York: Harper and Row, 1962), 76.

36. Critics have often taken note of the importance of color in *Tender Buttons*. Richard Bridgman, for instance, took note not only of the omnipresence of "words of transparency: glass, spectacle, eye glasses, carafe," but also of the predominance of a handful of colors, "especially versions of red-pink, scarlet, crimson, [and] rose" (126). More recently, feminist critics have tended to make a connection between these colors and female sexuality. For instance, Lisa Ruddick writes:

These poems in "Objects" depict the exchange, mutilation, and sexual suppression of the female body. On the other hand, let us think about "Red Roses" again. It contains an account of the erasure of sexuality, but it also has intensely sexual resonances that seem to belie this erasure. The poem, again, reads: RED ROSES. A cool red rose and a pink cut pink, a collapse and a sold hole, a little less hot." The progression from "cool" to "pink . . . pink," to "less hot," suggests arousal and release. The "collapse" in the middle could correspondingly allude to orgasm, after which things are "a little less hot." Indeed, if the word "sold" were not present to signal an economic issue, the sexual meaning might dominate." (206)

I find this sort of linkage more or less convincing, though I do not find (nor does anyone claim) that Stein's interest in color is exhausted by the motif of female sexuality.

37. Ludwig Wittgenstein, *Tractatus Logico-Philosophicus*, trans. D. F. Pears & B. F. McGuinness (1922; reprint, London: Routledge & Kegan Paul, 1978), 6.

38. Martin Heidegger, *Basic Writings* (New York: Harper and Row, 1977), 81.

39. Quoted in John Malcolm Brinnin, *The Third Rose: Gertrude Stein and Her World* (Boston: Little, Brown, 1959), 335.

40. Wittgenstein, 5.

41. Gertrude Stein, *Picasso* (1938; reprint, Boston: Beacon Press, 1959), 35. (Subsequent references to the text will be indicated by the abbreviation *Pic.*)

42. Jacques Derrida, *Writing and Difference*, trans. Alan Bass (Chicago: University of Chicago Press, 1978), ·280.

43. Heidegger, *Being and Time*, 89.

44. Hans-Georg Gadamer, *Truth and Method* (New York: Crossroad, 1985), 82.

45. The phrase is M. M. Bakhtin's in *The Dialogic Imagination*, trans. Caryl Emerson and Michael Holquist (Austin: University of Texas Press, 1983), 257.

46. Wittgenstein, 8. James also writes: "Even the advocates of an eternally identical Ego will confess that it must know its objects, *qua* changing, in and by and through changing states, affections, acts, or attitudes, which are modifications, however, superficial, of its identity." "On Some Omissions of Introspective Psychology," *Mind*, no. 33 (January, 1884), 9.

47. C. S. Peirce, *Selected Writings*, ed. Philip Wiener (New York: Dover, 1966), 124.

48. Wittgenstein, 8.

49. Wittgenstein, 71.

50. Paul de Man, *Allegories of Reading* (New Haven: Yale University Press, 1979), 129.

51. Stein, *A Primer*, 29.

52. Stein, *A Primer*, 29.

53. Quoted in Bridgman, 135–36.

54. Stein, *A Primer*, 25.

55. Stein, *A Primer*, 25.

56. Derrida, *Writing and Difference*, 295.

57. Derrida, *Dissemination*, trans. Barbara Johnson (Chicago: University of Chicago Press, 1981), 139.

58. Dodge continues,

> To name a thing is practically to create it & this is what your work is—real creation. It is almost frightening to come up against reality this way. I always get—I told you—the shivers when I read your things. And your palette is such a single one—the primary colors in word painting & you express every shade known and unknown with them. It is as new & strong & big as the post-impressionists in their way. I am perfectly convinced that it is the forerunner of a whole new epoch of new form and expression. (Quoted in *The Flowers of Friendship: Letters Written to Gertrude Stein*, ed. Donald Gallup [New York: Alfred A. Knopf, 1953], 52.)

59. Quoted in Richard Rorty, *Essays on Heidegger and Others* (Cambridge: Cambridge University Press, 1991), 116.

60. James, *A Pluralistic Universe* (1901; reprint, New York: Dutton, 1971), 125.

61. Quoted in Bridgman, 270.

62. Quoted in Bridgman, 270.

63. Stein, *Everybody's Autobiography*, 135.

64. In *Truth and Method*, Gadamer writes,

The work of [modern] art is conceived as an ontological event and the abstraction to which aesthetic differentiation commits it is dissolved. A picture is an event of presentation. Its relation to the original is so far from being a reduction of the autonomy of its being that, on the contrary, I had to speak, in regard to the picture, of an "increase in being." The use of concepts from the sphere of the holy seemed appropriate." (134)

65. See Carolyn Burke, "Gertrude Stein, the Cone Sisters, and the Puzzle of Female Friendship," in *Writing and Sexual Difference,* ed. Elizabeth Abel (Chicago: University of Chicago Press, 1982), 221–42; Harriet Scott Chessman, *The Public Is Invited to Dance: Representation, the Body, and Dialogue in Gertrude Stein* (Stanford: Stanford University Press, 1989); Marianne DeKoven, *A Different Language: Gertrude Stein's Experimental Writing* (Madison: University Of Wisconsin Press, 1983); Lisa Ruddick, *Reading Gertrude Stein* (Ithaca: Cornell University Press, 1990). Burke, for instance, writes:

Julia Kristeva's distinction between the semiotic and the symbolic modes of signification could . . . be applied in a discussion of Stein's early writing on women's relationships. The semiotic mode, in close relation to the unconscious, expresses the instinctual drives through the resources of rhythm, intonation, gesture, and melody. It is also . . . closely allied with the infant's pre-infant, pre-Oedipal (and presymbolic) attachment to the mother's body. Stein's enjoyment of the rhythmic sensations obtained through the minutely varied repetitions and variations of her early writing could be described as semiotic, in this sense. (238–39)

Chessman, meanwhile, is a little bit troubled by Kristeva's model, and offers (I think wisely) some words of caution:

Although this idea of a return to the mother and to a "presymbolic" maternal body is useful for an understanding of Stein, it is important to acknowledge the mythic elements inherent both in these approaches to Stein and in the theories about language in which they are grounded. Whether the myth finds definition in the utopian pre-Oedipal "life of immediate or raw perception" described by Ruddick or in the pleasurable sensations and rhythms of a nonsignifying mode, this pleasant place—the site of Stein's writing—acquires the status of a myth. Further, the concepts of both the pre-Oedipal and the presymbolic often acquire a dangerous element of essentialism, whereby the "maternal" or the "feminine" represent the utterly nonsignifying and bodily other. (4)

66. Quoted in Norman Bryson, *Looking at the Overlooked: Four Essays on Still Life Painting* (Cambridge: Harvard University Press, 1990), 175.
67. Bryson, 178.
68. Quoted in Bridgman, 327.
69. Stein, *Everybody's Autobiography,* 118.
70. Stein, *Everybody's Autobiography,* 118.
71. Stein, *Everybody's Autobiography,* 116.
72. Stein, *Everybody's Autobiography,* 115.
73. Quoted in Bridgman, 328.
74. Stein, *Everybody's Autobiography,* 154.
75. Derrida, *Writing and Difference,* 297.
76. David Lodge, *The Modes of Modern Writing* (London: Arnold, 1977), 153.
77. Roman Jakobson, quoted in David Lodge, "The Language of Modernist Fiction: Metaphor and Metonymy," in *Modernism,* eds. Malcolm Bradbury and James McFarlane (London: Penguin, 1983), 483.
78. Lodge, *The Modes of Modern Writing,* 152.

79. Roman Jakobson, "What Is Poetry," in *Selected Writings*, Vol. 2 (The Hague: Mouton, 1971), 742.

CHAPTER 4. ERNEST HEMINGWAY AND *IN OUR TIME*

1. Ernest Hemingway, *Selected Letters*, ed. Carlos Baker (New York: Scribner, 1981), 836. (Subsequent references to this volume will be indicated by the abbreviation SL.)

2. For studies of Hemingway's readings and influences, see Michael S. Reynolds, *Hemingway's Reading 1910–1940: An Inventory* (Princeton: Princeton University Press, 1981) and Mark Spilka, *Hemingway's Quarrel with Androgyny* (Lincoln: University of Nebraska Press, 1990). In the first, Reynolds offers "an inventory of those books, periodicals, and newspapers that Hemingway owned or borrowed between 1910 and 1940." In the second, Spilka selectively examines Hemingway's boyhood reading "to show how he was raised by a blend of feminine and masculine versions of manhood which later became submerged and dominant strains, respectively, in his published fiction" (5).

3. Ernest Hemingway, *In Our Time* (1925; reprint, New York: Scribner, 1970). The text includes the 1930 addition, "On the Quai at Smyrna." (Subsequent references to this volume will be indicated by page number[s] alone.)

4. Ernest Hemingway, interview by George Plimpton, in *Writers at Work: The "Paris Review" Interviews*, ed. Malcolm Cowley, 2nd ser. (New York: Viking, 1963), 233.

5. Gertrude Stein, *The Autobiography of Alice B. Toklas* (1933; reprint, New York: Vintage, 1961), 34. (Subsequent references to this text will be indicated by the abbreviation ABT.) Ernest Hemingway, *A Moveable Feast* (1964; reprint, New York: Bantam, 1973), 17. (Subsequent references to this volume will be indicated by the abbreviation MF.)

6. Ernest Hemingway, *A Moveable Feast* (1964; reprint, New York: Bantam, 1973), 17. (Subsequent references to this volume will be indicated by the abbreviation MF.)

7. Quoted in Jacqueline Tavernier-Courbin, "Ernest Hemingway and Ezra Pound," in *Ernest Hemingway: The Writer in Context*, ed. James Nagel (Madison: University of Wisconsin Press, 1984), 184.

8. Gertrude Stein, *Three Lives* (1909; reprint, New York: Vintage-Random House, 1936), 105.

9. Ernest Hemingway, *Three Stories and Ten Poems* (1923; reprint, Bloomfield Hills, Mich.: Bruccoli Clark Books, 1977), 3.

10. Quoted in James Mellow, *Charmed Circle* (1974; reprint, New York: Avon Books, 1982), 826.

11. Quoted in Michael Reynolds, "Hemingway's Stein: Another Misplaced Artist," *American Literature*, 55 (1983), 432.

12. Quoted in Reynolds, "Hemingway's Stein," 432.

13. Quoted in Michael Reynolds, ed., *Critical Essays on Hemingway's In Our Time* (Boston: G. K. Hall, 1983), 8.

14. Gertrude Stein, *What Are Masterpieces?* (1940; reprint, New York: Vintage-Random House, 1966), 98.

15. Hemingway always had some trouble articulating the connection between his work and that of the painters from whom he says he learnt. For instance, when George Plimpton asked him to explain the connection, his response appeared a little too much like a dodge:

I put in painters [in a list of "literary forbears"], or started to, because I learn as much from painters about how to write as from writers. You ask how this is done? It would take another day of explaining. I should think what one learns from composers and from the study of harmony and counterpoint would be obvious.

And in the infamous Lillian Ross portrait, standing before Cézanne's "Rocks— Forest of Fontainebleau," he also seemed to fumble for the connection:

I can make a landscape like Mr. Paul Cézanne. I learned how to make a landscape from Mr. Paul Cézanne by walking through the Luxembourg Museum a thousand times with an empty gut, and I am pretty sure that if Mr. Paul was around, he would like the way I make them and be happy that I learned from him. (*Portrait of Hemingway* [New York: Simon and Schuster, 1961], 60)

This is not to argue that Hemingway did not, in fact, learn anything of a technical nature from Cézanne. I think he did. But I do wish to make the point that (1) Stein introduced him to Cézanne—at least in the sense that he now began to deliberately direct his attention to the painter's work; and (2) his understanding of Cézanne's technical achievement, when not intuitive, was largely filtered through Stein's own understanding. This said, I should not argue with Emily Stipes Watts's conclusion:

Hemingway probably borrowed at least four methods from Cézanne for landscape descriptions: the use of a series of planes often cut across by a diagonal line, the careful delineation of even the most distant mountains and ridges, the emphasis upon volumes of space with the use of simple geometrical forms as the basis of definition, and the occasional use of color modulation. (*Ernest Hemingway and the Arts* [Urbana: University of Illinois Press], 40.)

16. Maurice Merleau-Ponty, *The Visible and the Invisible,* trans. Alphonso Lingis (Chicago: Northwestern University Press, 1968), 4.
17. Quoted in Linda Wagner, *Hemingway and Faulkner* (Metuchen, N.J.: The Scarecrow Press, 1975), 40.
18. "Naturalness" was another of those values extolled by Stein, and it seems likely that she also persuaded Hemingway of its importance. In *The Autobiography of Alice B. Toklas,* Stein tells the story of going to the Vollard gallery and, struck by the "naturalness" of a Matisse, purchasing it, despite the general laughter it seemed to provoke:

They [Stein and her brother, Leo] decided to go over to the salon and look at the picture again. They did. People were roaring with laughter at the picture and scratching at it. Gertrude Stein could not understand why, the picture seemed perfectly *natural*. The Cézanne portrait had not seemed natural, it had taken her some time to feel that it was *natural* but this picture by Matisse seemed to her perfectly *natural* and she could not understand why it infuriated everybody. Her brother was less attracted but all the same he agreed and they bought it. She then went back to look at it and it upset her to see them all mocking at it. It bothered her and angered her because to her it was so alright, just as later she did not understand why since the writing was all so clear and *natural* they mocked at and were enraged by her work. (35; emphasis added)

19. Ernest Hemingway, *Nick Adams Stories* (New York: Bantam, 1973), 219; emphasis added. The passage continues:

He could see the Cézannes. The portrait at Gertrude Stein's. She'd know it if he ever got things right. The two good ones at the Luxembourg, the ones he'd seen every day at the loan exhibit at Berhheim's. The soldiers undressing to swim, the house through the trees, one of the trees with a house beyond, not the lake one, the other lake one. The portrait of the bay. Cézanne could do people, too. But that was easier, he used what he got from the country to do people with. Nick could do that, too. People are easy. Nobody knew anything about them. If it sounded good they took your word for it. They took Joyce's word for it.

He knew just how Cézanne would paint this stretch of river. God, if he were only here to do it.

20. Quoted in Plimpton, 235.

21. Quoted in Sheldon N. Grebstein, *Hemingway's Craft* (Carbondale: Southern Illinois University Press, 1973), 155.

22. Susan F. Beegel, *Hemingway's Craft of Omission: Four Manuscript Examples* (Ann Arbor: UMI Research Press, 1988), 90.

23. Beegel, 11.

24. Ludwig Wittgenstein, quoted in Brian McGuinness, *Wittgenstein: A Life* (Berkeley: University of California Press, 1988), 288; Gertrude Stein, *Lectures in America* (1935; reprint, New York: Vintage, 1975), 236–37; Paul Cézanne, quoted in Dore Ashton, *A Fable of Modern Art* (Berkeley: University of California Press, 1991), 46; Martin Heidegger, *Being and Time,* trans. John Macquarrie and Edward Robinson (New York: Harper and Row, 1962), 76.

25. Ernest Hemingway, *The Garden of Eden* (New York: Scribner, 1986), 13.

26. Ludwig Wittgenstein, *Tractatus Logico-Philosophicus,* trans. C. K. Ogden (1922; reprint, London: Routledge, 1990), 189. (Subsequent refererences to this volume will be indicated by the abbreviation T.)

27. Paul Cézanne, in Joachim Gasquet's *Cézanne,* preface by John Rewald, introduction by Richard Shiff (London: Thames & Hudson, 1991), 154.

28. Ernest Hemingway, *Death in the Afternoon* (1932; reprint, New York: Scribner, 1960), 139. (Subsequent references to this volume will be indicated by the abbreviation DIA.)

29. Wittgenstein, quoted in McGuinness, 281.

30. Wittgenstein, *Philosophical Investigations,* trans. G. E. M. Anscombe (New York: Macmillan 1958), 128.

31. Wittgenstein, *Philosophical Investigations,* 129.

32. Wendolyn E. Tetlow's book-length *Hemingway's In Our Time: Lyrical Dimensions* (Lewisburg, Pa.: Bucknell University Press, 1992) does, in fact, make a full-scale claim for the book's poetic compression and unity:

> On the surface level, we can see that the chapters in *In Our Time* are linked by being numbered, by the presence of the character Nick Adams in eight of the pieces, by recurring images of birth, death, water, fishing, and walls, and by themes of violence and initiation. More deeply, though, the book's structure is lyrical. That is, it progresses by a succession of "tonal centers," "lyric centers," or "affects," to use Rosenthal's and Gall's terms, "centers of specific qualities, and intensities, of emotionally and sensuously charged awareness," which "reside in the *language of a passage* . . . rather than in the author's supposed feelings or those of a supposed 'speaker.'" The structuring—or the rhythm of feeling—of *In Our Time,* then, is similar to that of such poetic sequences as Ezra Pound's *Hugh Selwyn Mauberley* and T. S. Eliot's *The Waste Land,* works that progress tonally. (14)

33. Ernest Hemingway, "A Clean, Well Lighted Place," *The Fifth Column and the First Forty-nine Stories* (New York: Charles Scribner's Sons, 1938), 481. Of course, once again, the nothingness, in both the Stevens and Hemingway passages, speaks of something; "nothing" is not, perhaps never is, nothing.

34. Kenneth S. Lynn, *Hemingway* (New York: Simon and Schuster, 1987), 103.

35. Edmund Wilson, "Ernest Hemingway: Bourdon Gauge of Morale," *Atlantic Monthly* (July 1939), 396–418; and Malcom Cowley, introduction to *Portable Hemingway* (New York: Viking, 1944).

36. Ernest Hemingway, "The Art of Fiction," in Joseph M. Flora, *Ernest Hemingway: A Study of the Short Fiction* (Boston: G. K. Hall, 1989), 129–44.

37. Hemingway, "The Art of Fiction," 130–31.

38. Lynn, 103.

39. Susan Sontag, "The Aesthetics of Silence," in *A Susan Sontag Reader* (New York: Farrar, Straus, Giroux, 1982), 190.

40. Cézanne to J. Gasquet, quoted in Maurice Merleau-Ponty, *The Primacy of Perception* (Evanston, Ill.: Northwestern University Press, 1964), 159.

41. Barbara Herrnstein Smith, "Contingencies of Value," *Critical Inquiry,* 10 (1983), 14.

42. T. S. Eliot, "Tradition and the Individual Talent," in *Selected Prose of T. S. Eliot,* ed. Frank Kermode (New York: Harcourt, Brace, Jovanovich and Farrar, Straus and Giroux, 1975), 38.

43. Ernest Hemingway, *The Green Hills of Africa* (New York: Scribner, 1935), 26–27.

44. Quoted in Tetlow, 14.

45. Quoted in Carlos Baker, *Ernest Hemingway: The Writer As Artist,* 4th ed. (Princeton University Press, 1972), 64.

46. Quoted in Wagner, 38.

47. Quoted in Jeffrey Meyers, *Hemingway: A Biography* (New York: Harper & Row, 1985), 134.

48. Ernest Hemingway, "Introduction to Men at War," quoted in Beegel, 88.

49. Quoted in Meyers, 125.

50. Quoted in Ernest Hemingway, *88 Poems,* ed. Nicholas Geogiannis (New York: Harcourt, Brace & Jovanovich, 1979), xxiii–xxiv.

51. Michel Foucault, *The Order of Things: An Archaeology of the Human Sciences* (1971; reprint, New York: Vintage, 1973), 311.

52. Foucault, 311–12.

53. Paul de Man, *Allegories of Reading* (New Haven: Yale University Press, 1979), 111.

54. Quoted in De Man, 129.

55. Quoted in Baker, *Ernest Hemingway: The Writer as Artist,* 97.

56. Jacques Lacan, "God and the Jouissance of The Woman," in *Feminine Sexuality,* eds. Juliet Mitchell and Jacqueline Rose, trans., Jacqueline Rose (New York: Norton, 1985), 144. In place of "human," the original quotation has "woman."

57. Letter to Robert Morgan Brown, 14 July 1954, Humanities Research Center, Austin, Texas.

58. Upon this matter of a deliberate silence, Elias Canetti writes,

The man who maintains a deliberate silence knows exactly what should be left unspoken. Since, in practice, no one can remain silent forever, he has to decide what can be said and what cannot. The latter is what he really knows. It is more precise and also more precious. Silence not only guards it, but gives it greater concentration. He is forced to think about it every time he has to protect it. A man who says very little in any case always appears more concentrated than others; his silence leads one to suppose that he has more to conceal, that he is thinking of something secret. (Quoted in Denis Donoghue, *Warrenpoint* [New York: Alfred A. Knopf, 1990], 43–44.)

59. Ernest Hemingway, *The Garden of Eden,* 211.

60. Foucault, 133.

61. Quoted in Baker, *Ernest Hemingway: The Writer as Artist,* 4.

62. William James, *Pragmatism,* ed. A. J. Ayer (1907; reprint, Cambridge: Harvard University Press, 1978), 81.

63. William James, *Essays in Radical Empiricism,* ed. Richard J. Bernstein (1909; reprint, New York: Dutton, 1971), 24.

64. Quoted in Grebstein, 133–34.

65. James, *Pragmatism,* 62.

66. Milan Kundera, *The Unbearable Lightness of Being,* trans. Michael Henry Heim (New York: Harper & Row, 1984), 298.

67. T. S. Eliot, "Poetry and Propaganda," *Bookman* 70, no. 6 (February 1930), 601.

CHAPTER 5. WILLIAM CARLOS WILLIAMS AND *SPRING AND ALL*

1. William Carlos Williams, *Spring and All,* in *The Collected Poems of William Carlos Williams, vol. 1 (1909–1939),* eds. A. Walton Litz and Christopher MacGowan (New York: New Directions, 1986), 178; emphasis added. (All subsequent references to the text will be indicated by page number[s] alone.)

Previous readings of *Spring and All* include J. H. Miller, "Williams' *Spring and All* and the Progress of Poetry," *Daedalus,* 99 (1970): 415–29; Marjorie Perloff, *The Poetics of Indeterminacy: Rimbaud to Cage* (Evanston, Ill.: Northwestern University Press, 1983): 109–54; Henry M. Sayre, "Avant-Garde Dispositions: Placing *Spring and All* in Context"; Lisa Steinman, "Once More With Feeling: Teaching *Spring and All*"; and Thomas R. Whitaker, *Spring and All:* Teaching Us the Figures of Dance," *William Carlos Williams Review,* vol. 10, no. 2 (Fall 1984), 13–20; 7–12; 1–6.

In his article, Miller writes that *Spring and All* "is perhaps the most important single work by Williams" (415), an opinion with which I concur.

2. William Carlos Williams, *Selected Essays* (1954; reprint, New York: New Directions, 1969), 104; emphasis added.

3. Williams, *Selected Essays,* 67.

4. In *The Use of Poetry & The Use of Criticism* (1933; reprint, Cambridge: Harvard University Press, 1961), T. S. Eliot, the advocate of tradition, professes his own skepticism with the project of imagination:

> The words "intellect or imagination" strike me as a burking of the question: if there is a clear distinction between invention by exercise of intellect and invention by exercise of imagination, then two definitions are called for; and if there is no difference between intellectual and imaginative invention there can hardly be much difference between imagination and intellect. (48)

And:

> If . . . the difference between imagination and fancy amounts in practice to no more than the difference between good and bad poetry, have we done more than take a turn round Robin Hood's barn? It is only if fancy can be an ingredient in good poetry, and if you can show some good poetry which is the better for it; it is only if the distinction illuminates our immediate preference of one poet over another, that it can be of use to a practical mind like mine. (69)

5. John Slatin, " 'Something Inescapably Typical': Questions about Gender in the Late Work of William Carlos Williams and Marianne Moore," *William Carlos Williams Review,* vol. 14, no. 1 (Spring 1988), 101.

6. For studies of the influence of Dada upon Williams's work, see Dickran Taskijan, *Skyscraper Primitives: Dada and the American Avant-Garde, 1910–1925* (Middletown, Conn.: Wesleyan University Press, 1975); William Marling, *William Carlos Williams and the Painters, 1909–1923* (Athens: University of Ohio Press, 1982); Henry M. Sayre, *The Visual Text of William Carlos Williams* (Urbana: University of Illinois Press, 1983); and Peter Schmidt, *William Carlos Williams, The Arts, and Literary Tradition* (Baton Rouge: Louisana State University Press, 1988).

7. For a study of the visual accent in Williams's poetics, see Sayre, *The Visual Text of William Carlos Williams.*

8. For studies of the influence of Cubism upon Williams's work, see Bram Dijkstra, *The Hieroglyphics of a New Speech: Cubism, Stieglitz, and the Early Poetry of William Carlos Williams* (Princeton: Princeton University Press, 1969) and Peter Schmidt, *William Carlos Williams, The Arts, and Literary Tradition.*

9. Williams, *Imaginations,* ed. Webster Schott (New York: New Directions, 1971), 351–52; emphasis added.

10. Williams, *Selected Essays,* 229.

11. Williams, *Selected Essays,* 268.

12. Williams, *Selected Essays,* 268.

13. Williams, *Selected Essays,* 233.

14. William Carlos Williams, *Selected Letters,* ed. John C. Thirlwall (New York: McDowell, Obolensky, 1957), 311.

CHAPTER 6. MARIANNE MOORE AND *OBSERVATIONS*

1. Michel Foucault, *The Order of Things: An Archaeology of the Human Sciences* (1971; reprint, New York: Vintage, 1973), 239.

2. Marianne Moore, *The Complete Prose,* ed. Patricia C. Willis (New York: Viking, 1986), 157. (Subsequent references to this volume will be indicated by the abbreviation CP.)

3. Marianne Moore, interview by Donald Hall, in *Writers at Work: The "Paris Review" Interviews,* ed. George Plimpton, 2nd ser. (New York: Viking, 1963), 254–55.

4. *Writers at Work,* 273.

5. Marianne Moore, *The Complete Poems* (New York: MacMillan/Viking, 1981), 101.

6. *Writers at Work,* 254–55. Meanwhile, I think that Moore should agree with Denis Donoghue's understanding of the aesthetic as less fundamentally about action than perception. Donoghue writes,

[A]esthetics means perception, and . . . an aesthetic experience is just that, an experience of perception. A work of art is an object created for perception, and sequestered in that consideration from every other use to which it may be put. Suzanne Langer is right when she speaks of all artistic elements as "virtual, created only for perception." (*The Pure Good of Theory* [Oxford: Blackwell, 1992], 66.)

7. Marianne Moore, "Precision," 10, Moore Papers, Rosenbach Museum, Philadelphia.

8. Moore, "Precision," 10.

9. Marianne Moore, "Poetry and Criticism" (Cambridge, Mass.: Adams House & Lowell House Printers, 1965), n. pag.

10. Marianne Moore, "Monsieur Testes," unpublished essay [first draft, ca. 1952–56], 5, Moore Papers, Rosenbach Museum, Philadelphia.

11. Marianne Moore, *Observations* (New York: The Dial Press, 1925), 31. (Subsequent references to this volume will be indicated by page number[s] alone.)

12. "Monsieur Testes" [later draft], 4.

13. About the title, so reminiscent of T. S. Eliot's earlier *Prufrock and Other Observations* (1917), Moore wrote to him, when preparing for the publication of *Selected Poems* (1935) under his editorship,

> Despite the extreme amount of conscience I seem to have shown, in preparing the 1924 book I think I was erratic, or somnambulistic; it looks to me, that is to say, as if I had "quoted" things that were my own, and as if I had taken from you the titles, Observations, and Picking and Choosing.

Eliot wrote back, saying,

> I take it that the order which you give them [the poems] which is the same as in "Observations" (a title, by the way, to which you have better claim than I) is the order of composition.

Quoted in Bonnie Honigsblum, "MM's Revisions of 'Poetry,'" in *Marianne Moore: Woman and Poet,* ed. Patricia Willis [Orono, Me.: National Poetry Foundation, 1990], 198, 190.)

14. Marianne Moore, "Review of My Trip Abroad," 4, Moore Papers, Rosenbach Museum, Philadelphia.

15. Marianne Moore to William Carlos Williams, 12 May 1934, Moore Papers, Rosenbach Museum, Philadelphia.

16. T. S. Eliot, "Preface" to Marianne Moore, *Selected Poems* (New York and London, 1935), x.

17. Moore, *Complete Poems,* 267.

18. Norman Bryson, *Looking at the Overlooked: Four Essays on Still Life Painting* (Cambridge: Harvard University Press, 1990), 60.

19. Bryson, 65. Here Bryson is remarking specifically upon the work of Juan Sanchez Cotán, with the particular being used as illustrative of the general.

20. Quoted in Daniel L. Guillory, "Marianne Moore and Technology," in *Marianne Moore: Woman and Poet,* 89.

21. Review of *Ideas of Order,* by Wallace Stevens, *The Criterion,* 15 January 1936, 308.

22. Margaret Holley, *The Poetry of Marianne Moore: A Study in Voice and Value* (Cambridge: Cambridge University Press, 1987), 50.

23. Hugh Kenner, quoted in Jeffrey D. Peterson, "Notes in the Poem(s) 'Poetry,'" in *Marianne Moore: Woman and Poet,* 231.

24. Bonnie Costello, "Marianne Moore and the Sublime," *Sagetrieb,* 6, no. 3 (Winter 1987), 6.

25. Eliot, quoted in John M. Slatin, *The Savage's Romance* (University Park: Pennsylvania State University Press, 1986), 146.

26. Susan Sontag, *On Photography* (New York: Anchor Books, 1990), 149.

27. William Gaddis, *The Recognitions* (New York: Penguin, 1986), 309.

28. Stanley Cavell, "Being Odd, Getting Even: Threats to Individuality," in *Reconstructing Individualism: Autonomy, Individuality, and the Self in Western Thought,* eds. Thomas C. Heller, Morton Sosna, and David E. Wellbery (Stanford, Calif.: Stanford University Press, 1986), 309.

29. Cavell, 308.

30. Quoted in Holley, 1.
31. Valentine Cunningham, review of *Passion of the Mind,* by A. S. Byatt, *Times Literary Supplement,* 16 August 1991, 6.

Conclusion

1. Denis Donoghue, *Ferocious Alphabets* (New York: Columbia University Press, 1984), 66.
2. Marjorie Perloff, *The Dance of the Intellect* (Cambridge: Cambridge University Press, 1987), 21.
3. Quoted in Perloff, 2.
4. Quoted in Perloff, 49.
5. Hans-Georg Gadamer, *Truth & Method* (New York: Crossroad, 1985), 422. Meanwhile, W. J. T. Mitchell speaks of a like rule, that of "dialectical reversal, a process in which oppositions seem to change places." In *Iconology: Image, Text, Ideology* (Chicago: University of Chicago Press, 1987), 128.
6. J. Hillis Miller, *Poets of Reality* (Cambridge: Harvard University Press, 1965; reprint, New York: Atheneum, 1969), 224.
7. Marjorie Perloff, *The Poetics of Indeterminacy: Rimbaund to Cage* (Evanston, Ill.: Northwestern University Press, 1983), 61.
8. William Carlos Williams, *Spring and All,* in *The Collected Poems of William Carlos Williams, vol. 1 (1909–1939),* eds. A. Walton Litz and Christopher MacGowan (New York: New Directions, 1986), 202.
9. Martin Heidegger, *The Question Concerning Technology and Other Essays,* trans. William Lovitt (New York: Harper & Row, 1977), 128.
10. Heidegger, 129.
11. Williams, *Spring and All,* 235–36.
12. Heidegger, 132.
13. Gertrude Stein, *Lectures in America* (1935; reprint, New York: Vintage, 1975), 235.
14. Hans-Georg Gadamer, *The Relevance of the Beautiful and Other Essays,* trans. Nicholas Walker (Cambridge: Cambridge University Press, 1986), 119.
15. Gadamer, *The Relevance of the Beautiful,* 99.
16. Jacques Derrida, *The Truth of Painting,* trans. Ian McLeod (Chicago: University of Chicago Press, 1987), 110.
17. Williams, *Spring and All,* 178.
18. William Carlos Williams, *Imaginations,* ed. Webster Schott (New York: New Directions, 1970), 6.
19. Quoted in Craig Owens, "The Discourse of Others: Feminists and Postmodernism," in *The Anti-Aesthetic: Essays on Postmodern Culture,* ed. Hal Foster (Port Townsend, Wash.: Bay Press, 1983), 70.
20. Quoted in Donoghue, 31.
21. Derrida, *Positions,* trans. Alan Bass (Chicago: University of Chicago Press, 1981), 65.
22. Mitchell, 25.
23. Mitchell, 43.
24. Mitchell, 37.
25. Gertrude Stein, *Picasso* (1938; reprint, Boston: Beacon Press, 1959), 15.
26. Gregory L. Ulmer, "The Object of Post-Criticism," in *The Anti-Aesthetic,* 94.

Bibliography

Altieri, Charles. "'Ponderation' in Cézanne and Williams." *Poetics Today* 10, no. 2, (Summer 1989): 373–400.

Ashton, Dore. *A Fable of Modern Art.* Berkeley: University of California Press, 1991.

Baker, Carlos. *Hemingway: The Writer as Artist.* 4th ed. Princeton: Princeton University Press, 1972.

Bakhtin, M. M. *The Dialogic Imagination.* Translated by Caryl Emerson and Michael Holquist. Austin: University of Texas Press, 1983.

Barthes, Roland. *Camera Lucida.* Translated by Richard Howard. New York: Hill and Wang, 1981.

———. "The Death of the Author." In *The Rustle of Language.* Translated by Richard Howard. Berkeley: University of California Press, 1989.

———. *Image Music Text.* Translated by Stephen Heath. New York: Hill & Wang, 1977.

Baudrillard, Jean. "The Precession of Simulacra." In *Art After Modernism: Rethinking Representation,* edited by Brian Wallis. New York: New Museum of Contemporary Art, 1984.

Beardsley, Monroe C. and W. K. Wimsatt. *The Verbal Icon.* University of Kentucky Press, 1954.

Beegel, Susan F. *Hemingway's Craft of Omission: Four Manuscript Examples.* Ann Arbor: UMI Research Press, 1988.

Benjamin, Walter. *Illuminations.* Translated by Harry Zohn. New York: Schocken, 1969.

Bridgeman, Richard. *Gertrude Stein in Pieces.* New York: Oxford University Press, 1970.

Brinnin, John Malcolm. *The Third Rose: Gertrude Stein And Her World.* Boston: Little, Brown, 1959.

Bryson, Norman. *Looking at the Overlooked: Four Essays on Still Life Painting.* Cambridge: Harvard University Press, 1990.

Burke, Carolyn. "Gertrude Stein, the Cone Sisters, and the Puzzle of Female Friendship." In *Writing and Sexual Difference,* edited by Elizabeth Abel, 221–42. Chicago: University of Chicago Press, 1982.

Calinescu, Matei. *Five Faces of Modernity: Modernism, Avant-Garde, Decadence, Kitsch, Postmodernism.* Durham, N.C.: Duke University Press, 1987.

Cassirer, Ernst. *The Philosophy of Symbolic Forms.* Vol. 1. Translated by Ralph Manheim. 1923. Reprint, New Haven: Yale University Press, 1977.

Cavell, Stanley. "Being Odd, Getting Even: Threats to Individuality." In *Reconstructing Individualism: Autonomy, Individuality, and the Self in Western Thought,* edited by Thomas C. Heller, Morton Sosna, and David E. Wellbery, 278–312. Stanford, Calif.: Stanford University Press, 1986.

———. *In Quest of the Ordinary*. Chicago: University of Chicago Press, 1988.

Chai, Leon. *The Romantic Foundations of the American Renaissance*. Ithaca: Cornell University Press, 1987.

Chessman, Harriet Scott. *The Public Is Invited to Dance: Representation, the Body, and Dialogue in Gertrude Stein*. Stanford, Calif.: Stanford University Press, 1989.

Costello, Bonnie. "Marianne Moore and the Sublime." *Sagetrieb* 6, no. 3 (Winter 1987): 5–13.

Cowley, Malcom. Introduction to *Portable Hemingway*. New York: Viking, 1944.

Crary, Jonathan. *Techniques of the Observer: On Vision and Modernity in the Nineteenth Century*. Cambridge: MIT Press, 1990.

Cunningham, Valentine. Review of *Passion of the Mind* by A. S. Byatt. *Times Literary Supplement* (16 August 1991): 6.

Davidson, Donald. *Essays on Actions and Events*. Oxford: Clarendon Press, 1980.

DeKoven, Marianne. *A Different Language: Gertrude Stein's Experimental Writing*. Madison: University of Wisconsin Press, 1983.

De Man, Paul. *Allegories of Reading*. New Haven: Yale University Press, 1979.

———. *Blindness and Insight*. New York: Oxford University Press, 1971.

———. "The Epistemology of Metaphor." *Critical Inquiry* 5, no. 1 (Autumn 1978): 13–30.

———. "Hegel on the Sublime." In *Displacement: Derrida and After,* edited by Mark Krupnik, 139–53. Bloomington: Indiana University Press, 1983.

———. *Resistance to Theory*. Minneapolis: University of Minnesota Press, 1986.

Derrida, Jacques. *Dissemination*. Translated by Barbara Johnson. Chicago: University of Chicago Press, 1981.

———. "'Eating Well,' or the Calculation of the Subject: An Interview with Jacques Derrida." In *Who Comes After the Subject?,* edited by Eudardo Cadava, Peter Connor, and Jean-Luc Nancy, 96–119. New York: Routledge, 1991.

———. "How to Avoid Speaking." In *Language of the Unsayable,* edited by Sandford Budick and Wolfgang Iser, 3–70. New York: Columbia University Press, 1989.

———. *Positions*. Translated by Alan Bass. Chicago: University of Chicago Press, 1982.

———. *The Truth of Painting*. Translated by Ian McLeod. Chicago: University of Chicago Press, 1987.

———. *Writing and Difference*. Translated by Alan Bass. Chicago: University of Chicago Press, 1978.

Dewey, John. "The Influence of Darwin on Philosophy." In *Darwin,* edited by Philip Appleman, 305–14. New York: Norton, 1970.

Dijkstra, Bram. *The Hieroglyphics of a New Speech: Cubism, Stieglitz, and the Early Poetry of William Carlos Williams*. Princeton: Princeton University Press, 1969.

Donoghue, Denis. *Ferocious Alphabets*. New York: Columbia University Press, 1984.

———. *The Pure Good of Theory*. Oxford: Blackwell, 1992.

———. *Reading America*. New York: Alfred A. Knopf, 1987.

———. *The Sovereign Ghost*. Berkeley : University of California Press, 1976.

———. *Warrenpoint*. New York: Alfred A. Knopf, 1990.

Dowling, William C. "Intentionless Meaning." *Critical Inquiry* 9, no. 4 (June 1983): 784–89.

Eliot, T. S. *Knowledge and Experience in the Philosophy of F. H. Bradley*. London: Faber & Faber, 1964.

———. "Poetry and Propaganda." *Bookman* 70, no. 6 (February 1930).

———. Preface to *Selected Poems*, by Marianne Moore. New York and London, 1935.

———. *Selected Prose of T. S. Eliot*. Edited by Frank Kermode. New York: Harcourt, Brace, Jovanovich and Farrar, Straus and Giroux, 1975.

———. *The Use of Poetry & The Use of Criticism*. 1933. Reprint, Cambridge: Harvard University Press, 1961.

Emerson, Ralph. "Nature." In *Ralph Waldo Emerson: Essays & Lectures*. New York: Library of America, 1983: 5–49.

———. *The Selected Writings of Ralph Waldo Emerson*. Edited by Brooks Atkinson. 1940. Reprint, New York: Modern Library, 1968.

Feidelson, Jr., Charles. *Symbolism and American Literature*. 1953. Reprint, Chicago: University of Chicago Press, 1983.

Foucault, Michel. *The Archaeology of Knowledge*. Translated by A. M. Sheridan Smith. New York: Pantheon Books, 1972.

———. "Nietzsche, Genealogy, History." In *Language, Counter-Memory, Practice: Selected Essays and Interviews*. Ithaca: Cornell University Press, 1977.

———. *The Order of Things: An Archaeology of the Human Sciences*. 1971. Reprint, New York: Vintage, 1973.

———. "What Is an Author?" Translated by Josué V. Harari. In *The Foucault Reader*, edited by Paul Rabinow, 101–20. New York: Pantheon, 1984.

Frow, John. "Postmodernism and Literary History." In *Theoretical Issues in Literary History*, edited by David Perkins, 131–42. Cambridge: Harvard University Press, 1991.

Gadamer, Hans-Georg. *Truth and Method*. New York: Crossroad, 1985.

———. *The Relevance of the Beautiful and Other Essays*. Translated by Nicholas Walker. Cambridge: Cambridge University Press, 1986.

Gaddis, William. *The Recognitions*. New York: Penguin, 1986.

Gallup, Donald, ed. *The Flowers of Friendship: Letters Written to Gertrude Stein*. New York: Alfred A. Knopf, 1953.

Gasché, Rodolphe. "In-Difference to Philosophy: de Man on Kant, Hegel, and Nietzsche." In *Reading de Man Reading*, edited by Lindsay Waters and Wlad Godzich, 259–94. Minneapolis: University of Minnesota Press, 1989.

Gasquet, Joachim. *Cézanne*. With a preface by John Rewald and an introduction by Richard Shiff. London: Thames & Hudson, 1991.

Giddens, Anthony. "Action, Subjectivity, and Meaning." In *The Aims of Representation: Subject/Text/History*, edited by Murray Krieger, 159–74. New York: Columbia University Press, 1987.

Gombrich, E. H. *Art and Illusion*. 1960. Reprint, Princeton: Princeton University Press, 1972.

Grebstein, Sheldon N. *Hemingway's Craft*. Carbondale: Southern Illinois University Press, 1973.

Guillory, Daniel L. "Marianne Moore and Technology." In *Marianne Moore: Woman and Poet,* edited by Patricia Willis, 83–94. Orono, Me.: National Poetry Foundation, 1990.

Habermas, Jürgen. *The Philosophical Discourse of Modernity: Twelve Lectures.* Translated by Frederick Lawrence. Cambridge: MIT Press, 1987.

Hadas, Pamela. "Spreading the Difference: One Way to Read Gertrude Stein's *Tender Buttons.*" *Twentieth Century Literature* 24 (Spring 1978): 57–75.

Heidegger, Martin. *Basic Writings.* New York: Harper and Row, 1977.

———. *Being and Time.* Translated by John Macquarrie and Edward Robinson. New York: Harper and Row, 1962.

———. *The Question Concerning Technology and Other Essays.* Translated by William Lovitt. New York: Harper & Row, 1977.

Hemingway, Ernest. "The Art of Fiction." In *Ernest Hemingway: A Study of the Short Fiction,* edited by Joseph M. Flora, 129–44. Boston: G. K. Hall, 1989.

———. *Death in the Afternoon.* 1932. Reprint, New York: Scribner, 1960.

———. *88 Poems.* Edited by Nicholas Geogiannis. New York: Harcourt, Brace & Jovanovich, 1979.

———. *The Garden of Eden.* New York: Scribner, 1986.

———. *The Green Hills of Africa.* New York: Scribner, 1935.

———. Letter to Robert Morgan Brown, 14 July 1954, Humanities Research Center, Austin, Texas.

———. *A Moveable Feast.* 1964. Reprint, New York: Bantam, 1973.

———. *Nick Adams Stories.* New York: Bantam, 1973.

———. *In Our Time.* 1925. Reprint, New York: Scribner, 1970.

———. Interview by George Plimpton. In *Writers at Work: The "Paris Review" Interviews,* edited by Malcolm Cowley, 2nd ser. New York: Viking, 1963: 215–39.

———. *Selected Letters.* Edited by Carlos Baker. New York: Scribner, 1981.

———. *Three Stories and Ten Poems.* 1923. Reprint, Bloomfield Hills, Mich.: Bruccoli Clark Books, 1977.

Holley, Margaret. *The Poetry of Marianne Moore: A Study in Voice and Value.* Cambridge: Cambridge University Press, 1987.

Honigsblum, Bonnie. "MM's Revisions of 'Poetry.'" In *Marianne Moore: Woman and Poet,* edited by Patricia Willis, 185–222. Orono, Me.: National Poetry Foundation, 1990.

Howard, Leon. *Herman Melville.* Berkeley: University of California Press, 1951.

Hoy, David Couzens. "Foucault: Modern or Postmodern?" In *After Foucault,* edited by Jonathan Arac, 12–41. New Brunswick, N.J.: Rutgers University Press, 1988.

Hulme, T. E. "Humanism and the Religious Art." In *Speculations: Essays on Humanism and the Philosophy of Art,* edited by Herbert Read, 1–71. New York: Harcourt, 1924.

Hutcheon, Linda. *A Poetics of Postmodernism: History, Theory, Fiction.* London: Routledge, 1988.

Jakobson, Roman. "What Is Poetry." In *Selected Writings,* Vol. 2. The Hague: Mouton, 1971.

James, William. *Essays in Radical Empiricism* and *A Pluralistic Universe.* Edited by Richard J. Bernstein. 1909. Reprint, New York: Dutton, 1971.

————. *Pragmatism.* Edited by A. J. Ayer. 1907. Reprint, Cambridge: Harvard University Press, 1978.

————. *The Principles of Psychology.* 2 vols. New York: Henry Holt, 1893.

————. "On Some Omissions of Introspective Psychology." *Mind,* no. 33 (January 1884): 1–26.

Jameson, Fredric. "Wallace Stevens." In *Critical Essays on Wallace Stevens,* edited by Steven Gould Axelrod and Helen Deese, 176–91. Boston: G. K. Hall, 1988.

Johnson, Barbara. Interview by Imre Salusinszky. *Criticism in Society.* New York: Methuen, 1987: 150–75.

Joyce, James. *Ulysses.* New York: Random House, 1922. Reprint, New York: Random House, 1961.

Kant, Immanuel. *Critique of Pure Reason.* Translated by F. Max Muller. New York: Anchor-Doubleday, 1966.

Kermode, Frank. *History and Value.* Oxford: Clarendon Press, 1989.

Kern, Stephen. *The Culture of Time and Space, 1808–1918.* Cambridge: Harvard University Press, 1983.

Knapp, Steven and William Benn Michaels. "Against Theory." *Critical Inquiry* 8, no. 4 (Summer 1982): 723–42.

Kuklick, Bruce. *The Rise of American Philosophy: Cambridge, Massachusetts, 1860–1930.* New Haven: Yale University Press, 1977.

Kundera, Milan. *The Art of the Novel.* Translated by Linda Asher. New York: Grove Press, 1988.

————. *The Unbearable Lightness of Being.* Translated by Michael Henry Heim. New York: Harper & Row, 1984.

Lacan, Jacques. "God and the Jouissance of The Woman." In *Feminine Sexuality,* edited by Juliet Mitchell and Jacqueline Rose, and translated by Jacqueline Rose. New York: Norton, 1985: 137–48.

Lentricchia, Frank. *Ariel and the Police.* Madison: University of Wisconsin Press, 1988.

Lodge, David. "The Language of Modernist Fiction: Metaphor and Metonymy." In *Modernism,* edited by Malcolm Bradbury and James McFarlane, 481–96. London: Penguin, 1983.

————. *The Modes of Modern Writing.* London: Arnold, 1977.

Lynn, Kenneth S. *Hemingway.* New York: Simon and Schuster, 1987.

Lyotard, Jean-François. *The Postmodern Condition: A Report on Knowledge.* Translated by Geoff Bennington and Brian Massumi. Minneapolis: University of Minnesota Press, 1984.

Marling, William. *William Carlos Williams and the Painters, 1909–1923.* Athens: University of Ohio Press, 1982.

McGuinness, Brian. *Wittgenstein: A Life.* Berkeley: University of California Press, 1988.

Mellow, James. *Charmed Circle.* 1974. Reprint, New York: Avon Books, 1982.

Merleau-Ponty, Maurice. *The Primacy of Perception.* Evanston, Ill.: Northwestern University Press, 1964.

————. *The Visible and the Invisible.* Translated by Alphonso Lingis. Evanston, Ill.: Northwestern University Press, 1968.

Meyers, Jeffrey. *Hemingway: A Biography.* New York: Harper & Row, 1985.

Miller, J. Hillis. *Poets of Reality*. Cambridge: Harvard University Press, 1965. Reprint, New York: Atheneum, 1969.

———. "Williams' *Spring and All* and the Progress of Poetry." *Daedalus* 99, (1970): 415–29.

———. *Versions of Pygmalion*. Cambridge: Harvard University Press, 1990.

Mitchell, W. J. T. *Iconology: Image, Text, Ideology*. Chicago: University of Chicago Press, 1987.

Monk, Ray. *Ludwig Wittgenstein: The Duty of Genius*. New York: The Free Press, 1990.

Moore, Marianne. *Collected Poems*. 1951. Reprint, New York: Macmillan, 1979.

———. *The Complete Poems*. New York: MacMillan/Viking, 1981.

———. *The Complete Prose of Marianne Moore*. Edited by Patricia C. Willis. New York: Viking, 1986.

———. Interview by Donald Hall. In *Writers at Work: The "Paris Review" Interviews*, edited by Malcolm Cowley, 2nd ser., 61–87. New York: Viking, 1963.

———. Letter to William Carlos Williams, 12 May 1934, Moore Papers, Rosenbach Museum, Philadelphia.

———. "Monsieur Testes." Unpublished essay [first draft, ca. 1952–56], Moore Papers, Rosenbach Museum, Philadelphia.

———. *Observations*. New York: The Dial Press, 1925.

———. "Poetry and Criticism." Cambridge, Mass.: Adams House & Lowell House Printers, 1965.

———. "Precision," Moore Papers, Rosenbach Museum, Philadelphia.

———. "Review of My Trip Abroad," Moore Papers, Rosenbach Museum, Philadelphia.

———. Review of *Ideas of Order* by Wallace Stevens. *The Criterion*, 15 January 1936: 307–9.

Norris, Christopher. *Derrida*. Cambridge: Harvard University Press, 1987.

———. *Paul de Man: Deconstruction and the Critique of Aesthetic Ideology*. London: Routledge, 1988.

———. *What's Wrong With Postmodernism: Critical Theory and the Ends of Philosophy*. Baltimore: Johns Hopkins University Press, 1990.

Orvell, Miles. *The Real Thing: Imitation and Authenticity in American Culture, 1880–1940*. Chapel Hill: University of North Carolina Press, 1989.

Owens, Craig. "The Discourse of Others: Feminists and Postmodernism." In *The Anti-Aesthetic: Essays on Postmodern Culture*, edited by Hal Foster, 57–82. Port Townsend, Wash.: Bay Press, 1983.

Peirce, Charles. *Selected Writings*. Edited by Philip P. Wiener. New York: Dover, 1966.

Perkins, David. "Literary Classifications: How Have They Been Made?" In *Theoretical Issues in Literary History*, edited by David Perkins, 248–67. Cambridge: Harvard University Press, 1991.

Perloff, Majorie. *The Dance of the Intellect*. Cambridge: Cambridge University Press, 1987.

———. *The Poetics of Indeterminacy: Rimbaud to Cage*. Evanston, Ill.: Northwestern University Press, 1983.

Peterson, Jeffrey D. "Notes in the Poem(s) 'Poetry.'" In *Marianne Moore: Woman and Poet,* edited by Patricia Willis, 223–42. Orono, Me.: National Poetry Foundation, 1990.

Poirier, Richard. *Poetry and Pragmatism.* Cambridge: Harvard University Press, 1992.

Pound, Ezra. "Vorticism." The Fortnightly Review. 1 September 1914.

Randall, John. "The Changing Import of Darwin on Philosophy." In *Darwin,* edited by Philip Appleman, 314–25. New York: Norton, 1970.

Reynolds, Michael, ed. *Critical Essays on Hemingway's In Our Time.* Boston: G. K. Hall, 1983.

Reynolds, Michael S. *Hemingway's Reading, 1910–1940: An Inventory.* Princeton: Princeton University Press, 1981.

Reynolds, Michael. "Hemingway's Stein: Another Misplaced Artist." *American Literature* 55, no. 3 (1983): 431–34.

Robinson, Lillian S. "Sometimes, Always, Never: Their Women's History and Ours." *New Literary History.* (Winter 1990): 377–93.

Rorty, Richard. *Essays on Heidegger and Others.* Cambridge: Cambridge University Press, 1991.

———. "Foucault and Epistemology." In *Foucault: A Critical Reader,* edited by David Couzens Hoy. Oxford: Basil Blackwell, 1986.

———. *Philosophy and the Mirror of Nature.* Princeton: Princeton University Press, 1979.

Ross, Lillian. *Portrait of Hemingway.* New York: Simon and Schuster, 1961.

Ruddick, Lisa. *Reading Gertrude Stein: Body, Text, Gnosis.* Ithaca: Cornell University Press, 1990.

Sayre, Henry M. "Avant-Garde Dispositions: Placing *Spring and All* in Context." *William Carlos Williams Review* (Fall 1984): 13–20.

Sayre, Henry M. *The Visual Text of William Carlos Williams.* Urbana: University of Illinois Press, 1983.

Schmidt, Peter. *William Carlos Williams, The Arts, and Literary Tradition.* Baton Rouge: Louisana State University Press, 1988.

Scholes, Robert. *Protocols of Reading.* New Haven: Yale University Press, 1989.

Shattuck, Roger. *The Innocent Eye.* New York: Farrar, Straus & Giroux, 1984.

Shiff, Richard. *Cézanne and the End of Impressionism: A Study of the Theory, Technique, and Critical Evaluation of Modern Art.* Chicago: University of Chicago Press, 1984.

Slatin, John M. *The Savage's Romance.* University Park: Pennsylvania State University Press, 1986.

———. "'Something Inescapably Typical': Questions about Gender in the Late Work of William Carlos Williams and Marianne Moore." *William Carlos Williams Review* 14, no. 1 (Spring 1988): 86–103.

Smith, Barbara Herrnstein. "Contingencies of Value." *Critical Inquiry* 10, no. 1. (1983): 1–36.

Smith, Paul. *Discerning the Subject.* Minneapolis: University of Minnesota Press, 1988.

Sontag, Susan. "The Aesthetics of Silence." In *A Susan Sontag Reader.* New York: Farrar, Straus, Giroux, 1982.

———. *On Photography.* New York: Anchor Books, 1990.

Spilka, Mark. *Hemingway's Quarrel with Androgyny.* Lincoln: University of Nebraska Press, 1990.

Stein, Gertrude. *The Autobiography of Alice B. Toklas.* 1933. Reprint, New York: Vintage, 1961.

———. "Cultivated Motor Automatism." *Psychological Review* 5 (1898): 295–306.

———. *Everybody's Autobiography.* New York: Random House, 1937.

———. *Fernhurst, Q.E.D., and Other Early Writings.* Edited by Leon Katz. New York: Liveright, 1971.

———. *Geographical History of America.* 1936. Reprint, New York: Vintage, 1973.

———. *How Writing is Written.* Los Angeles: Black Sparrow Press, 1974.

———. *Lectures in America.* 1935. Reprint, New York: Vintage-Random House, 1962.

———. *The Making of Americans.* 1925. Reprint, New York: Something Else Press, 1966.

———. *Picasso.* 1938. Reprint, Boston: Beacon Press, 1959.

———. *Portraits and Prayers.* New York: Random House, 1934.

———. *A Primer for the Gradual Understanding of Gertrude Stein.* Edited by Robert Baartlett Haas. Los Angeles: Black Sparrow Press, 1971.

———. *Selected Writings of Gertrude Stein.* Edited by Carl Van Vechten. New York: Vintage, 1972.

———. *Tender Buttons.* 1914. Reprint, Los Angeles: Sun & Moon, 1991.

———. *Three Lives.* 1909. Reprint, New York: Random House, 1936.

———. *What Are Masterpieces?* 1940. Reprint, New York: Vintage-Random House, 1966.

Steiner, George. *Real Presences: Is There Anything in What We Say?* Chicago: University of Chicago Press, 1989.

Steiner, Wendy. *Exact Resemblance to Exact Resemblance: The Literary Portraiture of Gertrude Stein.* New Haven: Yale University Press, 1978.

Steinman, Lisa. "Once More With Feeling: Teaching *Spring and All.*" *William Carlos Williams Review* 10, no. 2 (Fall 1984): 7–12.

Stevens, Wallace. *The Necessary Angel: Essays on Reality and the Imagination.* New York: Vintage, 1951.

Stewart, Allegra. *Gertrude Stein and the Present.* Cambridge: Harvard University Press, 1967.

Tanner, Tony. *The Reign of Wonder.* Cambridge: Cambridge University Press, 1965.

Taskijan, Dickran. *Skyscraper Primitives: Dada and the American Avant-Garde, 1910–1925.* Middletown, Conn.: Wesleyan University Press, 1975.

Tavernier-Courbin, Jacqueline. "Ernest Hemingway and Ezra Pound." In *Ernest Hemingway: The Writer in Context,* edited by James Nagel, 179–200. Madison: University of Wisconsin Press, 1984.

Tetlow, Wendolyn E. *Hemingway's In Our Time: Lyrical Dimensions.* Lewisburg, Pa.: Bucknell University Press, 1992.

Thomas, Brook. *The New Historicism and Other Old-Fashioned Topics.* Princeton: Princeton University Press, 1991.

Tichi, Cecelia. "Women Writers and the New Woman." In *Columbia History of the United States,* edited by Emory Elliott, 589–606. New York: Columbia University Press, 1988.

Ulmer, Gregory L. "The Object of Post-Criticism." In *The Anti-Aesthetic: Essays on Postmodern Culture,* edited by Hal Foster, 83–110. Port Townsend, Wash.: Bay Press, 1983: 83–110.

Wagner, Linda. *Hemingway and Faulkner.* Metuchen, N.J.: The Scarecrow Press, 1975.

Walker, Cheryl. "Feminist Literary Criticism and the Author." *Critical Inquiry* 16, no. 3 (Spring 1990): 551–72.

Watts, Emily Stipes. *Ernest Hemingway and the Arts.* Urbana: University of Illinois Press, 1971.

Whitaker, Thomas R. "*Spring and All:* Teaching Us the Figures of Dance." *William Carlos Williams Review* 10, no. 2 (Fall 1984): 1–6.

White, Hayden. *Tropics of Discourse.* Baltimore: Johns Hopkins University Press, 1985.

Whitehead, Alfred North. *The Concept of Nature.* Cambridge: Cambridge University Press, 1920.

Williams, William Carlos. *Imaginations.* New York: New Directions, 1970.

———. *Selected Essays.* 1954. Reprint by New York: New Directions, 1962.

———. *The Selected Letters of William Carlos Williams.* Edited by John C. Thirlwall. New York: McDowell, Obolensky, 1957.

———. *Spring and All.* In *The Collected Poems of William Carlos Williams, vol. 1 (1909–1939),* edited by A. Walton Litz and Christopher MacGowan. New York: New Directions, 1986.

Wilson, Edmund. *Axel's Castle.* New York: Scribner, 1931.

———. "Ernest Hemingway: Bourdon Gauge of Morale." *Atlantic Monthly* (July 1939): 396–418.

Wittgenstein, Ludwig. *Philosophical Investigations.* Translated by G. E. M. Anscombe. 1958. Reprint. Oxford: Basil Blackwell, 1981.

Wittgenstein, Ludwig. *Tractatus Logico-Philosophicus.* Translated by C. K. Ogden. 1922. Reprint. London: Routledge, 1990.

Wittgenstein, Ludwig. *Tractatus Logico-Philosophicus.* Translated by D. F. Pears & B. F. McGuinness. 1922. Reprint, London: Routledge & Kegan Paul, 1978.

Woolf, Virginia. *To the Lighthouse.* 1927. Reprint. New York: Harcourt Brace Jovanovich, 1955.

Zukofsky, Louis. *Prepositions: The Collected Critical Essays of Louis Zukofsky.* New York: Horizon Press, 1968.

Index

Abel, Elizabeth, 229n. 65
Agee, James, 46
Alcott, Louisa May, 56
Althusser, Louis, 217n. 35
Altieri, Charles, 45
Anderson, Sherwood, 117, 119, 121
Appollinaire, Guillaume, 220n. 66
Arnold, Matthew, 163

Bach, Johann Sebastian, 89
Bacon, Francis, 32
Bain, Alexander, 61
Bakhtin, Mikhail, 139
Baroja, Pío, 168
Barthes, Roland, 27, 39, 46
Baudrillard, Jean, 39
Beardsley, Monroe C., 28
Beegel, Susan F., 128
Benjamin, Walter, 41, 46; Arcades Project, 218n. 43
Benveniste, Emile, 30
Berenson, Bernard, 117, 136, 138
Bergson, Henri, 82, 90
Berkeley, George, 60
Bernard, Emile, 219n. 52
Bible, 201
Blake, William, 206
Bloom, Harold, 180, 207
Borges, Jorge Luis, "Pierre Menard, Author of the Quixote," 27
Bosanquet, Bernard, 60
Bridgeman, Richard, 227n. 36
Bronowski Jacob, 183
Bryson, Norman, 111, 188, 219n. 49, 236n. 19
Buffon, Comte de, 58
Burke, Carolyn, 229n. 65
Burke, Edmund, 201, 203
Burke, Kenneth, 194

Calinescu, Matei, 220n. 63
Callaghan, Morley, 117

Canetti, Elias, 233n. 58
Carey, M. C., 201
Carlyle, Thomas, 76
Cassirer, Ernst, 54, 76
Cather, Willa, 43
Cavell, Stanley, 200, 224n. 75
Cervantes Saavedra, Miguel de, 135, 157; Don Quixote, 27
Cézanne, Paul, 122–25, 128–29, 133, 156, 168, 213, 219n. 52, 231nn. 15 and 18, 231–32n. 19
Chaplin, Charlie, 186
Chessman, Harriet Scott, 229n. 65
Chopin, Kate, 43
Coleridge, Samuel Taylor, 207
Conrad, Joseph, 186
Corbusier, Le (Charles-Édouard Jeanneret), 225n. 6
Costello, Bonnie, 196
Cowley, Malcom, 131
Craig, Gordon, 185
Crane, Hart, 47
Cuvier, Georges, 33

Dalston, D. F., "Blown," 193
Dante Alighieri, 185
Darr, Rev. J. W., 201
Darwin, Charles, 66, 185, 221n. 15; The Origin of Species, 57–60
Davidson, Donald, 28–29
DeKoven, Marianne, 229n. 65
De Man, Paul, 11, 19, 25, 29, 30, 39–42, 44, 79, 102, 141, 215n. 3; Resistance to Theory, 19, 23, 40, 41
Democritus, 201
Demuth, Charles, 156
Derain, André, 120
Derrida, Jacques, 30, 38, 79, 100, 107, 114, 212, 215n. 9, 217n. 26, 217n. 35, 225n. 5
Descartes, René, 32, 37, 62, 93
Dewey, John, 59

247

The Dial, 121, 122, 198
Dickinson, Emily, 206
Dijkstra, Bram, 235 n. 8
Dilthey, Wilhelm, 225 n. 6
Dodge, Mabel, 107, 228 n. 58
Dolittle, Hilda (H. D.), 187
Donoghue, Denis, 70, 235 n. 6; *Ferocious Alphabets*, 206–7
Dowling, William C. 81, 206
Duchamp, Marcel, 225 n. 6
Duns Scotus, John, 201

Eagelton, Terry, 216 n. 16
Edelstein, Marilyn, 216 n. 16
Einstein, Alfred, 38, 76, 184
El Greco, 156, 168
Eliot, T(homas) S(tearns), 78, 117, 156, 163, 187, 197, 206, 207, 208, 220 n. 66, 234 n. 4; *Burnt Norton*, 195; "Prufrock," 169; *Prufrock and Other Observations*, 236 n. 13; *Tradition and the Individual Talent*, 136; *The Waste Land*, 232 n. 32
Emerson, Ralph Waldo, 11, 49, 50–56, 62, 69, 70, 72, 74, 76, 158, 206, 207, 208; "Nature," 49–55

Fitzgerald, F. Scott, 124
Flaubert, Gustave, 156, 185, 200; *Trois Contes*, 122
Ford Madox Ford, 119
Forsyth, P. T., 201
Foucault, Michel, 28–39, 41, 97, 140, 147, 182, 217 n. 30; "Nietzsche, Genealogy, History," 37–38; *The Order of Things*, 31–37; "What Is an Author?," 28
France, Anatole, 158–59, 164, 168, 201
Freud, Sigmund 217 n. 35
Frow, John, 225 n. 6
Fry, Roger, 82

Gadamer, Hans-Georg, 79, 101, 228–29 n. 64
Gasché, Rodolphe, 41–42
Gasquet, J., 133
Giddens, Anthony, 216 n. 17
Gilman, Charlotte Perkins, 43
Gombrich, Ernst, 82
Green, Nicholas, 61
Greeff, Adele, 186

Gris, Juan, 156, 160, 168, 175, 177
Grosz, George, 183

Habermas, Jürgen, 38
Hadas, Pamela, 227 n. 32
Hall, Donald, 183
Hartley, Marsden, 44, 161; *Adventures in Art*, 168
Hawthorne, Nathaniel, 56
Hayden, Arthur, 201
Hazlitt, William, 201
Hegel, Georg Wilhelm Friedrich, 25, 60, 211, 221 n. 15; *Philosophy of History*, 201
Heidegger, Martin, 97–99, 101, 126, 128–29, 210, 217 n. 35, 224 n. 75; *Being and Time*, 97–98
Hemingway, Ernest, 12, 19, 27, 44–45, 47, 55–56, 69–70, 72, 74, 76–79, 117–51, 152, 153, 156–57, 162, 169, 180, 182, 183, 186, 189, 197, 198, 208–9, 210, 212, 213, 214, 225 n. 6, 230 n. 2, 231 n. 15, 231 nn. 18 and 19, 232 n. 33; "The Art of the Short Story," 131; "A Clean Well Lighted Place," 131; *Death in the Afternoon*, 131, 132, 137, 138, 140–41; *The Garden of Eden*, 129, 147; *In Our Time*, 11, 12, 13, 19, 26, 30, 31, 45, 48, 49, 117–51, 213, 232 n. 32; *Men Without Women*, 141; *A Moveable Feast*, 120, 124, 131, 136–37, 148; *Three Stories and Ten Poems*, 122; "Up in Michigan," 117, 120–21, 125; *In Our Time* chapters and stories: "The Battler," 142; "Big Two-Hearted River," 117, 123, 125, 131–32, 146, 148, 150; "Cat in the Rain," 142, 143; "Chapter II," 147," "Chapter III," 141; "Chapter IV," 141; "Chapter VIII," 141; "Chapter IX," 149; "Chapter X," 145, 147; "Cross-Country Snow," 142, 143; "The Doctor and the Doctor's Wife," 142, 143; "The End of Something," 142, 143; "Indian Camp," 143; "Mr. and Mrs. Elliot," 118, 120, 142; "My Old Man," 117, 143, 146; "On the Quai at Smyrna," 116; "Out of Season," 124–27, 142, 143; "Soldier's Home," 142, 143, 144; "The Three-Day Blow," 142, 143; "A Very Short Story," 142, 143

Hemingway, Hadley, 118
Hemingway, John Hadley Nicanor, 118
Heraclitus, 173
Holbein, Hans, 157, 168
Holley, Margaret, 193–94
Holmes, Jr., Oliver Wendell, 61
Homer, 156, 161, 168, 171
Howells, William Dean, 219 n. 46
Hoy, David Couzens, 34
Hulme, T. E., 70–74, 82, 154; *Specula-tions,* 12, 49, 71–74
Hume, David, 51–52, 56, 134, 221 n. 15
Hunt, Leigh, 201
Husserl, Edmund, 88

Isaiah, 201

Jakobson, Roman, 114
James, Alice, 43
James, Henry, 43, 126, 135, 157, 185, 201, 219 n. 46
James, William, 61, 63–70, 74, 75, 76, 82–83, 86, 90, 102, 109, 138, 156, 159, 175, 208, 222 n. 32, 226 n. 13, 228 n. 46; *Essays in Radical Empiricism,* 63, 66, 67; *A Pluralist Universe,* 63; Prag-matism, 12, 49, 63–66, 69, 148–49, 187; *Principles of Psychology,* 63, 67, 68, 69, 82
Jameson, Fredric, 39, 223 n. 39
Johnson, Barbara, 42
Jonas, Hans, 211
Joyce, James, 76, 117, 206, 225 n. 6, 232 n. 19

Kafka, Franz, 225 n. 6
Kandinsky, Wassily, 81
Kant, Immanuel, 51, 56–58, 88, 134, 220–21 n. 5, 221 nn. 9, 10, and 15, 222 n. 31; *Critique of Pure Reason,* 51, 57
Keats, John, 135, 207
Kenner, Hugh, 185, 193, 196, 206
Kermode, Frank, 207, 218 n. 45
Kern, Stephen, 58
Kipling, Rudyard, 117, 119
Knapp, Steven, "Against Theory," 81
Kreymborg, Alfred, 156, 168
Kristeva, Julia, 229 n. 65
Kuklick, Bruce, 58
Kundera, Milan, 28, 150

Kunitz, Stanley, 187

Lacan, Jacques, 217 n. 35
Laforgue, Jules, 82
Langer, Suzanne, 235 n. 6
Lardner, Ring, 117
Lawrence, D(avid) H(erbert), 122
Leavis, F(rank) R(aymond), 134
Lewis, Sinclair, 122
Lewis, Wyndham, 206
Liveright, Horace, 120, 130
Locke, John, 20, 51–52
Lodge, David, 114
London, Jack, 219 n. 46
Longfellow, Henry Wadsworth, 44, 172
Luke, 136
Lyell, Charles, 58
Lynn, Kenneth, 131–32
Lyotard, Jean-François, 38, 225 n. 6

Malevich, Kasimir, 81
Mallarmé, Stéphane, 225 n. 6
Marling, William, 235 n. 6
Marlowe, Christopher, 168
Marx, Karl, 217 n. 35
Matisse, Henri, 95–96, 156, 213, 231 n. 18
Maupassant, Guy de, 117, 135
Melville, Herman, 56, 221 n. 10
Mencken, H(enry) L(ouis), 122
Metaphysical Club, 61, 63
Michaels, Walter Benn, "Against The-ory," 81
Michelet, Jules, 48
Mies van der Rohe, Ludwig, 225 n. 6
Miller, J. Hillis, 41, 207, 209, 234 n. 1
Mitchell, W. J. T., 212, 237 n. 5
Moholy-Nagy, László, 220 n. 66
Mondrian, Piet, 81
Monet, Claude, 80–81, 156, 160, 168; *The Path through the Irises,* 80; *Water Lilies—Reflections of the Willow,* 80; *Water Lilies,* 80, 81
Moore, George Augustus, 187
Moore, Marianne, 44–45, 47, 55–56, 69–70, 72, 74, 76–79, 156, 165, 168, 170, 175, 178, 182–205, 206, 208–14, 225 n. 6, 235 n. 6; "The Accented Syl-lable," 193–94; *Complete Poems,* 196; "A Grave," 193; *Observations,* 11, 12, 13, 19, 27, 30, 31, 45, 48, 49, 182–205, 213, 236 n. 13; *Selected Poems,* 187,

236n. 13; "The Student," 184; *Observations* poems: "Bowls," 201; "The Bricks are Fallen Down . . .," 188; "Critics and Connoisseurs," 191; "Dock Rats," 199; "England," 197, 203; "An Egyptian Pulled Glass Bottle in the Shape of a Fish," 198; "In the Days of Prismatic Color," 189, 192, 196, 202; "Marriage," 196, 201–2; "The Monkey Puzzler," 200; "New York," 187; "Novices," 203; "An Octopus," 189, 203; "The Past is the Present," 186, 204; "People's Surroundings," 189–90, 199; "Peter," 192, 199; "Picking and Choosing," 184, 203, 236n. 13; "Poetry," 186, 187, 192, 196, 203; "Reinforcements," 188; "Silence," 197; "Snakes, Mongooses . . . Charmers and The Like," 189; "When I Buy Pictures," 186, 187, 189

Morrell, Lady Ottoline, 21
Mueller, Heiner, 43
Mumford, Lewis, 46
Munsterberg, Hugo, 86

Nadia, Marcia, 165
Nancy, Jean-Luc, 30
Newton, Isaac, 59–60, 75, 146, 153
Nietzsche, Friedrich Wilhelm, 37, 141, 217n. 35
Norris, Christopher, 215n. 2, 225n. 5
Norris, Frank, 84

Ortega y Gasset, José, 69; *The Dehumanization of Art,* 113

Parsons, Aluah, 201
Pascal, Blaise, 112
Pater, Walter, 197
Paul, Sherman, 53
Peirce, Charles, 60–63 passim, 102, 222n. 32
Perkins, David, 219n. 46
Perloff, Marjorie, 206–9, 234n. 1; *The Dance of the Intellect,* 206–7
Picasso, Pablo, 95, 108–110, 156
Plato, 73, 87, 134, 157
Plimpton, George, 119, 124, 125, 230n. 15
Pliny, 201

Poe, Edgar Allan, 156, 168
Pope, Alexander, *Rape of the Lock,* 201
Poirier, Richard, 222n. 32, 226n. 13
Pound, Ezra, 75, 77, 117, 121, 137, 156, 168, 185, 192, 193, 206–9, 213, 220n. 66; *Cathay,* 168; "Approaches to Paris," 44; *Cantos,* 207; "A Few Don'ts by an Imagiste," 185; Hugh Selwyn Mauberley, 232n. 32; "In a Station of the Metro," 76
Proust, Marcel, 69, 76
Purvis, Margaret Blake, 165

Randall, John, 57
Reese, Albert, 185
Reynolds, Joshua, 111
Reynolds, Michael, 230n. 2
Ricoeur, Paul, 216n 17
Rilke, Rainer Maria, 123
Robinson, Edwin Arlington, 44
Robinson, Lillian, 218n. 42
Rorty, Richard, 37, 60, 221–22n. 15, 222n. 31
Rosenfeld, Paul, 47
Ross, Lillian, 231n. 15
Rousseau, Henri, 191
Royce, Josiah, 60
Ruddick, Lisa, 226–27n. 22, 227n. 36, 229n. 65
Ruskin, John, 82, 186

Sandburg, Carl, 168
Sayre, Henry M. 234n. 1, 235n. 6
Schmidt, Peter, 235nn. 6 and 7
Schoenberg, Arnold, 225n. 6
Scholes, Robert, 38
Scribner, Charles, 135
Seurat, Georges, 48
Shakespeare, William, 104, 135, 156, 157, 161, 166, 168, 171, 176, 192; *The Tempest,* 201
Shattuck, Roger, 80–82
Shelley, Percy Bysshe, 135
Shiff, Richard, 220n. 67
Slatin, John, 165
Smith, Barbara Herrnstein, 134
Smith, Paul, 43–44
Solomon, Leon M., 83
Sontag, Susan, 48, 197; *The Aesthetics of Silence,* 132; *On Photography,* 220n. 66
Sorley, Hamilton, "Barrabas," 193
Spilka, Mark, 230n. 2

Steiner, George, 27
Stein, Gertrude, 44–45, 47, 55–56, 69–70, 72, 74–79, 80–116, 117–125, 128, 148, 152, 153, 162, 169, 175, 180, 182, 183, 186, 187, 189, 197, 198, 203, 204, 208–9, 210, 212, 213, 214, 225n. 6, 226n. 13, 226–27n. 22, 227n. 32, 228n. 58, 229n. 65, 231nn. 15, 18 and 19; "Ada," 95; *The Autobiography of Alice B. Toklas*, 27, 97, 119–20; *Everybody's Autobiography*, 83; *Fernhurst*, 84, 88; *Four Saints in Three Acts*, 100; *The Geographical History of America*, 93–96, 99; *Geography and Plays*, 122; *Lectures in America*, 92, 93, 103–6; *A Long Gay Book*, 91–92; *The Making of Americans*, 84–96, 105, 107, 112, 118, 119; "Matisse," 95, 96; "Picasso," 95; *Picasso*, 108–10; *Q.E.D.*, 84, 85, 88; *Tender Buttons*, 11, 12, 13, 19, 26, 27, 30, 31, 45, 48, 81, 96, 97–108, 110–16, 187, 211, 213, 227n. 36; *Three Lives*, 85–90, 107, 121,122, 226n. 8; *How Writing is Written*, 86, 90, 92, 93, 96, 103: *Tender Buttons* sections and still lifes: "Apple," 116; "A Book," 81; "A Box," 97, 99, 110, 116; "A Chair," 98; "A Cutlet," 98; "Food," 112, 116; "A Little Bit of A Tumbler," 106; "A Long Dress," 98, 116; "A Mounted Umbrella," 98; "Objects," 106, 116; "Orange," 115; "A Piano," 101; "A Plate, 116," "A Piece of Coffee," 97; "A Purse," 115; "A Red Hat," 114; "Roastbeef," 100; "Rooms," 101; "Salad," 115; "Salmon," 116; "Sauce," 115; "Sausages," 111; "A Seltzer Bottle," 110; "A Shawl," 81; "A Substance in A Cushion," 98; "A Table," 81, 101; "Water Raining," 98
Stein, Leo, 227n. 32, 231n. 18
Steinman, Lisa, 234n.1
Stevens, Wallace, 24–25, 27, 70, 78, 139, 194, 206–9, 215n. 6, 219n. 52, 228n. 39, 232n. 33; "As Before," 193; "The Credences of Summer," 44; *Harmonium*, 191; *The Necessary Angel*, 20, 24; "Nuances of a Theme by Williams," 74; "The Snow Man," 131
Stieglitz, Alfred, 48

Sullivan, Louis, 44
Sutherland, Donald, 89
Swinburne, Algernon Charles, 135

Tanner, Tony, 149
Taskijan, Dickran, 235n. 6
Tetlow, Wendolyn E., 232n. 32
Thomas, Brook, 218n. 40
Thoreau, Henry David, 56, 203
Tichi, Cecelia, 219n. 46
Toklas, Alice B., 27, 118
Tolstoy, Lev, 117, 135, 157
Transatlantic Review, 119
Trilling, Lionel, 69
Trollope, Anthony, 201
Tuille, Monsieur de, 120
Turgenev, Ivan Sergeevich, 117, 135
Twain, Mark, *Huck Finn*, 117

Ussher, Bishop James, 58

Valéry, Paul, 185–86
Velázquez, Diego Rodriguez de Silva, *Las Meninas*, 37
Vendler, Helen, 207
Voltaire, 192

Walker, Cheryl, 29
Watts, Emily Stipes, 231n. 15
Webern, Anton von, 225n. 6
Webster, Daniel, 201
Wells, H(erbert) G(eorge), 122
Weston, Edward, 44, 46–48
Wharton, Edith, 43
Whitaker, Thomas R., 234n. 1
White, Hayden, 91
Whitehead, A(lfred) N(orth), 74–75
Whitman, Walt, 56, 70, 156, 162, 168, 170, 191; "Crossing Brooklyn Ferry," 169
Whittier, John Greenleaf, 44
Williams, William Carlos, 19, 44–45, 47, 48, 55–56, 69–70, 72, 74–79, 123, 152–81, 182, 183, 186, 189, 192, 194, 195, 197, 198, 204, 205–14, 220n. 66, 225n. 6; *Collected Poems*, 203; *Spring and All*, 11, 12, 13, 26, 27, 30, 31, 45, 48, 49, 152–81, 210, 213; "Struggle of Wings," 197
Wimsatt, W. K., "The Intentional Fallacy," 28

Wilson, Edmund, 76, 118, 121, 147; "Ernest Hemingway: Bourdon Gauge of Morale," 131

Wittgenstein, Ludwig, 20, 35, 36, 99–100, 102–3, 128–31, 200, 215nn. 5, 7, 8, and 9, 219n. 46; *Philosophical Investigations,* 20, 21, 23, 35, 36, 130; *Tractatus Logico-Philosophicus,* 21–27, 30, 35, 63, 99, 103, 105, 128–131, 197, 215–16n. 10

Woolf, Virginia, 45, 76
Wright, Chauncey, 61
Wright, Richard, 226n. 13
Wundt, Wilhelm, 75

Xenophon, 185

Zukofsky, Louis, 75, 77, 213; *Prepositions,* 44